THE COMING

of the GLORY

HOW THE HEBREW SCRIPTURES
REVEAL THE PLAN OF GOD

VOLUME II
THE PREEXILIC YEARS:
AMOS TO JEREMIAH

EILEEN MADDOCKS

The Coming of the Glory
How the Hebrew Scriptures Reveal the Plan of God
Volume II The Preexilic Years: Amos to Jeremiah

ISBN: 978-1-954102-06-4
Library of Congress Control Number: 2020935114

Printed in the United States of America

First Printing: 2022
Edited by Geraldine Maddocks Whitfield and John Irvin
Interior design by Michael Grossman
Cover design by Dragan Bilic

SOMETHING OR OTHER PUBLISHING
Brooklyn, Wisconsin 53521
Info@SOOPLLC.com

For bulk orders e-mail: Orders@SOOPLLC.com

Books by Eileen Maddocks

1844: Convergence in Prophecy for Judaism, Christianity, Islam and the Bahá'í Faith (2018)

The Coming of the Glory: How the Hebrew Scriptures Reveal the Plan of God, Volume I Göbekli Tepe to Elijah (2020)

The Coming of the Glory: How the Hebrew Scriptures Reveal the Plan of God, Volume II The Preexilic Years: Amos to Jeremiah (2022)

Contents

Acknowledgments

MAJOR WRITING PROJECTS NEED a lot of help. This trilogy is now two-thirds completed, and upon completion, it will have been a ten-year endeavor. Only because of my sister, Geraldine Maddocks Whitfield, have I arrived this far. She painstakingly read and reread the manuscript, chapter by chapter, and greatly improved the flow and vocabulary. She urged me forward with endless encouragement and loving patience.

Wade Fransson, my publisher (Something Or Other Publishing, or SOOP), has supported my efforts wholeheartedly. We share a deep love and respect for the Bible and can talk endlessly as kindred spirits about biblical interpretation and history.

JoAnn Gometz patiently corrected tortured sentence constructions and taught me the difference between "might" and "may." John Irvin, editor and proofreader for SOOP, labored with the fine points of vocabulary, grammar, and punctuation in this research-heavy manuscript.

Deanna McCollum, Leslie King, Ethel Van Zanten, and Serena Rushford, who have been friends for many years, contributed to reviewing the manuscript and submitting helpful comments.

Dragan Bilic did a truly excellent job with the book cover design and interior design.

The SOOP team worked innumerable hours to bring this volume to publication. Thank you Jesús E. Bracho, Marketing Manager; Diana Vidal, Operations Manager; and Beth Rule, Director of Publications.

Writing is a lonely pursuit. I give heartfelt thanks to friends in this country and around the world for their encouragement and prayers.

Foreword

WHY IS THE HEBREW Bible important to us today? Why do we continue to read and study chapters and verses about kings and prophets—dead for three or four millennia—and their tales of murder and intrigue, of plagues and famines, of Assyrian and Babylonian battles, and the dispensations and covenants laid before them by God?

Volume II of *The Coming of the Glory: How the Hebrew Scriptures Reveal the Plan of God* continues our journey of understanding, helping us to grasp the elusive thread of comprehension that ties together the unfolding of God's unending revelation. Follow the author's journey as she takes the reader further along a path of awareness that travels through the warp and woof of an increasingly comprehensive and profound biblical tapestry. Page by page, the mystery of the overarching narrative of God's Covenant with mankind unravels, thus allowing us to comprehend the principle that all religions come from God and are one, and that we are on a continuum with neither a beginning nor an end—treading a transcendent byway at the edge of a shoreless sea.

How do we acquire a link to the unknowable essence that is God? Is it possible by faith alone? Perhaps. But mostly, we learn through recognizing His Prophets and their messages. From man's beginning— long before the written word—the Prophets and their teachings were shared within a family or tribe through oral traditions and stories told around a fire. Those stories, often preserved as parables, were punctuated by images drawn with a finger in the dirt. Only later, when record-keeping was manifested by symbolic cuneiform marks, pictographs, and hieroglyphs, and then evolved into writing as literature, were the scriptures and histories of the Prophets finally recorded for posterity.

Frequently our knowledge of early divine teachers is provided by archaeological evidence such as the ruins of a stone temple, a bronze age idol, or a clay figure in the dust. For example, Volume I presented the wonders of the paleolithic temple site Göbekli Tepe, which was a monumental undertaking to express spirituality before the Neolithic revolution began in the Middle East. It is only recently, through the accessibility and examination of the printed Hebrew Bible, the New Testament, and the Qur'án, that we could link the Prophets of God as a continuous narrative. There is a thin, but very distinct, dividing line between what is history and what is theology in these scriptures and chronicles.

The Dispensation of Moses was unique because manifest within it was a phenomenon called the Hebrew prophets. Often referred to as the canonical prophets, they were called by God to be His mouthpieces in ministries dedicated to the spiritual renewal of the Mosaic Covenant. It is through their chronicles that we further our understanding of God's guidance that they brought to the time and place in which they lived, both in Israel and Judah. Nor were the Hebrew prophets limited to the period of their missions; they also foretold the coming of future Prophets of God and the signs by which they could be recognized. The prescience of the Hebrew prophets hinted of a universality that binds man's progressive spiritual evolution.

Scholars investigating the catalog of redolent place names such as the Land of Canaan, the Promised Land, Eretz Israel, and the Holy Land must be able to connect that land and its people to the deep-seated messages of those prophets. The years that led to the Exile in the sixth century BCE were grim; however, the preexilic Hebrew prophets offered comfort in the future. They foresaw ahead twenty-five centuries and beyond with prophecies addressed to us today. A close study of the books of the Hebrew prophets divulges how they revealed God's plan for humanity now.

Traversing the unending continuum, we learn from a closer look at the growth of this prophetic tree that the events in the Hebrew Bible only occupy rings at its outer edge. Our peregrination to unravel its mysteries is resumed with our study of this volume, furthering our reach beyond our material sensibility to grasp the transcendental nature of our existence. It is our spiritual reality combined with the existential that defines us as human beings and links our souls. Archaic stories like Elijah's struggle with Baal for the souls of man on the slopes of Mount Carmel illustrate a never-ending journey and a return to that mountain in its most recent glory, ushering in the Prophet of God for this day and age.

G. L. HOGENSON, co-author of *Roy C. Wilhelm: Servant to the Servants*

Introduction

WELCOME BACK, READERS OF the first volume of *The Coming of the Glory: How the Hebrew Scriptures Reveal the Plan of God.* Those of you who have not read the first volume are urged to do so before starting the second because it lays the foundation for this one. The introduction to Volume 1 also presents the history and beliefs of the Bahá'í Faith, which are related to some of the prophecies that will be discussed. In addition, that introduction explains the cycles, spiritual seasons, and other concepts to which references continue throughout the second and third volumes.

This trilogy started with exploring the early evolution of spiritual consciousness suggested by excavations of the Paleolithic hunter-gatherer site Göbekli Tepi, located between the Tigris and Euphrates Rivers in today's southeastern Turkey; the Neolithic site Çatalhöyük, located in south-central Turkey; and the Mesopotamian city-states along the Tigris and Euphrates Rivers. Most probably, these swift advances in human civilization in the Middle East were triggered by divine Messengers whose names have been lost to history. Progress continued with the missions and legacies of Adam, Noah, Abraham, and Moses, all of Whom, according to Bahá'í understanding, were Prophets of God sent to educate humanity. The days of the judges with the emergence of the schools of the prophets came with Israelite settlement in Canaan. Then came the rise of the united kingdom with its three fabled kings—Saul, David, and Solomon—and its subsequent split into two kingdoms, Israel and Judah. The early prophets warned the Israelite kings of the errors of their ways, usually to no avail.

INTRODUCTION

The first volume ended with the *still small voice* heard by the prophet Elijah. The Israelite perception of God as a "storm god" in the Mesopotamian tradition was evidenced by Mount Sinai covered with billowing smoke while the mountain trembled violently, with the sound of a trumpet for further effect (Exodus 19:18–19), when Moses ascended the mount to receive the Ten Commandments. Elijah himself was rather noisy when he summoned God to light his altar when confronting the priests of Baal, but towards the end of his ministry, Elijah heard the voice of God within himself, as did the Hebrew prophets who followed him.

We now move into the era of the writing prophets, that is, those Hebrew prophets whose work was preserved in scrolls, or books, that were named after them. Amos and Hosea were the first of the writing, classical prophets, and both of their missions took place in the northern kingdom of Israel. There they warned of the Assyrian threat, which they saw as divine punishment for forsaking the spiritual teachings of Mosaic law. The northern kingdom fell to the Assyrians in 722 BCE.

First Isaiah, Micah, Hosea, Zephaniah, Nahum, Habakkuk, and Jeremiah counseled and warned their kings and the people of defeat at the hands of the Babylonian empire as divine retribution for disobedience to the spiritual laws of the Mosaic Covenant. The southern kingdom fell to the Babylonians in stages, each resulting in deportations of Judahites to the Babylonian empire. The end came in 587 BCE with the fall of Jerusalem, when further deportations to Babylon swelled the number of Israelites living in the Exile. The third volume covers the postexilic years and the prophets Ezekiel, Obadiah, Second and Third Isaiah, Haggai, Zechariah, Joel, Malachi, and Daniel.

A basic history of ancient Israel is woven throughout this trilogy, aided by timeline charts and maps. The prophets' missions are entwined with Israelite history and can only be fully understood by putting them within its context. This historical backdrop is given in a chronological and systematic manner.

The search continues throughout this volume for references to the Glory of God, which is the Arabic translation for Bahá'u'lláh, the

Prophet of the Bahá'í Faith. The British scholar Stephen Lambden found mentions of "the glory of the Lord" and "the Glory of God" thirty-six times in the Hebrew Bible.[1] From Genesis through Malachi, the Hebrew Bible abounds with prophecies about the coming of Jesus Christ and His return, the coming of the Glory. Other terms and titles may refer to the Báb and the Bahá'í Era, also known as the Bahá'í Cycle (see Appendices A, B, and C).

Key words in our search will also be *justice* and *judgment*. All the Hebrew prophets pummeled away at these two key concepts of the Mosaic Dispensation. The biblical scholar Gary Selchert wrote:

> Centuries before Jesus, Peter and Paul, the social order of the Israelite tribes was legislated, adjudicated and enforced in accordance with the Covenant and Law of Moses. While not world-embracing in its vision, the Mosaic order is certainly our original example of a divine standard of justice.[2]

The spiritual verity of justice was stressed repeatedly by Moses and succeeding Prophets. Bahá'u'lláh wrote: *"The essence of all that We have revealed for thee is Justice, is for man to free himself from idle fancy and imitation, discern with the eye of oneness His glorious handiwork, and look into all things with a searching eye."*[3]

THE MIDDLE EAST LEGACY OF DIVINATION AND PROPHECY

The Israelites were confronted in Canaan with the Middle Eastern traditions of seers, priests, astrologers, and diviners of all sorts, and with polytheism and human sacrifice. However, Mosaic law put a damper on this scene. *"Let no one be found among you who sacrifices their son or daughter in the fire, who practices divination or sorcery, interprets omens, engages in witchcraft, or casts spells, or who is a medium or spiritist or who consults the dead"* (Deut. 18:10–11). Only three methods of divination were sanctioned in the Pentateuch— dreams, prophets, and the Urim and Thummim. However, the struggles between obedience to Mosaic law and the enticement of idolatrous practices were a constant in Israelite history and the backdrop to the prophets' admonitions.

Individual sensitivity to the divine voice developed, in accordance with Mosaic strictures, into a phenomenon known as the Hebrew prophets, a phenomenon extraordinary in its dramatic depiction of failure to adhere to the law of God and the consequences. The earlier prophets, named and unnamed, often belonged to schools or guilds known as the "sons of the prophets" and lived in communities under a leader such as Samuel or Elijah. There were two types of prophetic guilds—those that trained prophets for service in temples or at hilltop shrines, and those that trained prophets for service in the royal court. The court prophets were often portrayed as sycophants because prophecy was their livelihood, and prophecies that flattered their kings and successfully endorsed their wars could ensure their jobs. When court prophets agreed upon a certain outcome, but the future event didn't coincide, the group could insulate individual prophets from royal wrath. However, an independent prophet like Micaiah, who aroused royal anger by giving truthful accounts, had no protection within a group (see Chapter 2).

AUTHENTICITY OF THE HOLY SCRIPTURES

Discussion of the Bible and biblical scholarship inevitably prompts the question: How authentic is the Bible?

Shoghi Effendi addressed this question when he wrote, "The Bible is not *wholly* authentic, and in this respect is not to be compared with the Qur'án, and should be wholly subordinated to the authentic writings of Bahá'u'lláh."[4] He further noted, "Except for what has been explained by Bahá'u'lláh and 'Abdu'l-Bahá, we have no way of knowing what various symbolic allusions in the Bible mean."[5] Later, the Universal House of Justice provided assurance about the divine care and protection given the Holy Scriptures:

> The Bahá'ís believe that God's Revelation is under His care and protection and that the essence, or essential elements, of what His Manifestations intended to convey has been recorded

and preserved in Their Holy Books. However, as the sayings of the ancient Prophets were written down sometime later, we cannot categorically state, as we do in the case of the Writings of Bahá'u'lláh, that the words and phrases attributed to Them are Their exact words.[6]

Perhaps this care and protection were extended to the Hebrew prophets who spoke for God and whose divinely inspired words have spoken to hearts and minds for thousands of years. They not only labored to renew the Mosaic Dispensation, but they also caught glimpses of future Dispensations.

SYMBOLISM, METAPHORS, AND ALLUSIONS

As discussed in Volume 1, the Word of God has often been shrouded in various forms of symbolism, metaphors, and allusions. What was the reason? Bahá'u'lláh explained the purpose when He wrote:

Know verily that the purpose underlying all these symbolic terms and abstruse allusions, which emanate from the Revealers of God's holy Cause, hath been to test and prove the peoples of the world; that thereby the earth of the pure and illuminated hearts may be known from the perishable and barren soil. From time immemorial such hath been the way of God amidst His creatures, and to this testify the records of the sacred books.[7]

Abdu'l-Bahá, after speaking with a Christian audience about the multi-faceted meanings and ramifications of *"The Word was with God,"* cautioned: *"The intention of this explanation is to show that the Words of God have innumerable significances and mysteries of meanings—each one a thousand and more."*[8]

In other words, spiritual treasures are not presented on proverbial silver trays. The seeker must be willing to investigate and ponder before he can claim the treasures.

The truth lies within symbolism, metaphors, and allusions, yet we must remember that meanings are limitless. Bahá'u'lláh wrote to an

INTRODUCTION

Islamic mufti (legal expert) in Akka, *"Know assuredly that just as thou firmly believest that the Word of God, exalted be His glory, endureth forever, thou must, likewise, believe with undoubting faith that its meaning can never be exhausted."*[9]

It's also important to keep in mind that, to a certain extent, the Prophets spoke to the people within the context of their culture and within the framework of their history as they perceived it. In these instances, their remarks cannot be taken as verifications of traditional or biblical history. The preeminent early Bahá'í scholar Mírzá Abu'l-Faḍl Gulpáypání emphasized that the prophets and Manifestations of God were sent "to guide the nations, to improve their characters, and to bring the people nearer to their Source and ultimate Goal."[10] He then clarified that they were not sent as historians, astronomers, philosophers, or natural scientists. Therefore, the prophets have indulged the people in regard to their historical notions, folk stories, and scientific principles, and have spoken to them according to these. They conversed as was appropriate to their audience and hid certain realities behind the curtain of allusion.[11]

For example, the peoples' literal belief in Noah's flood could wait for another day for a symbolic interpretation, a day when the gradual forces of education and a broadening worldview had taken hold. Other situations, such as the corruption, greed, and opposition of the Jewish priesthood to Jesus, had to be confronted head-on. *"Woe to you, teachers of the law and Pharisees, you hypocrites! You clean the outside of the cup and dish, but inside they are full of greed and self-indulgence"* (Matt. 23:25).

THE CONCEPT OF DIVINE TIME

The subject of prophecy raises reasonable questions in the minds of rational people. How can anyone know the future? If God gave man free will, how can future events be known? Does man not have the will and capacity to create his own destiny? If something is predestined, isn't that unfair? Has God been micromanaging human affairs in ways that render human effort futile?

Perhaps the best approach to the enigma of divine time and prophetic time is to remember that this is God's world. He created it with all the natural laws that run it, and He has been intimately and continuously involved with His creation. He created time and space, but they are experienced quite differently for us on earth than in the infinite number of worlds of God. 'Abdu'l-Bahá illustrated divine time as follows:

> *In the world of God, there is no past, present, or future: All of these are one. So when Christ said, "In the beginning was the Word,"* He meant that it was, is, and shall be; for in the world of God there is no time. Time holds sway over the creatures but not over God. So in the prayer where Christ says, "Hallowed be Thy name",** the meaning is that Thy name was, is, and shall be hallowed. Again, morning, noon, and evening exist in relation to the earth, but in the sun there is neither morning, nor noon, nor evening.*[12]
> * John 1:1
> ** Matt. 6:9, Luke 11:2

Our concept of time—expressed as past, present, and future—might be described as only a tool for use on earth because in the worlds of God *there is no past, present, and future.* They are one. The linear time upon which we depend to understand our world and live our lives is not applicable to the worlds of God. 'Abdu'l-Bahá sympathized with our problem of understanding the idea of no past, present, or future. *"Know that it is one of the most abstruse questions of divinity that the world of existence—that is, this endless universe—has no beginning."*[13] And 'Abdu'l-Bahá elaborated on this concept when He wrote:

> *For God the beginning and the end are one and the same. Similarly, the reckoning of days, weeks, months, and years—of yesterday and today—is made with respect to the earth; but in the sun such things are unknown: There is neither yesterday, nor today, nor tomorrow, neither months nor years—all are equal. Likewise, the Word of God is sanctified above all these conditions and exalted beyond every law, constraint, or limitation that may exist in the contingent world.*[14]

INTRODUCTION

Does predetermination play a role in prophecy? Here's how 'Abdu'l-Bahá approached that question:

> *The knowledge of a thing is not the cause of its occurrence; for the essential knowledge of God encompasses the realities of all things both before and after they come to exist, but it is not the cause of their existence. This is an expression of the perfection of God.*
>
> *As to the pronouncements which, through divine revelation, have issued from the Prophets regarding the advent of the Promised One of the Torah, these likewise were not the cause of Christ's appearance. But the hidden mysteries of the days to come were revealed to the Prophets, who thus became acquainted with future events and who proclaimed them in turn. This knowledge and proclamation were not the cause of the occurrence of these events.*
>
> *In the same way, the record and mention of a thing in the Scriptures is not the cause of its existence. The Prophets of God were informed through divine revelation that certain events would come to pass. For instance, through divine revelation they came to know that Christ would be martyred, which they in turn proclaimed. Now, did their knowledge and awareness cause the martyrdom of Christ? No: This knowledge is a sign of their perfection and not the cause of His martyrdom.*
>
> *Through astronomical calculations, the mathematicians determine that at a certain time a solar or lunar eclipse will occur. Surely this prediction is not the cause of the eclipse. This of course is merely an analogy and not an exact image.*[15]

WRITING AND EDITING CONSIDERATIONS

Every effort was made to provide the context for all cited verses within their sources, within the continuity of the Hebrew experience and the socioeconomic conditions of the times. Excerpts from Bahá'í texts are provided to enhance understanding of various prophetic utterances. My own opinions are noted as such.

Unless noted otherwise, the *New International Version* (NIV) of the Bible is used throughout.

The title *Hebrew Bible* is used instead of the *Old Testament* because it is more accurate and respectful. The Old Testament is only *old* when it is paired with the New Testament and when its relevance is considered secondary to the coming of Jesus. As you progress through the volumes, you will discover how relevant the Hebrew Bible is to our times.

The acronyms BCE (before the Common Era) and CE (Common Era) are used instead of BC and AD.

Quotations from the Sacred Scriptures of all faiths are given in italics, including those from the three Central Figures of the Bahá'í Faith—the Báb, Bahá'u'lláh, and 'Abdu'l-Bahá. For Bahá'ís, the writings of the Central Figures are considered authoritative, as are the interpretations of Shoghi Effendi and the elucidations of the Universal House of Justice. All other interpretations of Scripture presented here are matters of opinion, offered as contributions to thought and understanding.

The book of Exodus introduces the term Yahweh (YHWH) for God, which was used for several centuries. I've used God for consistency, with the understanding that God and Yahweh are interchangeable.

The ancient people whose history the Hebrew Bible tells are called Israelites; Israelis, in contrast, are citizens of the modern state of Israel. The term *Jews* did not come into use until postexilic times when the former kingdom of Judah became the Persian province of Yehud.

The Manifestations of God, as understood in the Bahá'í teachings, are referred to as Prophets with a capital "P." A small "p" indicates the classical prophets. Pronouns referring to the Prophets and the central figures of the Bahá'í Faith are also capitalized.

Many chronologies of the kings of Israel and Judah have date variances with other chronologies. The earlier the reign, the higher is the probability of inaccuracy of as much as ten years for the earlier kings and two or three years for some of the later kings. Coregencies and rival reigns muddle the historical calendar considerably, not to mention that the two kingdoms used different methods of noting the dates of royal accessions and deaths. The factors involved in the dated chronologies of these kings can be found in the article "Has the chronology of the Hebrew kings been finally settled?" by Leslie McFall.[16]

INTRODUCTION

Concerning the dates of the prophets, it is immensely helpful that many of their books state the names of the kings who reigned during their missions or mentioned battles and natural catastrophes recorded in history, such as the vision Amos saw *"concerning Israel two years before the earthquake, when Uzziah [786–746] was king of Judah and Jeroboam [783–735] son of Jehoash was king of Israel"* (Amos 1:1). This was a major earthquake that has been dated by geologists to within a ten-year timeframe.

Unfamiliarity with the Hebrew Bible is not a barrier to understanding the material covered. Readers are encouraged to keep a Bible handy or to refer to Bible Gateway online (www.biblegateway.com).

This work is also written with the conviction that it is important to know the Bible because it speaks to us today. 'Abdu'l-Bahá admonished, *"You must know the Old and New Testaments as the Word of God."*[17] That says it all.

Charts

Chart of the Kings and Named Prophets*

Rulers of united kingdom	Approx. dates of reign	Prophets
Saul	c. 1030–1010	Samuel Medium at Endor
David	c. 1010–970	Nathan Gad
Solomon	c. 970–930	

CHARTS

The Divided Kingdoms

Kings of Israel	Approx. years BCE	Prophets of Israel	Kings of Judah	Approx. years BCE	Prophets of Judah
1. Jeroboam I (first three years united kingdom	930–910	Ahijah			
			1. Rehoboam	931–913	Shemaiah
			2. Abijah	913–911	
			3. Asa	911–870	Azariah Hanani – Asa, Jehoshaphat
2. Nadab	910-909				
3. Baasha	909–886	Jehu			
4. Elah	886-885				
5. Zimri	885				
6. Omri	885-874				
7. Ahab	874-853	Micaiah Elijah			
		Elisha – Ahaziah through Jehoash (Joash)	4. Jehoshaphat	870–848	Jehu Jahaziel Eliezer
8. Ahaziah	853-852				
9. Jehoram (Joram)	852-841		5. Jehoram (Joram)	848-841	
			6. Ahaziah	841	
10. Jehu	841-814		7. Athaliah	841–835	
			8. Joash	835–796	
11. Jehoahaz (Joahaz)	814–798				
12. Jehoash (Joash)	798-782				
			9. Amaziah	796–767	
13. Jeroboam II	782-753	Jonah (to Nineveh)			

The Divided Kingdoms

Kings of Israel	Approx. years BCE	Prophets of Israel	Kings of Judah	Approx. years BCE	Prophets of Judah
			10. Uzziah (Azariah)	767–740	First Isaiah – last year of Uzziah's reign through Jotham, Ahaz, and Hezekiah, possibly into Manasseh
14. Zechariah	747	during the 750s	11. Jotham	738-732	
15. Shallum	747	Hosea – Jeroboam II to Hoshea			
16. Menahem	747–737				
17. Pekahiah	737–735	Oded			Micah – Jotham, Ahaz, and Hezekiah, 730s to the 690s
18. Pekah	735–732				
			12. Ahaz	732-716	
19. Hoshea	732–722		13. Hezekiah	732-716	
Fall to Assyria in 722			14. Manasseh	716–697	
			15. Amon	642–640	
			16. Josiah (Josias)	640–608	Hulda – Josiah
			17. Jehoahaz (Joahaz)	608	Nahum – Josiah Zephaniah – Josiah
			18. Jehoakim	608–597	Habakkuk – Josiah, Jehoakim, 609–598
			19. Jehoiachin	597–	Jeremiah – Josiah through Zedekiah, and Gedaliah, governor
			20. Zedekiah	597–586	Uriah

CHARTS

Exilic and Postexilic Prophets, Plus Ezra and Nehemiah, with Approximate Dates	
Daniel	606–534
Ezekiel	596–574
Second Isaiah	No dates available, lived in the exile
Obadiah	Early sixth century soon after the fall of Jerusalem in 586
Haggai	Late sixth century
First Zechariah	520–518, the second year of the reign of Darius through his fourth year
Third Isaiah	About 520 to 500, or later
Ezra	The second half of the fifth century, starting the seventh year of the reign of Artaxerxes I, King of Persia, 457 BCE
Nehemiah	The second half of the fifth century, starting the twentieth year of the reign of Artaxerxes I, King of Persia, about 444 BCE
Second Zechariah	Perhaps a century after First Zechariah
Joel	Late fifth century or possibly early fourth
Malachi	Mid-fifth century or possibly later

* The above chart was inspired by the one constructed by Jonathan Petersen, content manager for Bible Gateway, that was posted on July 17, 2017. It does not include the various regencies and coregencies. A few changes were made by Maddocks according to her understanding of the chronologies, and she readily admits that no chart of the dated chronologies is entirely correct.
https://www.biblegateway.com/blog/2017/07/
updated-chart-of-israels-and-judahs-kings-and-prophets/

Maps

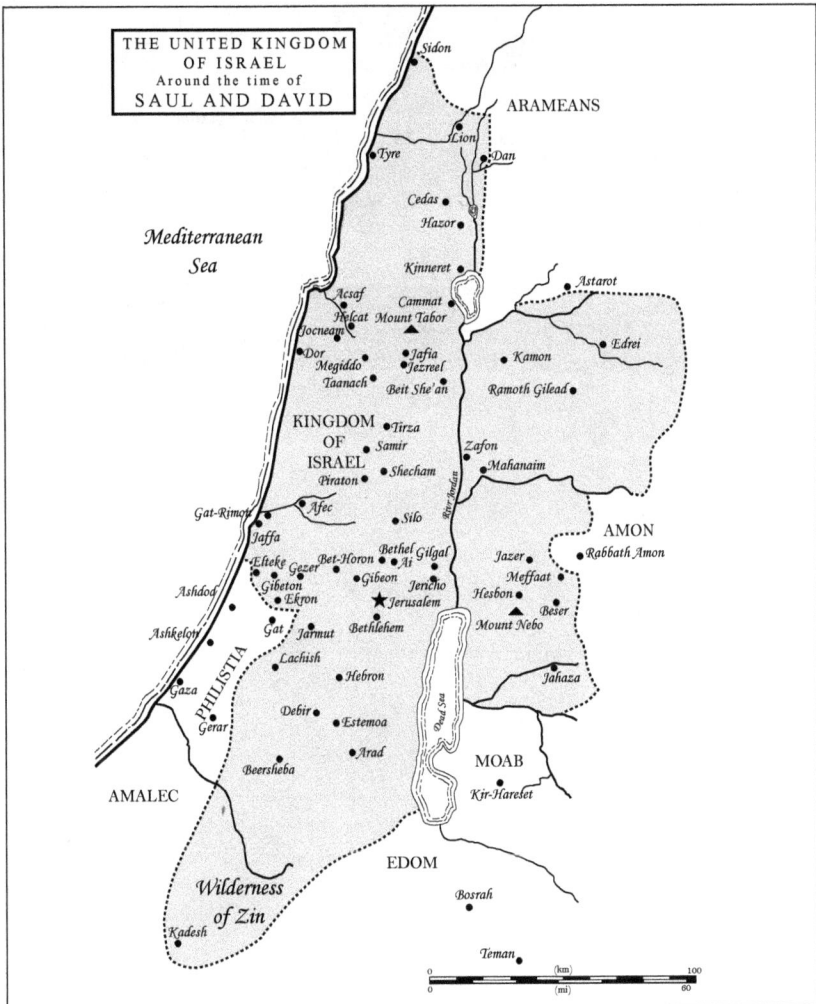

THE UNITED KINGDOM
OF ISRAEL
Around the time of
SAUL AND DAVID

Mediterranean
Sea

ARAMEANS

Sidon

Lion

Tyre

Dan

Cedas

Hazor

Kinneret

Astarot

Acsaf

Cammat
Mount Tabor

Helcat

Jocneam

Jafia

Kamon

Edrei

Dor

Jezreel

Megiddo

Taanach

Beit She'an

Ramoth Gilead

KINGDOM
OF
ISRAEL

Tirza

Samir

Zafon

Piraton

Shecham

Mahanaim

Gat-Rimon

Afec

Silo

AMON

Jaffa

Bethel
Ai

Gilgal

Jazer

Rabbath Amon

Efteke

Gezer

Bet-Horon

Gibeon

Jericho

Meffaat

Ashdod

Gibeton

Hesbon

Ekron

Jerusalem

Beser

Ashkelon

Gat

Jarmut

Bethlehem

Mount Nebo

Lachish

Gaza

PHILISTIA

Debir

Hebron

Jahaza

Gerar

Estemoa

Dead Sea

Arad

MOAB

Beersheba

Kir-Haretet

AMALEC

EDOM

Wilderness
of Zin

Bosrah

Kadesh

Teman

(km) 100

(mi) 60

River Jordan

MAPS

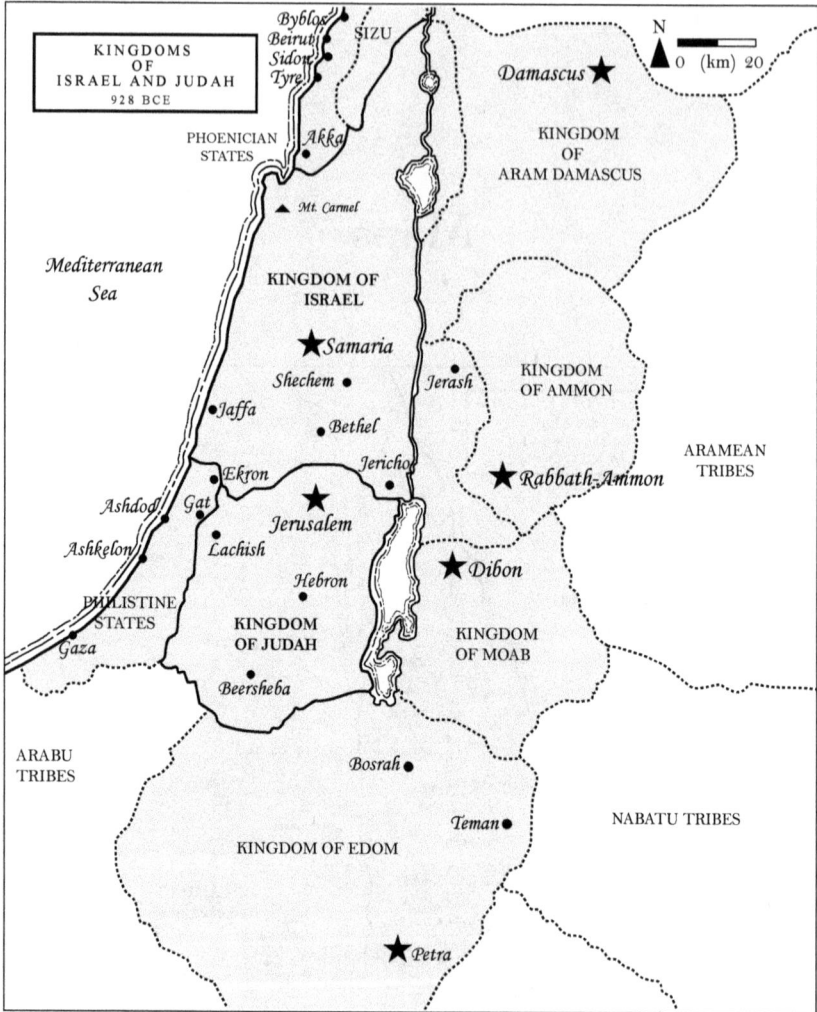

KINGDOMS
OF
ISRAEL AND JUDAH
928 BCE

Byblos
Beirut
Sidon
Tyre
SIZU

Damascus ★

PHOENICIAN
STATES

Akka

KINGDOM
OF
ARAM DAMASCUS

▲ Mt. Carmel

Mediterranean
Sea

KINGDOM OF
ISRAEL

★Samaria

Shechem ●

Jerash ●

KINGDOM
OF AMMON

ARAMEAN
TRIBES

● Jaffa

● Bethel

Jericho ●

★Rabbath-Ammon

Ekron ●

Ashdod Gat ●

★
Jerusalem

Ashkelon ●

Lachish ●

● Dibon

Hebron
●

PHILISTINE
STATES

KINGDOM
OF JUDAH

KINGDOM
OF MOAB

Gaza

● Beersheba

ARABU
TRIBES

Bosrah ●

Teman ●

NABATU TRIBES

KINGDOM OF EDOM

★Petra

N
▲ 0 (km) 20

Chapter 1

The Writing Prophets

No comprehensive definition of the Israelite prophet is possible.
The persons conventionally included in
this category appear to have
manifested great diversity of character and function.

R. N. WHYBRAY

THE HEBREW PROPHETS PLAYED a unique role in Israelite history for many centuries from the thirteenth or twelfth century BCE until the fifth. Among the earliest recorded prophets, and the first identified by name, was Balaam, whose story is found in the book of Numbers. He was not an Israelite, but he did recognize the one God.

The narrative states that the Moabite king, Balak, was afraid of the Israelites who camped on the plains of Moab after defeating the Amorites on the way to their incursion into the land of the Canaanites. He sent the elders of Moab and Midian to summon Balaam and ask him to put a curse on the Israelites. Balaam was a diviner for hire, while Balak's name meant "devastator" or "one who lays waste."[2]

Balaam was found and an offer was made. After Balaam settled in for the night, God came to him and asked who the men were. Balaam responded that they told him of a people that had come out of Egypt and covered the face of the land. These men had asked Balaam to put a curse on these intruders. *"But God said to Balaam, 'Do not go with them. You*

1

must not put a curse on those people, because they are blessed'" (Num. 22:12). The next morning, Balaam told the elders to go back to their own country *"for the LORD has refused to let me go with you"* (22:13).

Balaam must have had a sterling reputation with his curses because Balak sent another delegation of officials to repeat the request for an even higher payment. Balaam replied that not even for all the silver and gold in Balak's palace could he act against the command of the Lord. That night, God came to Balaam and told him, *"Since these men have come to summon you, go with them, but do only what I tell you"* (22:20). Balaam was to embark on his education as a prophet, not a diviner.

Enter the donkey that Balaam saddled the next morning for the trip to Moab. Three times on the trip the donkey saw an angel of the Lord blocking their way and tried to avoid it by stopping, and three times Balaam beat his donkey.

> *Then the Lord opened the donkey's mouth, and it said to Balaam, "What have I done to you to make you beat me these three times?"*
>
> *Balaam answered the donkey, "You have made a fool of me! If only I had a sword in my hand, I would kill you right now."*
>
> *The donkey said to Balaam, "Am I not your own donkey, which you have always ridden, to this day? Have I been in the habit of doing this to you?"*
>
> *"No," he said.*
> (Num. 22:28–30)

Then the Lord opened Balaam's eyes and he saw an angel who was blocking the way and told him to go with the men but to speak only what God told him. Upon arrival in Moab, Balaam forewarned Balak that this was the case, but Balak was adamant. He would have the Israelites cursed. Balaam asked that seven altars be prepared for the sacrifice of one bull and one ram on each of them. While the offering was being made, Balaam went off by himself to a barren height after telling Balak, *"Perhaps the Lord will come to meet with me. Whatever he reveals to me I will tell you"* (23:3). And the Lord indeed came to Balaam with a message and said, *"Go back to Balak and give him this word"* (23:5). Balaam returned to the Moabite officials:

> *And he took up his parable, and said, Balak the king of Moab hath brought me from Aram, out of the mountains of the east, saying, Come, curse me Jacob, and come, defy Israel.*
>
> *How shall I curse, whom God hath not cursed? or how shall I defy, whom the Lord hath not defied?*
>
> *For from the top of the rocks I see him, and from the hills I behold him: lo, the people shall dwell alone, and shall not be reckoned among the nations.*
>
> *Who can count the dust of Jacob, and the number of the fourth part of Israel? Let me die the death of the righteous, and let my last end be like his!*
>
> (Num. 23:7–10, KJV)

Balaam had been shown the separation of the Israelites from other people because they held the station of the chosen people. As Jewish history unfolded over thousands of years, the Jews did live in increasing separation from others, whether in their united or divided kingdoms or in exile in the Diaspora (the dispersion of the Jews from the Holy Land after the Babylonian and Roman conquests). In recent history, the modern state of Israel has existed relatively alone among the nations but, against all odds, Israel won its War of Independence in 1948–49, the Six-Day War of 1967, and the Yom Kippur War of 1973. Also standing relatively alone, Israel has withstood intifadas from the West Bank and missile barrages from Gaza and Lebanon while slowly succeeding in developing global trade relations and diplomatic recognition with some Arab and other countries that had historically been hostile.

Balak was not happy with Balaam's message and did not give up, so again a sacrifice was offered. Balaam withdrew to receive the word of God, and again he returned to the Moabite officials. Balaam delivered quite a condemnation to Balak for wishing it were not so.

God is not a man, that he should lie; neither the son of man, that he should repent: hath he said, and shall he not do it? or hath he spoken, and shall he not make it good?

Behold, I have received commandment to bless: and he hath blessed; and I cannot reverse it.

He hath not beheld iniquity in Jacob, neither hath he seen perverseness in Israel: the Lord his God is with him, and the shout of a king is among them.

God brought them out of Egypt; he hath as it were the strength of an unicorn.

Surely there is no enchantment against Jacob, neither is there any divination against Israel: according to **this time** *it shall be said of Jacob and of Israel,* **What hath God wrought!**

Behold, the people **shall rise up as a great lion,** *and lift up himself as a young lion: he shall not lie down until he eat of the prey, and drink the blood of the slain.*

(Num. 23:19–24, KJV, emphasis added)

How clearly spoken! Not only was there to be no enchantment or divination against the Israelites but it would be said of them, *What hath God wrought!* This famous verse was the first telegraphic message sent by Samuel Morse, which was sent on May 24, 1844. Because of the "coincidence" that this verse was sent the day after the Báb declared His mission, it appears that this verse from over three thousand years ago was alluding to the declaration of the Báb to His first disciple the previous evening. The term *this time* is also understood to mean the latter days, or the time of the end, which started in 1844 with the return of the Christ spirit embodied in the Báb.

To *rise up as a great lion* is suggestive of the formation of the modern state of Israel. Lions are mentioned many times in the Hebrew Bible in various descriptive and metaphorical contexts. The tribe of Judah was traditionally symbolized by a lion, dating from the day Jacob called his twelve sons together *that I may tell you that which shall befall you in* **the last days** (Gen. 49:1, KJV, emphasis added). Addressing his son Judah, Jacob said, *"Judah is a lion's whelp: from the prey, my son, thou art gone up: he stooped* *down, he couched as a lion, and as an old lion, who shall rouse him up?"* (Gen. 49:9, KJV, emphasis added).

The term *the last days* is another reference to 1844. The ten tribes of Israel were lost in dispersal throughout the Assyrian empire. The tribe of Judah was predominant in the southern kingdom of Judah. The Israelites, later called the Jews, who survived throughout the centuries in the Diaspora, were primarily descendants of the tribe of Judah and, to a lesser extent, of the tribes of Simeon and Benjamin, which had largely assimilated into the tribe of Judah.

After the third set of altars was built and sacrifices made, Balaam knew what to say and do without asking. Now he understood that God could not be contacted through divination and enchantments but only through faith and prayer. Balaam set his face to the wilderness, and the spirit of God came upon him. He saw the prosperity of the land and spoke, *"Blessed is he that blesseth thee, and cursed is he that curseth thee"* (Num. 24:9, KJV).

A frustrated Balak and an illumined Balaam parted ways, but not before Balak's parting shot that he would have promoted Balaam to great honor had he cooperated, and Balaam's parting prophecy, *"I shall see him, but not now: I shall behold him, but not nigh: there shall come a **Star** out of Jacob, and a **Sceptre** shall rise out of Israel..."* (24:17, KJV, emphasis added). The *Star* might refer to the Star of Bethlehem announcing the birth of Jesus Christ. Perhaps the *Sceptre* denotes the moral authority of Jesus because His kingdom was not of this world.

The six-pointed Star of David, which is often called the Shield of David, emerged in the seventeenth century CE as a symbol of Jewish identity and Judaism. The Star of David is now emblazoned on the flag of Israel. Jews were forced by the Nazis to wear a yellow star on their clothing. The Holocaust so chastened the "civilized" world that it hastened the establishment of the independent state of Israel. Modern Israel has wielded the authority of the *Sceptre* to both militarily protect the state and to safeguard freedom of religion to all persons living there. The *Sceptre* might also be a symbol of the spiritual authority of the Bahá'í Faith, which emanates from Mount Carmel in Israel through the Universal House of Justice.

5

THE WRITING PROPHETS

OTHER EARLY PROPHETS

Schools or guilds of prophets, known as the "sons of the prophets," emerged early in Hebrew history. They could be roving bands, but they often lived in communities under leaders such as Samuel, Elijah, and Elisha. Since the days of Moses, there had also been cult prophets associated with priests and shrines and, later, with the Jerusalem Temple. The court prophets, such as Nathan, appeared with the united monarchy. One of the first and best-remembered preaching prophets of record was Elijah, who directly addressed and chastised King Ahab and the court prophets (see Vol. 1, Chapter 13).

During the early years of Israelite history, there were solitary prophets whose names were not given but who were remembered as men of God. Such was the case of the prophet who delivered God's message to the priest Eli, whose two sons and heirs were corrupt and unfit to take their father's place:

> *Now a man of God came to Eli and said to him, "This is what the Lord says: 'Did I not clearly reveal myself to your ancestor's family when they were in Egypt under Pharaoh?'*
>
> *"And what happens to your two sons, Hophni and Phinehas, will be a sign to you—they will both die on the same day. I will raise up for myself a faithful priest, who will do according to what is in my heart and mind. I will firmly establish his priestly house, and they will minister before my anointed one always."'*
> (1 Sam. 2:27, 34–35)

Samuel, who had been dedicated to God by his mother as a small boy, was in training under Eli. The Lord was with Samuel as he matured to manhood. Upon Eli's death, Samuel became the leader of Israel.

A named prophet often appeared just once in a narrative. The book of 1 Kings relates how the prophet Ahijah was divinely directed to tell Jeroboam, a well-regarded construction foreman, that he was to succeed King Solomon as monarch of the northern kingdom of Israel (1 Kings 11:29–31). Rehoboam (931–913), son of Solomon, set out to do battle

6

with Jeroboam (930–910 BCE), who was leading a rebellion against him in the north when a prophet named Shemaiah delivered to Rehoboam a message from God dissuading him from that course of action.

> *But this word of God came to Shemaiah the man of God: "Say to Rehoboam son of Solomon king of Judah, to all Judah and Benjamin, and to the rest of the people, 'This is what the Lord says: Do not go up to fight against your brothers, the Israelites. Go home, every one of you, for this is my doing.'" So they obeyed the word of the Lord and went home again, as the Lord had ordered.* (1 Kings 12:22–24)

Despite the special place that the Hebrew prophets held in Israelite society, this was a rare example of the people following a prophet's advice. Rehoboam sacrificed a major piece of his kingdom to do so. The two kingdoms would engage in battle with each other in the decades ahead, and then they would reverse course to become allies to battle other enemies.

Why would God prefer that the kingdom be divided? Perhaps the reason was that the experiences of the two kingdoms and their people were needed as stern examples of the perils of ignoring their Covenant with God and His laws. Ultimately these two kingdoms would provide far more effective teaching examples and theological perplexities than one kingdom, Israel, could have within one hundred and eighty-five years. The Hebrew experience was a major event in human religious history. Judah added more than a hundred and thirty years to the Israelite regnal experience and to the era of the Hebrew prophets. Imagine Hebrew history without First Isaiah and Jeremiah! Those years of Judah, together with Israel's, would contribute greatly to human spiritual growth.

THE PROPHET MICAIAH

The prophet Micaiah caused a commotion and much royal distress. King Jehoshaphat of Judah (870–848 BCE) was allied with King Ahab (874–853) of Israel in a fight against Ramoth Gilead, a city east of the Jordan River in Gilead. Because no decision about warfare could be made without divine guidance, Ahab summoned his four hundred court prophets and asked them if he would triumph. They vociferously and unanimously replied that the Lord would deliver Ramoth Gilead into Ahab's hands. However, Jehoshaphat was suspicious and asked for a second opinion. Ahab answered that there was only one other prophet through whom they could inquire of the Lord, *"but I hate him because he never prophesies anything good about me, but always bad. He is Micaiah son of Imlah"* (1 Kings 22:8).

A messenger went to summon Micaiah and told him that the other prophets were all predicting success for the king, so he had better play it safe and agree with them. But Micaiah replied, *"As surely as the Lord lives, I can tell him only what the Lord tells me"* (22:14). Bravely spoken. But upon meeting Ahab, a much-intimidated Micaiah initially echoed the four hundred. Ahab remonstrated, *"How many times must I make you swear to tell me nothing but the truth in the name of the Lord?"* (22:16). So, Micaiah found his courage and replied forthrightly in contradiction to the court prophets, *"I saw all Israel scattered on the hills like sheep without a shepherd, and the Lord said, 'These people have no master. Let each one go home in peace'"* (22:17). Ahab was embarrassed in front of Jehoshaphat and moaned that Micaiah never prophesied anything good about him, only the bad.

Micaiah then explained his prophecy to the kings. He had seen the Lord sitting on His throne with the multitudes of heaven. *"And the Lord said, 'Who will entice Ahab into attacking Ramoth Gilead and going to his death there?' One suggested this, and another that. Finally, a spirit came forward, stood before the Lord and said, 'I will entice him ... I will go out and be a deceiving spirit in the mouths of all his prophets'"* (22:20, 22). And by the leave of the Lord, this spirit did so. As Micaiah told Ahab, *"So now the Lord has put a deceiving spirit in the mouths of all these prophets of yours. The Lord has decreed disaster for you"* (22:23). Ahab and Jehoshaphat attacked Ramoth Gilead anyway and Ahab was killed in the battle. Nothing further was written about Micaiah, whom Ahab had put in prison with *"nothing but bread and water until I return safely"* (22:27). It was not noted whether Micaiah died in prison or was released by the next king.

The prophet Elijah appeared during the reign of Ahab and alternately assisted and challenged him and his two sons and heirs, Jehoram (852–841), who was murdered after eleven years, and Ahaziah (841), who died within a year or two of injuries from a fall. Jehu, an army officer, became the next king. The adventures and misadventures of the hapless kings of Israel continued until the Assyrian conquest of Samaria in 722 BCE and were entwined with the anecdotal prophets and then with Amos and Hosea.

THE CLASSICAL PROPHETS

The last phase of biblical Hebrew prophecy, the classical prophets, also known as the canonical prophets because their books were put in the canon of the Hebrew Bible, began in the eighth century BCE and lasted through the fifth. The accounts of the earlier prophets such as Nathan, Micaiah, Elijah, and Elisha had been preserved as anecdotes within a large narrative context. It was a significant development when collections of individual prophets' speeches were put into written form and preserved as named books, although often not during the times of the prophets themselves.

The biblical scholar William Schniedewind notes that, ironically, the earliest of the four writing prophets—Isaiah, Micah, Amos, and Hosea—were not writers at all.

By calling them "writing" prophets, they are contrasted with figures like Nathan or Elijah, who do not have independent books. But in the books ascribed to them, the early writing prophets are rarely portrayed as having *written* anything. God commands them to speak, not to write. There are no books in their books! Writing is a marginal activity for the eighth-century prophets. So who wrote their books? The prophetic books of Isaiah, Micah, Amos, and Hosea contain superscriptions that place them in the second half of the eighth century BCE. These superscriptions point to the editorial activity of collecting prophetic oracles. Although the superscriptions are widely regarded as later additions to the prophetic literature, they do seem to accurately place the prophets historically.[3]

None of the superscriptions in these four prophetic books mentions any king after Hezekiah (715 and 686 BCE), which indicates that these books were likely compiled and edited during his reign. Schniedewind commented that they supported the Davidic monarchy.

As David Noel Freedman, professor of biblical studies at the University of California, San Diego, has suggested, "the collection of the books of the four prophets were assembled during the reign of Hezekiah, to celebrate and interpret the extraordinary sequence of events associated with the Assyrian invasion of Judah and investment of Jerusalem, along with the departure of the Assyrian army and the deliverance of that city." Ultimately, all of these books support the Davidic monarch, and Hezekiah's scribes would have had good reason to collect them.[4]

The use of writing was the purview of royal courts and the priesthood. Priestly scribes would not have been inclined to preserve the words of prophets who castigated them. The role of writing became more central for later prophets such as Jeremiah, Ezekiel, and Zachariah, which reflected the rising rate of literacy in the seventh century and beyond. Indeed, Jeremiah had a scribe who was identified as Baruch ben Neriah.

A significant departure of the classical prophets from the professional prophets is that the former were called by God, not trained in schools. The intensity of the voices of these independent prophets compelled attention and the preservation of their words. Their personalities and voices are each distinctly evident in their books. This factor lends veracity to their words having been adequately preserved and the original documents used at least partially, or even primarily, as the foundation of the final books bearing their names. It's probable that followers formed schools to preserve the prophets' legacies, which resulted in the books we have today that have earned their place among the world's greatest literature.

The classical prophets are generally divided into major and minor groups for rather practical reasons. Isaiah, Jeremiah, and Ezekiel are categorized as major prophets because their books are the largest and the three of them fit on one scroll. The twelve minor prophets, whose books could fit on another scroll, are Hosea, Joel, Amos, Obadiah, Jonah, Micah, Nahum, Habakkuk, Zephaniah, Haggai, Zechariah, and Malachi. The sixteenth prophet, Daniel, is considered a major prophet by Christians but not by Jews.

The Hebrew Bible consists of three sections—the Torah (the five books of Moses, or the Pentateuch), the Nevi'im (the prophets), and the Ketuvim (the writings). The book of Daniel is included in the Ketuvim.

Counting the actual number of prophets gets complicated when one considers that the book of Isaiah was written by three or more individuals and the book of Zechariah by two.

Only the prophet Jonah preached outside the Holy Land because God sent him to Nineveh in Mesopotamia, hundreds of miles from the kingdom of Israel. Only two of the prophets—Amos and Hosea—preached in Israel, although Amos was a native of Judah.

The prophets can generally be divided between preexilic and postexilic. Six of the prophets appeared in preexilic Judah—First Isaiah, Micah, Zephaniah, Nahum, Habakkuk, and Jeremiah. However, Daniel was reportedly deported to Babylon in 605 BCE and Ezekiel in 597. They could be considered both preexilic and postexilic. Jeremiah was primarily preexilic, but he survived the fall of Jerusalem to the Babylonians in 597 and was forced by circumstances beyond his control to continue prophesying during the early postexilic months or perhaps as long as a couple of years. The postexilic prophets were Obadiah, Haggai, Second and Third Isaiah, First and Second Zechariah, Malachi, and Joel.

Called by God and answerable only to God, these prophets usually found themselves in opposition to the court and the priesthood. Their mandate was to bring the people back into their covenantal relationship with God. Justice and holiness were the main factors in Mosaic law, the warp and woof of God's laws. The prophets hammered these teachings home and exposed the corruption of their times. Though they confronted the rulers and the priestly establishment, they never fomented revolution. God would handle the aberrancies of their time in His own good time.

The prophets' relationships with their kings were intriguing. Traditionally in the Middle East, kings were demi-gods to be worshipped or, at the very least, to be considered the major conduit through whom the will of the gods was made known. But the Israelite prophets, although loyal to their kings, insisted that no king had any claim to divinity. A monumental achievement of the Israelite people had been the founding of a society based not on the rule of a god-king, or of any king, but on a covenant between God and His people. This was especially true during the age of the judges that preceded the first anointed king, Saul. Royalty was neither exempt from the obligations of the Mosaic Covenant nor free of the wrath of the prophets.

This new wave of educated and eloquent prophets came from varied backgrounds. They used pantomime, props, oratory, allegories, cryptic allusions, and forthright statements that could be denied, but not easily ignored. They spoke not only to kings and priests but also to the people at large. For the first time in known religious prophecy, prophecies were given of the destruction of an entire nation as punishment for its sins, although usually this fate could be avoided through repentance. One particular exception came from Jeremiah, who maintained that the fate of Judah and her conquest by the Babylonians could not be avoided. But regardless of how severe the coming catastrophes might be, there would always be survivors.

These prophets were the followers of Moses, the Prophet for their time. The Bahá'í Faith distinguishes between the Prophets of God who are followed and the lesser prophets who follow Them. The Prophets of God each brought a new Dispensation, a new Book (whether written or oral), and new social and religious laws for their times. Their essential radiance was like the sun. 'Abdu'l-Bahá contrasted this with the nature and role of the Hebrew prophets, whose station was contingent rather than independent.

12

They acquire divine grace from the independent Prophets and seek the light of guidance from the reality of universal prophethood. They are like the moon, which is not luminous and radiant in and of itself but which receives its light from the sun.

The universal Prophets Who have appeared independently include Abraham, Moses, Christ, Muḥammad, the Báb, and Bahá'u'lláh. The second kind, which consists of followers and promulgators, includes Solomon, David, Isaiah, Jeremiah, and Ezekiel. For the independent Prophets are founders; that is, They establish a new religion, recreate the souls, regenerate the morals of society, and promulgate a new way of life and a new standard of conduct. Through Them a new Dispensation appears and a new religion is inaugurated. Their advent is even as the springtime, when all earthly things don a new garment and find a new life.

As to the second kind of Prophets, who are followers, they promulgate the religion of God, spread His Faith, and proclaim His Word. They have no power or authority of their own, but derive theirs from the independent Prophets.[5]

Each of the Hebrew follower-prophets received a divine call, known as the call narrative, that authorized him to speak for God within the Mosaic Dispensation. Some of the prophets accepted the call unquestioningly and others reluctantly. The call was not for a singular event, but for a commitment that could last a year or a lifetime. Once they accepted their missions, these prophets were under divine compulsion to deliver God's messages.

The prophets' messages were always spoken in the name of God; therefore, logically, they could only be the truth, however disturbing or disparaging. For this reason, the prophets were relieved of personal responsibility for their words and were entitled to prophetic immunity, that is, protection from persecution and worse. Enforcement of this protection was uneven. Isaiah and Jeremiah were persecuted and imprisoned at various times, and it has been traditionally believed that the anecdotal prophet Zechariah was stoned to death upon the order of Jehoash (Joash) (835–796) after warning the people that their disobedience to the Lord's commands would bring His wrath (2 Chron. 24:20–21; Matt. 23:25).

The fearlessness and zealotry in these prophets' undivided loyalty to God and their missions were extraordinary, especially considering that they worked alone and stood alone against tremendous opposition. A few of them were contemporaries but no evidence of collaborative or even friendly relationships between them have survived.

Standing alone, though, did not mean that a prophet's words were heard by only a few. On the contrary! There were places where a prophet could reach hundreds of people a day, from where his words could be spread far and wide. Those places were the city gates, the Temple courtyard, and the hilltop shrines. Cities were fortified and access was often limited to one gate, although Jerusalem had several. The city gate was not only the way in and out of the city. It was also a marketplace, the tax collector's office, and the courtroom. The king and city elders heard petitions and gave pronouncements at city gates. What better place to attract attention and challenge conventional beliefs?

The prophets served as divinely appointed messengers who were raised up in times of moral decline and apostasy. Inevitably, there were serious clashes between them and the kings, the priests, and the court prophets. Despite the tense atmosphere, desperate kings would sometimes consult these irksome prophets in times of national peril. Although the prophets showed an uncanny understanding of geopolitics, their guidance was always to trust in God because diplomatic and military alliances made without trust in God, or in disobedience to His counsel given through the prophet, would always fail. These were not the talking points that would influence the powers at court. The prophets were united in their warnings first about the Assyrian empire and, later, the Babylonian, two menaces on the horizon the likes of which the Israelites had never faced. The kingdoms of Israel and Judah had mostly fought each other or small bordering tribal entities. Now the kingdoms faced imperial armies and the specter of utter destruction and exile. The prophets attributed these threats entirely to the collapse of moral standards, disobedience to the Mosaic Covenant, and idolatry. The worship of Molech was especially abhorrent because of its child sacrifices by fire in the valley of Hinnom, which could be seen from Jerusalem. The worship of Asherah, also called Astarte, was a close second. She was an ancient Middle Eastern fertility goddess that the Canaanites had adopted from Mesopotamia. There was also the worship of the starry host and all sorts of imaginary deific beings. Incredibly, places in Solomon's Temple had been set aside for idolatrous worship.

Were Israel and Judah any more sinful than the nations around them? That was not the point, even though idolatry, sacred prostitution, child sacrifice, and social inequity were the norm throughout the Middle East. The Mosaic Dispensation, though, had fostered a spiritual, benevolent civilization that put the Israelites ahead of their neighbors (see commentary on the Covenant Code, the Holiness Code, and the Deuteronomic Code, Chapter 9 in Vol. 1). The bar had been set high with the admonition to be holy. *"The Lord said to Moses, 'Speak to the entire assembly of Israel and say to them: Be holy because I, the Lord your God, am holy'"* (Lev. 19:1–2).

'Abdu'l-Bahá summarized the station of the Hebrews when he stated: *"Moses established laws and ordinances that conferred new life upon the people of Israel and led them to attain the highest degree of civilization at that time."*[6] The Hebrews had been chosen to receive the Mosaic Revelation during whose spring and summer they achieved the highest level of social and spiritual development at that time, and this factor made their failings far more grievous than those of their neighbors (see Appendix D for 'Abdu'l-Bahá's talk on the divine seasons). That is why the prophets excoriated the people for their sins. Jesus would later explain, *"From everyone who has been given much, much will be demanded; and from the one who has been entrusted with much, much more will be asked"* (Luke 12:48).

Some of the prophets' predictions came to pass relatively quickly, such as the fall of the kingdoms of Israel and Judah to the Assyrians and Babylonians, respectively. But some of their prophecies were so far into the future that I call them "far future," "distant future," and "time shifts." Many prophecies were layered and had more than one meaning, and sometimes the prophets moved suddenly from the present to the far future. In the prophets' books, these time shifts often pop up unexpectedly, bookended by comments about their present time.

The books of the prophets were not intended to be historical records, although oftentimes they were quite accurate in that respect. They represented a religious and theological perspective in deeply emotional, compassionate tones and often in poetic, expressive literary forms. The prophets' anguish bleeds through. At times they seem like haunted beings.

Abraham Heschel (1907–1972 CE), a Polish-born American rabbi and one of the leading Jewish theologians and philosophers of the twentieth century, encapsulated the voice of the prophets as God's expression of rage at mankind's behavior.

> The prophet is a man who feels fiercely. God has thrust a burden upon his soul, and he is bowed and stunned at man's fierce greed. Frightful is the agony of man; no human voice can convey its full terror. Prophecy is the voice that God has lent to the silent agony, a voice to the plundered poor, to the profaned riches of the world. It is a form of living, a crossing point of God and man. God is raging in the prophet's words.[7]

Heschel also emphasized the iconoclastic aspects of the prophets. "The prophet is an iconoclast, challenging the apparently holy, revered, and awesome. Beliefs challenged as certainties, institutions endowed with supreme sanctity, he exposes as scandalous pretensions."[8]

The eschatological content relating to death, judgment, and the fate of humankind was high hyperbole that was sometimes used in desperate circumstances to wake up the people. The impending judgment of God was not presented in conversational tones! Likewise, the promises of a postexilic restoration of the people to their homeland were not afterthoughts. The restoration of the remnant was a theme presented many times to keep hope alive.

Each prophet was profoundly individual in fulfilling his mission, a factor that makes generalizations about the prophets difficult. But each was far more than a messenger, or an enlightened, insightful soul. He was in communion with God to the extent that he was given glimpses of the world through God's eyes. Again, Heschel cast light on the perplexities of the prophets.

> The prophet does not judge the people by timeless norms, but from the point of view of God. Prophecy proclaims what happened to God as well as what will happen to the people. In judging human affairs, it unfolds a divine situation. Sin is not only the violation of a law, it is as if sin were as much a loss to God as to man. God's role is not spectatorship but involvement. He and man meet mysteriously in the human deed. The prophet cannot say man without thinking God.
>
> Therefore, the prophetic speeches are not factual pronouncements. ... not objective criticism or the cold proclamation of doom. He dwells on God's inner motives, not only upon His historical decisions. He discloses *a divine pathos*, not just a divine judgment.
>
> The divine pathos is the key to inspired prophecy.[9]

The era of the writing prophets waned during the fifth century after the Jews had reestablished themselves in Judah and rebuilt Jerusalem and the Temple following their return from the Exile. The ruling trilogy of kings, prophets, and the priesthood of former times was reduced by the end of the fifth century to one authority—the priesthood—and that is why the priesthood was so powerful during the time of Jesus.

The classical prophets not only gave consolation and hope for millennia, but they also delivered prophecies relevant to our time. How best can we approach the nature of prophecy in the Bible? The biblical scholar Michael Sours wrote that prophecy goes beyond prediction.

> Prophecy is not merely about prediction—it is not merely a divine or magical knowledge of things that should and/ or would come about in the future. Prophecy is about God's

17

promises, and these promises teach us important things about the nature of God and the purpose of life. Biblical prophecy teaches that God is a personal God, a God who cares about humankind, Who makes promises and keeps them. Prophecy calls attention to God's presence, and awareness of this can provide an important confirmation of faith. From what prophecies say about the future, humanity is reminded of where it is headed and what it can attain through faith and obedience—its spiritual potential and destiny.[10]

Sours also wrote succinctly about that all-important biblical concept—redemption.

The prophecies, as recorded in the great Biblical tradition, also give meaning to the history of humankind. This history is one of "redemption." That is, there is a divine plan running through human history. Redemptive history is a theme common to the Bible, the Qur'án, and other Scriptures; it is also one of the main themes of *The Book of Certitude* (see *God Passes By*, 139). Some events may be cyclical or recurring, like a wheel, such as the rise and fall of civilizations and the successive appearances of divine Messengers; but this wheel is also moving in a particular direction—toward the redemption of humankind.[11]

One can wonder why so much divine energy was put into the era of the Hebrew prophets. Once a Dispensation of God passes through its summer and enters the fall and winter of its degradation, this process is not reversed. There are always laudable reform movements within the religion of a Dispensation, but they don't ultimately succeed. The process of the divine seasons will not be annulled. The next Dispensation has been scheduled, and a normal process of divine continuity will resume the process of educating humanity.

So why was so much divine energy put into the era of the Hebrew prophets? To ponder answers to this question, we must consider that the

Hebrew prophets were divinely shown far beyond their times to speak to the world today.

One can also ponder whether the prophets "failed" because they didn't succeed in significantly renewing the Mosaic Covenant, although a few hearts and minds were touched and lives were changed. I believe they succeeded grandly in their larger purpose. Rather than saving the Israelites from conquest by the Assyrians and the Babylonians, the prophets prompted the first known example of a people accepting catastrophe as just punishment for their sins. The prophets' teachings of Mosaic ethics and morality were not only preserved for the ages but were spread around the world and have been venerated to this day.

In addition, it became apparent to me that, except for Jonah, all the classical prophets, to one extent or another, foretold the coming of future Manifestations of God, especially the Báb and Bahá'u'lláh.

Chapter 2

Jonah – A Most Reluctant Prophet

Adam hid in the Garden of Eden.
Moses tried to substitute his brother.
Jonah jumped a boat and was swallowed by a whale...
Man likes to run from God. It's a tradition.

MITCH ALBUM

THE BOOK OF JONAH is short with forty-eight verses in four chapters. Rather than focusing on Jonah's mission to transmit the words of God, His warnings and encouragements, Jonah's saga concentrates primarily on himself and his all-too-human character defects as he grapples with obedience to God and his own inclinations. Jonah's story is an allegory rather than an ancient remembrance of events; it is a metaphoric tale of divine mercy rather than prophetic oracles. Jonah insists arrogantly on divine wrath with no understanding that no man could bear God's wrath and His justice, without a measure of mercy and hope.

There is consensus among biblical scholars that the book of Jonah was written sometime between the sixth and fourth centuries BCE, a time when the Hebrews were trying to comprehend the tragedy of the Exile. The tone of this book is so different from the other prophetic books that it has sometimes been considered a parody or satire of the Hebrew prophets and even a depiction of an antiprophet or antihero.

This book has no superscription or historical marker that would place it in the time of any specific king. The only reference to a man named Jonah outside the book of Jonah is found in 2 Kings 14:25: *"He [Jeroboam II of Israel, 788–747], was the one who restored the boundaries of Israel from Lebo Hamath to the Dead Sea, in accordance with the word of the LORD, the God of Israel, spoken through his servant Jonah son of Amittai, the prophet from Gath Hepher."* This Jonah may have been a court prophet who assisted the king to expand his kingdom.

The eighth-century Jonah may have been the subject of the book of Jonah since his call identified him as the son of Amittai. *"The word of the LORD came to Jonah son of Amittai: 'Go to the great city of Nineveh and preach against it, because its wickedness has come up before me'"* (Jonah 1:1–2). Or his name could have been borrowed from 2 Kings to establish him as a historical figure.

Jonah's call was forthright and surprising. He was the only Hebrew prophet who was assigned to work outside the kingdoms of Israel or Judah and, in this case, in the heart of the enemy. Nineveh, the capital of the dreaded Assyrian empire, was in upper Mesopotamia, and today it lies partially under the city of Mosul, Iraq. Nineveh was the largest Mesopotamian city with an estimated population of 120,000.[2] It was the capital of the Assyrian empire from the early ninth century BCE until its demise in the late seventh. Archeologists have determined that the city wall surrounding Nineveh was seven and a half miles long and had eighteen monumental gates. A vast system of canals brought water to the city and the fields.

Sennacherib (704–681), the nemesis of King Hezekiah of Judah (727–698 BCE) as we shall see in Chapter 6, built a massive palace in Nineveh. He was a hydraulic engineer at heart and designed a complex system of canals that not only extended agricultural land around Nineveh but also supplied water to the city and its innumerable parks, gardens, and orchards. The Assyriologist Gwendolyn Leick expressed the common belief among archeologists and historians of Assyria that "The 'Hanging Gardens of Babylon' are much more likely to refer to Sennacherib's complex artificial plantations and waterworks in Nineveh."[3]

However, within a few decades, the Assyrian empire was crumbling. It was defeated in 612 by a coalition of enemies that included the Babylonians. A dying Nineveh hung on during the Babylonian and Persian empires and then faded from history. A small mound remained within the city limits that was eventually occupied by a mosque built within the remains of a Christian monastery. This mound was known as Tell Nebi Yunus, the Mount of the Prophet Jonah, who, according to tradition, was buried there.[4]

God is the central character of the text, although Jonah provides most of the action as he deals with a great storm, a huge fish, a miraculous plant, a voracious worm, and a scorching east wind. God acts and Jonah reacts in a flawed manner. At one point he rises to the best within himself and fulfills his mission, after which we see him flounder when God forgives the Ninevites.

THE NUMBER THREE

Jonah was the one exception to the classical prophets who either accepted their call without hesitation or after only initial resistance. Jonah bluntly refused. He *"ran away from the Lord and headed for Tarshish. He went down to Joppa, where he found a ship bound for that port. After paying the fare, he went aboard and sailed for Tarshish to flee from the Lord"* (Jonah 1:3).

Jonah could run but he couldn't hide. The violent storm that arose could be a symbol of Jonah's spiritual crisis, his inner turmoil at defying God, through which he blissfully slept. The sailors prayed to their gods and threw overboard everything they could to lighten the ship's load, but to no avail. The next step was to cast lots with the crew to discover who was responsible for the storm. The lot fell to Jonah, who answered their questions by explaining, *"I am a Hebrew and I worship the Lord, the God of heaven, who made the sea and the dry land"* (1:9). The sympathetic sailors asked what they could do to calm the seas, and Jonah took responsibility. *"Pick me up and throw me into the sea,"* he replied, *"and it will become calm. I know that it is my fault that this great storm has come upon you"* (1:12). Was this a brave motion to sacrifice his life for others? Or was it the first of several times when Jonah would express a preference for death over life if life meant having to work through his spiritual issues?

The sailors hurled Jonah overboard while beseeching the Lord not to hold them accountable for killing an innocent man. The sea grew calm, and Jonah was given an opportunity to reflect and repent. *"Now the Lord provided a huge fish to swallow Jonah, and Jonah was in the belly of the fish **three days and three nights"*** (1:17, emphasis added).

Rabbi R. Baruch, an Israeli Orthodox rabbi, wrote a commentary on the symbolic meaning of the number three in Scripture:

> The number "three" is one of the most significant numbers in the Scriptures. Its primary purpose is for the sake of revealing or documenting something as fact (testing in order to validate something). It is also connected to the outcome of the will of G-d. One of the most famous occurrences for the number three is found in the Book of Jonah, where Jonah is in the belly of the fish "three days and three nights." A major aspect of the Book of Jonah is that the prophet was fleeing from the presence of HaShem [G-D]. Instead of Jonah going to Nineveh as G-d had commanded, the prophet desired not to obey this commandment, even if it meant that his relationship with G-d would be destroyed. HaShem decided to test in order to see if Jonah really preferred to end his relationship with G-d rather than go to Nineveh. By placing Jonah in the belly of the fish for three days and three nights, it would be revealed whether it was true that Jonah wanted to end his relationship with G-d over this commandment to go to Nineveh. It is most significant that immediately after (in the next verse) the reader is informed that Jonah was in the belly of the fish for three days and three nights. What does Jonah do? The text states that Jonah prayed to the L-rd his G-d from within the fish. Hence, the three days and three nights ultimately revealed, proved, or documented that what Jonah said he wanted was not true. One could also say that Jonah was tested for those

three days and three nights and the test results showed that he did not want to end his relationship with G-d and in the end Jonah went to Nineveh.[5]

A Catholic approach to the number three is similar. An article by Michael E. Hunt on the Agape Catholic Bible Study website states, "In sacred Scripture, the number three represents that which is solid, real, substantial, and something in its completeness. This number operates as a 'sign-post' in Scripture study for the reader to 'pay attention' to the significance of the next event."[6]

Several usages of the number three in the Hebrew Bible illustrate these symbolic meanings. Moses stretched out his hand toward the sky and total darkness covered Egypt for three days. Saul searched for his father's lost donkeys for three days before meeting with the seer Samuel, who anointed him the first king of Israel. Three years after the death of Solomon, his heir Rehoboam considered for three days his decision that led to rebellion and the separation of the united kingdom into two. Jonah's *three days and three nights* were referred to by Jesus in response to the request for a sign from some Pharisees.

> *He answered, "A wicked and adulterous generation asks for a sign! But none will be given it except the* **sign of the prophet Jonah.** *For as Jonah was three days and three nights in the belly of a huge fish, so* **the Son of Man will be three days and three nights in the heart of the earth.** *The men of Nineveh will stand up at the judgment with this generation and condemn it; for they repented at the preaching of Jonah, and now something greater than Jonah is here."*
> (Matt. 12:39–41, emphasis added)

The *sign of Jonah* could have been an alert to Jesus's followers about the full three days after His crucifixion (see below). In addition, an extra day would have assisted them to attain stability in their faith, to contemplate Jesus's teachings on an internalized, stronger level than before realized. His followers would have more fully realized that Jesus was the

Messiah, the Prophet of God, to the point where they could arise in steadfast service to Him without His physical presence.

Jesus's statement that *the Son of Man will be three days and three nights in the heart of the earth* flags a question. How does the time from the crucifixion to the resurrection as told in the Gospels, lasting from Friday midday through Sunday at the ninth hour, equal three full days and nights? Even though it does not, this discrepancy has been mostly ignored. Let's examine it.

All four Gospels record the early morning crowing of a rooster (Matt: 26:74, Mark 14:72, Luke 22:60, John 18:27) while Jesus was being interrogated by Caiaphas, the high priest. Following this, Jesus was taken to Pontius Pilate for interrogation and judgment. Jesus was then forced to carry the cross to Golgotha where He was crucified. The Gospels of Matthew, Mark, and Luke note darkness that started at noon and lasted until three in the afternoon. There were three hours of darkness.

The synoptic Gospels also agree that Jesus expired at three in the afternoon on a Friday before the Sabbath (Matt. 27:45–46, Mark 15:34, and Luke 23:44–46). Only the Gospel of John sheds light on the disparity between *three days and three nights* and the two days and two nights recorded in the other three Gospels.

> *When he had received the drink, Jesus said, "It is finished." With that, he bowed his head and gave up his spirit.*
>
> *Now it was the day of Preparation, and the next day was to be a **special Sabbath**. Because the Jewish leaders did not want the bodies left on the crosses during the Sabbath, they asked Pilate to have the legs broken and the bodies taken down.*
> (John 19:30–31, emphasis added)

In the Jewish calendar, there were seven sabbath days called high days such as Shavuot (Feast of Weeks) and Yom Kippur (Day of Atonement), and these did not usually coincide with the weekly sabbaths that run from Friday sunset to Saturday sunset. Passover always started at sundown on the 15th of the month of Nisan and ended the following sundown. Jesus could have been martyred on the 17th of Nisan, which fell on a Wednesday the year of the crucifixion, with Mary Magdalene going to His temporary resting place after the weekly Sabbath had ended at sundown on Saturday.

THE PSALM OF JONAH

Jonah's sojourn in the fish could be likened to a womb where he was given the time he needed to prepare for a new life. His moment of truth was expressed in prayer known as the Psalm of Jonah. *"In my distress I called to the Lord, and he answered me. From deep in the realm of the dead I called for help, and you listened to my cry"* (Jonah 2:2). Jonah admitted that he had been banished from the sight of the Lord, *"yet I will look again toward your holy temple"* (2:4). His faithlessness and disobedience to the Lord had taken him low in the opposite direction taken by Moses and Elijah. *"To the roots of the mountains I sank down; the earth beneath barred me in forever. But you, Lord my God, brought my life up from the pit"* (2:6). Jonah lamented and then gave thanks for redemption not yet granted and vowed that he would embrace his mission. Absent was repentance.

> *"When my life was ebbing away,*
> *I remembered you, LORD,*
> *and my prayer rose to you,*
> *to your holy temple.*

> *"Those who cling to worthless idols*
> *turn away from God's love for them.*
> *But I, with shouts of grateful praise,*
> *will sacrifice to you.*
> *What I have vowed I will make good.*
> *I will say, 'Salvation comes from the LORD.'"*

> *And the LORD commanded the fish, and it vomited Jonah onto dry land.*
> (Jonah 2:7–9)

The biblical writer James L. Crenshaw commented on Jonah's inadequate, even laughable, repentance:

> The weighty message does not exclude humor: on hearing Jonah's facile confession that deliverance belongs to the Lord, the fish throws up. This entire psalm is a devastating mockery of Israelite piety as it is exemplified by this dubious prophet whose sole concern was his reputation for accuracy of prediction or a restriction of divine compassion to Israel.[7]

After the vomiting episode, Jonah was again given the call. *"Then the word of the LORD came to Jonah a second time: 'Go to the great city of Nineveh and proclaim to it the message I give you'"* (3:1–2). By sending Jonah to a foreign people who were bitter enemies of the Hebrews, God showed His concern for a people other than His chosen, the Hebrews. Here is a theme of divine universalism that went far beyond Israelite nationalism. Jesus would later say, *"I have other sheep that are not of this sheep pen. I must bring them also. They too will listen to my voice, and there shall be one flock and one shepherd"* (John 10:16). Jonah's sojourn in the belly of a big fish describes the hell of separation from God and of hell being a state of mind.

A MISSION AND THE NUMBER FORTY

It's recorded that it took Jonah three days to walk through Nineveh (presumably after two or three months of travel to get there). However, since he could have walked around the outside wall of Nineveh within less than a day, the number three again seems to be used symbolically.

The message that Jonah proclaimed was the shortest in recorded Hebrew prophetic history: *"**Forty more days** and Nineveh will be overthrown"* (3:4, emphasis added). But it was effective. *"The Ninevites believed God. A fast was proclaimed, and all of them, from the greatest to the least, put on sackcloth"* (Jonah 3:5). Even the king accepted Jonah's words and rent his robes, dressed in sackcloth, sat in the dust, and issued a proclamation to the citizens of Nineveh.

"By the decree of the king and his nobles:

Do not let people or animals, herds or flocks, taste anything; do not let them eat or drink. But let people and animals be covered with sackcloth. Let everyone call urgently on God. Let them give up their evil ways and their violence. Who knows? God may yet relent and with compassion turn from his fierce anger so that we will not perish."
(Jonah 3:7–9)

The number forty may be a key concept in this allegory. Rabbi Geoffrey Dennis, an American rabbi of Reform Judaism, wrote that "Forty appears many times in the Bible, usually designating a time of radical transition or transformation."[8] Rabbi Baruch agreed. "The number forty expresses a change or transition."[9] And Hunt expressed a similar Catholic viewpoint. "This number [forty] is recognized as an important number both on account of the frequency of its occurrence and with the uniformity of its association as a time of consecration and as a period of trial."[10] Moses spent forty days on Mount Sinai with the Lord and the Israelites spent forty years in the wilderness before they were allowed to enter Canaan. Elijah traveled forty days from Beersheba to Mount Horeb (Mount Sinai) to ask for guidance from the Lord. Jesus retreated to the wilderness for forty days after His baptism before He started His ministry. Bahá'u'lláh was in exile for forty years.

With one sentence, Jonah was more successful than any of the other Hebrew prophets. Nineveh was saved. *"When God saw what they did and how they turned from their evil ways, he relented and did not bring on them the destruction he had threatened"* (Jonah 3:10). But Jonah did not celebrate this divine mercy.

Jonah had sat down outside the city wall to wait and see what happened. He sulked in anger when the Ninevites were forgiven and spared. Jonah's defiance reemerged as he recalled his first response to the Lord's calling. He prayed, *"Isn't this what I said, LORD, when I was still at home? That is what I tried to forestall by fleeing to Tarshish. I knew that you are a gracious and compassionate God, slow to anger and abounding in love, a God who relents from sending calamity. Now, LORD, take away my life, for it is better for me to die than to live"* (4:2–3). Jonah professed preference for death rather than life because he could not rejoice in God's mercy. He wallowed in anger and self-pity because the prophecy he had proclaimed had not come true. God had promised one thing and done another, causing Jonah to lose face with the Ninevites. Not only that, but now Jonah had a theological problem. Can God be totally trusted based on what man sees of Him? Can faith in God—His plan, mercy, and goodness—be absolute no matter what happens?

The Lord probed Jonah's anger. *"Is it right for you to be angry?"* (4:4). The Lord had provided a leafy plant to grow over Jonah to give him shade, which improved his mood. But the next day the Lord had delivered a worm that chewed the plant so that it withered. *"When the sun rose, God provided a scorching east wind, and the sun blazed on Jonah's head so that he grew faint. He wanted to die, and said, 'It would be better for me to die than to live'"* (4:8). This was petulant Jonah's second expressed wish to die, and the third soon followed.

> But God said to Jonah, *"Is it right for you to be angry about the plant?"*
>
> *"It is,"* he said. *"And I'm so angry I wish I were dead."*
>
> But the LORD said, *"You have been concerned about this plant, though you did not tend it or make it grow. It sprang up overnight and died overnight. And should I not have concern for the great city of Nineveh, in which there are more than a hundred and twenty thousand people who cannot tell their right hand from their left—**and also many animals?"***
>
> (Jonah 4:9–11, emphasis added)

It's fascinating that God mentions *animals* as a factor in His decision for mercy. The book of Genesis states that humanity was given dominion over the fish, birds, and animals, both domestic and wild, when God said: *"Let us make mankind in our image, in our likeness, so that they may rule over the fish in the sea and the birds in the sky, over the livestock and all the wild animals, and over all the creatures that move along the ground"* (Gen. 1:26).

The Lord expressed to Jonah His concern not only for the people of Nineveh but also for *many animals.* Is dominion being changed to nurturance? Is there a hint here of animal rights? 'Abdu'l-Bahá commented on reverence for all forms of life.

> *"Briefly, it is not only their fellow human beings that the beloved of God must treat with mercy and compassion, rather must they show forth the utmost loving-kindness to every living creature. For in all physical respects, and where the animal spirit is concerned, the selfsame feelings are shared by animal and man."*[11]

The Qur'án presents a short version of Jonah's story that matches the biblical version and ends with *"And they believed; so We permitted them to enjoy (their life) for a while"* (Qur'án, 37:148, Ali Yusuf translation).

The major themes running through the books of the Hebrew prophets are judgment and mercy, punishment, and forgiveness. Let's see how these themes unfolded in the ministries of the other prophets in the days of the divided kingdoms.

Chapter 3

Israel Severed from Judah

If a kingdom is divided against itself, that kingdom cannot stand.
If a house is divided against itself, that house cannot stand.

MARK 3:24–25

THE YEARS OF THE united kingdom (c. 1030–933 BCE) were recorded in books 1 and 2 Samuel and 1 Kings, which biblical scholars estimate were written at least three hundred years afterward. By then, the united monarchy was a nostalgic memory comparable to the Camelot of Arthurian legends, a golden age in the memory of the Hebrew people. What followed led to conquests, ruin, deportations, and the Exile. David and Solomon became larger than life and the telling of their exploits and accomplishments took on a devotedly nationalistic fervor.

There is much difference of opinion among biblical scholars about the historical accuracy of biblical depictions of the united kingdom. At one extreme, everything in the Hebrew Bible is accepted as literal truth, and at the other, there is denial that the united monarchy ever existed. Critical biblical scholarship, which started evolving during the late nineteenth century, considers other areas of scholarly study such as archeology, history, and ancient written languages. The discipline of historical archeology emerged, which studies places, objects, and issues where written records and oral traditions can inform and contextualize artifacts and cultural material. This approach can both complement and conflict with archeological evidence found at a particular site.

Archeological studies in the Holy Land went through a process from early archeologists striving to "prove the Bible" to their modern colleagues considering scientific, literary, historical, anthropological, linguistic, and other factors. Most archeologists, like most biblical scholars, take the middle ground concerning David and Solomon. For example, the archeologists and biblical historians Israel Finkelstein and Neil Asher Silberman affirm the historicity of David and Solomon but doubt that their place in history was as fabled as portrayed in legend:

> It is now clear that Iron Age Judah enjoyed no precocious golden age. David and his son Solomon and the subsequent members of the Davidic dynasty ruled over a marginal, isolated, rural region, with no signs of great wealth or centralized administration. It did not suddenly decline into weakness and misfortune from an era of unparalleled prosperity. Instead, it underwent a long and gradual development over hundreds of years. David and Solomon's Jerusalem was only one of a number of religious centers within the land of Israel; it was surely not acknowledged as the spiritual center of the entire people of Israel initially.[1]

While accepting the historicity of David and Solomon, Finkelstein and Silberman warn about circular reasoning—using the Bible narrative as the basis for archeological interpretation and then using an interpreted archeological site as proof of the Bible's historical accuracy. They wrote that "it is clear today that the archaeological proofs of the conquests of David were illusory."[2] The Israeli archeologist Hillel Geva reported that Jerusalem had a population of only about two thousand inhabitants during Solomon's reign.[3]

There was another element that caused the memories of David and Solomon to shine resplendently throughout the ages, an intangible light that was probably interpreted in patriotic, militaristic, and materialistic terms. However, this light issuing forth from the united kingdom was spiritual in nature. 'Abdu'l-Bahá gave insight into this phenomenon. He explained that there are two kinds of prophets—independent Prophets who bring a new Dispensation and a new religion, and secondary prophets who are followers and promulgators of the Dispensation for their day, which *"includes Solomon, David, Isaiah, Jeremiah, and Ezekiel. They have no power or authority of their own, but derive theirs from the independent Prophets."*[4]

Regardless of having had two prophet-kings, the united kingdom was cleaved into the two kingdoms of Israel and Judah about 930 BCE, two or three years after the accession of Solomon's son Rehoboam (933–913). Ten of the twelve tribes of Israel rejected Rehoboam and only the tribes of Judah and Simeon (and half of Benjamin) in the south remained loyal to him. Despite his supposed wisdom, Solomon had caused much stress and resentment with his extensive building projects that required conscripted laborers. Rehoboam continued in like vein and rebellion ensued.

The short version of the story is that the assembly of Israel went to Rehoboam and said to him, *"Your father put a heavy yoke on us, but now lighten the harsh labor and the heavy yoke he put on us, and we will serve you"* (1 Kings 12:4). Rehoboam consulted the elders who had served Solomon, who replied, *"If today you will be a servant to these people and serve them and give them a favorable answer, they will always be your servants"* (12:7). Rehoboam rejected this advice and followed that of his young friends to get tough. He said, *"My father made your yoke heavy; I will make it even heavier. My father scourged you with whips; I will scourge you with scorpions"* (12:14). The people revolted and Rehoboam fled back to Jerusalem to gather an army to fight the insurgency.

The prophet Shemaiah, titled *the man of God*, received a message that the continuation of the united kingdom was not God's plan. He reported to Rehoboam, *"This is what the LORD says: Do not go up to fight against your brothers, the Israelites. Go home, every one of you, for this is my doing"* (12:22–24).

Amazingly, the message was obeyed. Such was the respect the Hebrews usually accorded their prophets, at least in the early days. This directive may have been divine justice to relieve the northerners from the tyranny of Jeroboam. It may have been a divine strategy to greatly increase the years of dramatic unfoldment of the prophets' mission, which were part of God's plan not only for the Israelites but for us today.

KINGS OF THE KINGDOM OF ISRAEL

The royal history of Israel was filled with instability and idolatry, mayhem and murder. Israel had nineteen kings from about 927 BCE to its demise in 722. There were three singleton reigns and five dynasties, the longest-lived of which lasted five generations. At least seven kings were assassinated, usually by army officers. More than once a royal heir had his male relatives murdered to secure his throne. Most of these rulers earned the epitaph that they *"did what was evil in the LORD's sight"* or similar wording, perhaps reflections of revisionist scribes of exilic times.

These kings provided much fodder for the prophets' rhetorical fires. King Jeroboam of Israel erected golden calves for worship in Bethel and Dan. When he was about to make an offering at the pagan altar at Bethel, a *man of God* appeared and proclaimed: *'Altar, altar! This is what the LORD says: A son named Josiah will be born to the house of David. On you he will sacrifice the priests of the high places who make offerings here, and human bones will be burned on you.' That same day the man of God gave a sign: 'This is the sign the LORD has declared: The altar will be split apart and the ashes on it will be poured out'"* (1 Kings 13:2–3).

The famous reformist king of Judah, Josiah (640–608), crossed the border into Israel about a hundred years after Israel fell, and about three hundred years after Jeroboam had erected the idolatrous altar at Bethel. It was recorded that Josiah ordered that the altar built by Jeroboam at a high place be demolished and burned along with an Asherah pole (2 Kings 23:15).

Another independent prophet, Jehu, is recorded as countering the idolatry of Baasha (909–886), the third king of Israel, with blistering words from the Lord. *"So I am about to wipe out Baasha and his house, and I will make your house like that of Jeroboam son of Nebat. Dogs will eat those belonging to Baasha who die in the city, and birds will feed on those who die in the country"* (1 Kings 16:3–4).

Baasha was the army officer who killed Nadab (910–909), son of Jeroboam, and then killed all of Jeroboam's descendants. Baasha's son and successor, Elah (886–885), was reportedly killed by an army general. And so it went, with few exceptions, through a couple of hundred years of regnal atrocities and military clashes with neighbors until Assyrian incursions caught the attention of the last kings.

Israel had only one reformist king of record, the like-named Jehu (841–814), an army officer anointed by one of Elisha's prophet-followers to succeed Jehoram and to destroy the house of Ahab, which he did. Jehu also ordered that the prophets of Baal be killed and their temple in Samaria destroyed. It was subsequently used as a latrine. But Jehu seems to have been half-hearted in his fight against idolatry. *"However, he did not turn away from the sins of Jeroboam son of Nebat, which he had caused Israel to commit—the worship of the golden calves at Bethel and Dan"* (2 Kings 10:29). In recognition of his effort, the Lord told Jehu that his descendants would sit on the throne of Israel to the fourth generation. But Jehu *"did not keep the law of the LORD, the God of Israel"* (10:31). Therefore, true to the biblical theme of divine reward and punishment, *"the LORD began to reduce the size of Israel"* (10:32) by allowing the Arameans to seize territory.

It is written of Jehoahaz (814–798), son of Jehu, that he sought the Lord's favor and was able to defeat the Arameans, and the Israelites lived in their own homes as before. *"But they did not turn away from the sins of the house of Jeroboam, which he had caused Israel to commit; he continued in them. Also, the Asherah pole remained standing in Samaria"* (2 Kings 13:6). Jehoash (798–782) did no better. *"He did evil in the eyes of the Lord and did not turn away from any of the sins of Jeroboam son of Nebat, which he had caused Israel to commit; he continued in them"* (13:11).

Jeroboam II (782–753) is considered by biblical historians to have been an excellent king who regained the former boundaries of Israel and brought peace and prosperity to Israel. His son Zechariah (753–752) was assassinated six months into his reign by Shallum (752), an army officer, who in turn met the same fate at the hands of Menahem (752–742), yet another army officer. The mighty Assyrian empire then invaded a weakened Israel during Menahem's reign, leaving him with few options.

Assyria had consolidated its power over northern Mesopotamia by the early ninth century and then its armies marched west. By the mid-eighth century, the Assyrian menace posed a direct threat to the small states to the west, including Israel and Judah. Sometimes Assyria asserted its hegemony through threats that induced voluntary submission to vassal status. Other times Assyria forced submission to vassal status through total conquest, marked by mass deportations to other parts of the empire and corresponding resettlements in the conquered areas by populations from other regions of the empire. But this does not capture the terror of Assyrian brutality. Countries and peoples who resisted the Assyrians, and failed, faced gruesome punishment. Not only were their cities destroyed and their lands devastated, but the people suffered mass-scale impalements, flayings, beheadings, and slavery. These terrors were recorded in Assyrian records and carved as reliefs on obelisks and seals. Assyria was the most ferocious empire ever seen, even by the standards of that time. Its very name became a byword for vicious cruelty and atrocity. Assyrian armies struck terror in the hearts of everyone standing in their line of march.

Menahem chose voluntary submission and Israel became a vassal state. The chronicle of his reign states that he gave Tiglath-pileser III one thousand talents of silver to gain his support and strengthen his own hold on the kingdom of Israel. The silver was raised by levying fifty shekels of silver upon the wealthiest people in the land for an annual tribute.[5] Predictably, this yearly levy caused much resentment from the wealthy, who undoubtedly got the money from the sweat of the lower classes.

The social and religious fabric of the country was severely stressed by vassalage. Monarchical stability was shattered by serial regnal assassinations. Menahem's son and heir, Pekahiah (740), was murdered by Pekah (740–732), a military officer, who lasted a few years until he was assassinated by Hoshea (732–722). The kingdom was in chaos.

Serial encroachments by the Assyrians into the kingdom of Israel started about 740 and ended with the capture of Samaria, the capital city of Israel, in 722. Their invasion of 732 had cost the kingdom its northern valleys and the Galilee area. Many of its inhabitants were deported and resettled throughout the empire at that time. Finkelstein and Silberman explained this breakdown and its consequences as follows:

> The delicate balance of economic independence and political alliance with, or subservience to, Assyria gradually broke down.
>
> The series of violent dynastic upheavals at Samaria could not have come at a more dangerous time. Great changes were taking place in Mesopotamia. In 745—precisely after two kings were assassinated in Samaria—the ambitious governor of the great Assyrian city of Calah in the Tigris valley revolted against his own overlords and began the process of transforming Assyria into a brutal and predatory state.
>
> This new king, Tiglath-pileser III (also known by his Babylonian name, Pul, in the Hebrew Bible) began nothing less than a thorough revamping of the Assyrian empire— primarily in its relations to its former vassals, which would now be much more directly controlled. In 738 BCE, he led his army westward on a great threatening campaign, in which he succeeded in cowering Assyria's formerly semi-independent vassals with unprecedented economic demands.[6]

The Assyrian empire had a longstanding policy of forcibly resettling conquered peoples not only to reduce rebellion but to develop and strengthen the empire. *"In the ninth year of Hoshea, the king of Assyria captured Samaria and deported the Israelites to Assyria. He settled them in Halah, in Gozan on the Habor River and in the towns of the Medes"* (2 Kings 17:6). Halah was north of Nineveh, and the towns of the Medes were far east of the Tigris River.

The deportations from Israel dispersed the ten northern tribes, which were never mentioned again in the Hebrew Bible. That is why they are commonly referred to as the "lost tribes of Israel."

Much mythology and even messianic expectations have been tied to these ten tribes. However, it is more realistic to understand that because the ten tribes were dispersed throughout the Assyrian empire, they lost their identity through assimilation into local cultures.

Simultaneously, reverse deportations brought populations from the Assyrian empire into newly conquered areas. The poorer Israelites who were left behind to work the land probably intermarried with the newcomers. The Samaritans mentioned in the Gospels were descendants of people resettled in Israel who converted to the religion of Moses.

Hoshea, the last king of Israel, continued the payment of tribute to Assyria for five years, but then he foolishly and secretly sought an alliance with Egypt for revolt. The successor to Tiglath-pileser III, Shalmaneser (727–722), discovered the conspiracy and invaded Israel. Samaria was under siege for three years until it fell in 722 to Sargon II (722–705). Assyrian cuneiform sources state that 27,290 people were deported from Samaria. An inscription written in cuneiform states:

> The inhabitants of Samerina, who agreed [and plotted] with a king [hostile to] me, not to do service and not to bring tribute [to Aššur] and who did battle, I fought against them with the power of the great gods, my lords. I counted as spoil 27,280 (error for 27,290) people, together with their chariots, and gods, in which they trusted. I formed a unit with 200 of [their] chariots for my royal force. I settled the rest of them in the midst of Assyria. I repopulated Samerina more than before. I brought into it people from countries conquered by my hands. I appointed my eunuch as governor over them. And I counted them as Assyrians.[7]

The book of 2 Kings relates the sins of Israel that led to their defeat and exile by the Assyrians. For example:

> *All this took place because the Israelites had sinned against the Lord their God, who had brought them up out of Egypt from under the power of Pharaoh king of Egypt. They worshiped other gods and followed the practices of the nations the Lord had driven out before them, as well as the*

practices that the kings of Israel had introduced. The Israelites secretly did things against the LORD their God that were not right. From watchtower to fortified city they built themselves high places in all their towns. They set up sacred stones and Asherah poles on every high hill and under every spreading tree.
(2 Kings 17:7–10)

The first two canonical prophets, Amos and Hosea who preached in the kingdom of Israel, had warned that the sins of the people would lead to the demise of their kingdom. First Isaiah of Judah counseled Ahaz (732–716) during the Assyrian threats and Hezekiah (716–697) during the Assyrian depredations of Judah and the aborted siege of Jerusalem. Other prophets, Micah and Jeremiah in particular, counseled and warned the kings, priests, and people of Judah of a fate similar to that of the northern kingdom. They had an uphill battle.

Chapter 4

Amos – Yet You did not Return to Me

But let justice roll on like a river,
righteousness like a never-failing stream!

Amos 5:24

AMOS AND HOSEA WERE the first of the writing prophets, each with
a ministry in the northern kingdom of Israel. They both irritated and
angered the sovereigns, priests, and nobility with razor-sharp warnings
and rebukes.

The question arises about how authentic the prophets' books are in
their final form. *The Oxford Bible Commentary* notes that "marked differences
between individual prophetic books and circumstantial details (e.g., the
description of Amos as *nōqēd* [sheep farmer] in 1:1) perhaps point to the
survival of ancient historical elements."[1] In fact, surprising confirmations
of biblical data have been discovered. For example, a seal was found in
2018 during archeological excavations under the old city of David in Jerusalem. The seal was inscribed in ancient Hebrew "to Natan-Melech, the
King's Servant."[2] Natan-Melech is mentioned in 2 Kings 23:11: *"They
were in the court near the room of an official named Nathan-Melek."* In addition,
as mentioned earlier, we know that the Bible, the Word of God, has been
under the care and protection of God throughout the centuries.

It is written that Amos was a shepherd and a dresser of sycamore trees[3]
in Tekoa, a small village in Judah about seven miles south of Jerusalem when

43

the call came to him in the form of a vision. *"The words of Amos, one of the shepherds of Tekoa—the vision he saw concerning Israel two years before the earthquake, when Uzziah [786–746] was king of Judah and Jeroboam [782–735] son of Jehoash was king of Israel"* (Amos 1:1). Geologists estimate that this earthquake, with its epicenter in Syria, struck Israel and Judah sometime between 760 and 750 BCE at a magnitude of 7.8 to 8.2 on the Richter scale.[4]

Amos was sent from Judah in the south to Israel in the north, specifically to Bethel and Samaria. Bethel had a major site for idolatrous worship that had been instituted by Jeroboam I (931 to 910). It seems that Amos set forth without hesitation on a mission believed to have lasted only a year or two. He described a prophetic dynamic of intimacy with God thus:

> *Surely the Sovereign LORD does nothing*
> *without revealing his plan*
> *to his servants the prophets.*
>
> *The lion has roared—*
> *who will not fear?*
> *The Sovereign LORD has spoken—*
> *who can but prophesy?*[5]
> (Amos 3:7–8)

In the time of Amos, both the kingdoms of Israel and Judah had long-reigning kings—Jeroboam II (782–753) in the north, and Amaziah (796–767) and Uzziah (767–740) in the south. It had been a time of prosperity. But trouble was brewing. The people had drifted far from the Mosaic teachings, and the Assyrian empire had extended as far as Damascus to the north, stopping there only to consolidate its gains before pushing south. Amos warned mightily of Israel's impending doom if it did not reform and adhere to the Mosaic Covenant.

THE SYMBOLOGY OF CARMEL

The first recorded prophecy from Amos, found immediately after the introduction, was extraordinary in farseeing twenty-six centuries into the future. *"The LORD will roar from Zion, and utter his voice from Jerusalem; and the habitations of the shepherds shall mourn, and the top of Carmel shall wither"* (Amos 1:2, KJV). Zion was a hill south of Mount Moriah (the Temple Mount) where a Jebusite fortress of the same name was conquered by David and renamed the City of David. Bahá'u'lláh wrote about the significance of Mount Carmel relative to Amos 1:2.

A few months before Bahá'u'lláh passed from this world, He wrote a letter called *Epistle to the Son of the Wolf.* "The Wolf," so named by Bahá'u'lláh, was a high Persian official who issued the death sentence for two wealthy Bábí brothers who were known for their philanthropies and excellent characters. The "son of the Wolf" assisted his father in this ignoble deed which ended in their brutal execution. The two brothers are remembered in Bahá'í history as the King of Martyrs and the Beloved of Martyrs, and as the Twin Shining Lights. Bahá'u'lláh addressed this epistle to the son of the Wolf. After noting the foretellings of His coming by David and Isaiah, Bahá'u'lláh quoted Amos 1:2 and explained the significance of Carmel, the *Hill of God.*

> Amos saith: *"The LORD will roar from Zion, and utter His Voice from Jerusalem; and the habitations of the shepherds shall mourn, and the top of Carmel shall wither."* Carmel, in the Book of God, hath been designated as **the Hill of God, and His Vineyard.** It is here that, by the grace of the Lord of Revelation, the **Tabernacle of Glory** hath been raised. Happy are they that attain thereunto; happy they that set their faces towards it. And likewise He saith: *"Our God will come, and He will not be silent."*[6] (emphasis added)

Bahá'u'lláh thus clarified that Amos was referring to His coming. The biblical meaning of the tabernacle was the portable tent where it was believed that God resided with the stone tablets of the Ten Commandments. In writing about the last years of Bahá'u'lláh's life, Shoghi Effendi mentioned that He visited Mount Carmel in Haifa, which was across the bay from Akka, four times. Shoghi Effendi explained that the tent raised there for His stays was called the *Tabernacle of Glory.*

In that same year [1890] Bahá'u'lláh's tent, the *"Tabernacle of Glory,"* was raised on Mt. Carmel, *"the Hill of God and His Vineyard,"* the home of Elijah, extolled by Isaiah as the *"mountain of the LORD,"* to which *"all nations shall flow."* Four times He visited Haifa, His last visit being no less than three months long. In the course of one of these visits, when His tent was pitched in the vicinity of the Carmelite Monastery, He, the *"LORD of the Vineyard,"* revealed the Tablet of Carmel, remarkable for its allusions and prophecies. On another occasion, He pointed out Himself to 'Abdu'l-Bahá, as He stood on the slopes of that mountain, the site which was to serve as the permanent resting-place of the Báb, and on which a befitting mausoleum was later to be erected.[7] (emphasis added)

Bahá'u'lláh wrote that the *Law of God* would issue from Zion.

> *The time foreordained unto the peoples and kindreds of the earth is now come. The promises of God, as recorded in the holy Scriptures, have all been fulfilled.* **Out of Zion hath gone forth the Law of God,** *and Jerusalem, and the hills and land thereof, are filled with the glory of His Revelation. Happy is the man that pondereth in his heart that which hath been revealed in the Books of God, the Help in Peril, the Self-Subsisting.*[8] (emphasis added)

When Bahá'u'lláh wrote *Out of Zion hath gone forth the Law of God,* He was undoubtedly referring to His Revelation, whose covenant would be fulfilled by the establishment of the Universal House of Justice with its Seat located on Mount Carmel. His Most Holy Book, the *Kitáb-i-Aqdas,* the Book of Laws, would be published by the Universal House of Justice.

Why would *the habitations of the shepherds mourn, and the top of Carmel wither?* Shepherds are ecclesiastical authorities, and ecclesiastics seldom recognize a Prophet of God but may live to later mourn their blindness. A withered top of Mount Carmel would represent a spiritual past that was rocky and dry. Speaking literally, Mount Carmel was also rocky and dry. However, since the early twentieth century, the portion of Mount Carmel that is owned by the Bahá'ís has been gradually transformed into verdant greenery and gardens.

As explained in Chapter 5, the symbolic meaning of Zion evolved over the centuries to mean the Holy Land in general and Mount Carmel in particular. Jerusalem would come to signify the new, or renewed, Word of God that would issue from Zion.

Such a rich tableau for exploration and contemplation is offered in just one verse from Amos!

VERDICTS FOR SURROUNDING NATIONS AND JUDAH AND ISRAEL

Amos uttered themes of divine universalism and even of universal crimes at a time when each country, and often each city, had its own god and its own rules of conduct. He condemned neighboring countries for what we would call war crimes, but which were standard military conduct for the times. Here are excerpts, all of which begin with *This is what the LORD says:*

> *"For three sins of Damascus,*
> *even for four, I will not relent.*
> *Because she threshed Gilead*
> *with sledges having iron teeth,*
> *I will send fire on the house of Hazael*
> *that will consume the fortresses of Ben-Hadad."*
> (Amos 1:3–4)

> *"For three sins of Gaza,*
> *even for four, I will not relent.*
> *Because she took captive whole communities*
> *and sold them to Edom,*
> *I will send fire on the walls of Gaza*
> *that will consume her fortresses."*
> (1:6–7)

"For three sins of Tyre,
  even for four, I will not relent.
Because she sold whole communities of captives to Edom,
  disregarding a treaty of brotherhood,
I will send fire on the walls of Tyre
  that will consume her fortresses."
(1:9–10)

"For three sins of Edom,
  even for four, I will not relent.
Because he pursued his brother with a sword
  and slaughtered the women of the land,
because his anger raged continually
  and his fury flamed unchecked,
I will send fire on Teman
  that will consume the fortresses of Bozrah."
(1:11–12)

"For three sins of Ammon,
  even for four, I will not relent.
Because he ripped open the pregnant women
  of Gilead
  in order to extend his borders,
Her king[e] will go into exile,
  he and his officials together," says the LORD.
(1:13, 15)

"For three sins of Moab,
  even for four, I will not relent.
Because he burned to ashes
  the bones of Edom's king,
I will send fire on Moab
  that will consume the fortresses of Kerioth."
(2:1–2)

The above nations were being held accountable not for breaking their own laws, but for inhumane conduct that was against God's law, even though they were ignorant of it. Judah and Israel would receive worse punishment because they had the benefit of the Mosaic Dispensation but rejected the law of the Lord.

> *"For three sins of Judah,*
> > *even for four, I will not relent.*
> *Because they have rejected the law of the Lord*
> > *and have not kept his decrees,*
> > *because they have been led astray by false gods*
> > *the gods their ancestors followed,*
> *I will send fire on Judah*
> > *that will consume the fortresses of Jerusalem."*
>
> (2:4–5)

> *"For three sins of Israel,*
> > *even for four, I will not relent.*
> *They sell the innocent for silver,*
> > *and the needy for a pair of sandals...*
> *They lie down beside every altar*
> > *on garments taken in pledge.*
> > *In the house of their god*
> > *they drink wine taken as fines...*
> *I brought you up out of Egypt*
> > *and led you forty years in the wilderness*
> > *to give you the land of the Amorites.*
> *"I also raised up prophets from among*
> > *your children*
> > *and Nazirites from among your youths.*
> *Is this not true, people of Israel?"*
> *declares the Lord.*
> *"But you made the Nazirites drink wine*
> > *and commanded the prophets not to prophesy.*

"Now then, I will crush you
as a cart crushes when loaded with grain."
(2:6, 8, 10–13)

Eight times Amos used *three sins … even for four* as a rhetorical device. Three does not mean the number of sins but is a statement that sin was committed, and four could represent even greater sins that triggered the limit of God's patience.

Amos did not specify the source of the punishment to come, which would be Assyria, whose forces would defeat Damascus about twenty years later in the late 730s BCE. From there the Assyrians would conquer the northern kingdom in 722 and reduce the neighboring kingdoms to vassal status, undoubtedly with typical Assyrian cruelties that fulfilled Amos's prophecies of their fate.

CRIES FOR JUSTICE

The writing prophets lived in an agrarian society where the principle of patrimonial inheritance had given way to land grants from the king, which produced estates owned by people who mostly lived at court. During this transition, small landowners often fell on hard times and were forced to sell their lands, thus creating a class of dependent and impoverished tenant farmers. The landless worked as day laborers who surrendered their cloaks in the morning as collateral for their labor and retrieved them at night with their day's pay. There was a small middle class of artisans and merchants. Increasing demands of the monarchies for taxes, farm goods, and labor stressed the middle and lower classes while the economic elite sported the wealth and luxuries made possible by the trade routes that went through the Holy Land. The result was social and economic corruption built on the exploitation of the poor.

Amos raised the cry for justice, as did all the succeeding prophets, in accordance with the Ten Commandments and the Mosaic law codes that emphasized justice as protection for the poor and less fortunate and as a social equalizer (see Vol. 1, Chapter 6, for discussion on the Code of Hammurabi, the Ten Commandments, the Covenant Code, the

Holiness Code, and the Deuteronomic Code). Amos spoke with acerbic anger and barbed diatribes against injustice and social inequity, and he warned of dire punishment to come.

> *Hear this word, you cows of Bashan on Mount Samaria,*
> > *you women who oppress the poor and crush the needy*
> > *and say to your husbands, "Bring us some drinks!"*
> *The Sovereign LORD has sworn by his holiness:*
> > *"The time will surely come*
> > *when you will be taken away with hooks,*
> > *the last of you with fishhooks.*[9]
>
> (Amos 4:1–2)

Amos continues in like vein and then reminds the people of their history, that they had been *like a burning stick snatched from the fire,* but that they had not returned to their Lord.

> *"I have sent among you the pestilence after the manner of Egypt: your young men have I slain with the sword, and have taken away your horses; and I have made the stink of your camps to come up unto your nostrils: yet have ye not returned unto me, saith the LORD.*
>
> *I have overthrown some of you, as God overthrew Sodom and Gomorrah, and ye were as a firebrand plucked out of the burning: yet have ye not returned unto me, saith the LORD.*
>
> *Therefore thus will I do unto thee, O Israel: and because I will do this unto thee, prepare to meet thy God, O Israel.*
>
> *For, lo, he that formeth the mountains, and createth the wind, and declareth unto man what is his thought, that maketh the morning darkness, and treadeth upon the high places of the earth, The LORD, The God of hosts, is his name.*
>
> (4:10–13, KJV)

Surprisingly, Amos did not launch into a warning such as, *"You only have I chosen of all the families of the earth; therefore I will punish you for all your iniquities"* (3:2). Instead, verse 4:13 seems to have leaped thousands of years ahead to the nineteenth century CE. The eminent scholar Adib Taherzadeh (1921–2000) believed that Amos was speaking of Bahá'u'lláh in verse 13 when he wrote as follows:

Amos, another prophet of Israel, referred to Bahá'u'lláh in Constantinople when he said:

> *For, lo, he that formeth the mountains, and createth the wind, and declareth unto man what is his thought, that maketh the morning darkness, and treadeth upon the high places of the earth, The Lord, The God of hosts, is his name. (4:13, KJV)*

In one of His tablets revealed in Akka, Bahá'u'lláh states that this prophecy refers to Him, that it concerns the year eighty (1280 A.H., 1863 CE), and that the 'high places of the earth' are Constantinople and the Holy Land (Mount Carmel). Furthermore, alluding to Mírzá Yaḥyá [an inveterate enemy of Bahá'u'lláh] whose title was Ṣubḥi-i-Azal (Morning of Eternity), He asserts that through His power the untrue morn was completely darkened.[10]

Amos railed against those who turned justice into bitterness and cast righteousness to the ground by depriving the poor of justice in the courts. He condemned the practice of levying a grain tax on poor farmers. Landowners no longer left the harvest gleanings for the poor but harvested and sold them. Crooked practices in the marketplace did not escape Amos's attention, such as skimping on the measure, boosting the price, and using dishonest scales. Amos condemned those who sell *"the innocent for silver and the needy for a pair of sandals,"* and who *"trample on the heads of the poor as on the dust of the ground and deny justice to the oppressed"* (2:6, 7). He denounced the rich, who were oblivious to the plight of the poor or to Israel's defiance of the covenant.

> *You lie on beds adorned with ivory*
> *and lounge on your couches.*

You dine on choice lambs
    and fattened calves.
You strum away on your harps like David
    and improvise on musical instruments.
You drink wine by the bowlful
    and use the finest lotions,
        but you do not grieve over the ruin of Joseph.
Therefore you will be among the first to go into exile;
    your feasting and lounging will end.
(6:4–7)

Divine retribution would come. Amos repeatedly gave explicit warnings such as, *"For the LORD God Almighty declares, 'I will stir up a nation against you, Israel, that will oppress you all the way from Lebo Hamath to the valley of the Arabah'"* (6:14). He accurately foretold the destruction of the kingdom of Israel, but he did not specify Assyria as the cause. Lebo Hamath was a northern border marker, and the valley of the Arabah was a barren depression in the Jordan River valley that ran from Mount Hermon in the north to the Gulf of Akaba.

Amos led the procession of prophets to come who would denounce the religious commemorations and sacrificial worship that had become a mockery of their original spiritual intent. Here is one of his many laments.

"I hate, I despise your religious festivals;
    your assemblies are a stench to me.
Even though you bring me burnt offerings and grain offerings,
    I will not accept them.
Though you bring choice fellowship offerings,
    I will have no regard for them.
Away with the noise of your songs!
    I will not listen to the music of your harps.
But let justice roll on like a river,
    righteousness like a never-failing stream!"
(5:21–24)

There is no uncertainty in the rebukes from Amos about worship made contemptible by sin.

DARKNESS IN THE DAY OF THE LORD

The first mention of the day of the Lord from a Hebrew prophet is found in the book of Amos.

> *"Woe to you who long*
>> *for the **day of the Lord**!*
> *Why do you long for **the day of the Lord**?*
>> *That day will be darkness, not light.*
> *It will be as though a man fled from a lion*
>> *only to meet a bear,*
> *as though he entered his house*
>> *and rested his hand on the wall*
>> *only to have a snake bite him.*
> *Will not the **day of the Lord** be darkness, not light—*
>> *pitch-dark, without a ray of brightness?"*
> (Amos 5:18–20, emphasis added)

Was Amos speaking of the day of the Lord marked by a new Prophet of God? Such a day brings turmoil and spiritual suffering as each soul is confronted with the choice of remaining with tradition or embracing the new—and the implications of each choice. Amos may have been referring to the coming of Jesus, Whose last hours did bring an episode of darkness. Amos elaborated on this theme of darkness as follows:

> ***"In that day,"*** *declares the Sovereign Lord,*
> *"I will make **the sun go down at noon***
>> ***and darken the earth in broad daylight."***
> (8:9, emphasis added)

Amos seems to speak of the darkness that occurred during the last three hours of the crucifixion of Jesus. It was reported that witnesses saw *the sun go down at noon and darken the earth in broad daylight.* The Gospel of Mark states, *"At noon, darkness came over the whole land until three in the afternoon"* (Mark 15:33); the Gospel of Matthew says, *"From noon until three in the afternoon darkness came over all the land"* (Matt. 27:45); and the Gospel of Luke records, *"It was now about noon, and darkness came over the whole land until three in the afternoon, for the sun stopped shining. And the curtain of the temple was torn in two"* (Luke 23:44–45).

Perhaps the three hours of darkness occurred, but with no historical record of this event, the darkness could symbolize the darkness brought by Jesus's martyrdom. The tearing of the Temple curtain signified that the Mosaic Dispensation had been replaced by that of Jesus.

Amos could also have been referring to the darkness brought on by the martyrdom of another Prophet of God, the Báb. In this case, literal darkness was witnessed by thousands of people when the Báb was publicly executed. He faced His martyrdom by firing squad in the city of Tabriz, Persia, at noon on July 9, 1850 CE. *"The very moment the shots were fired, a gale of exceptional severity arose and swept over the whole city. A whirlwind of dust of incredible density obscured the light of the sun and blinded the eyes of the people. The entire city remained enveloped in that darkness from noon till night."*[11]

CONFRONTATION WITH THE PRIEST AMAZIAH

Not surprisingly, Amos incurred the wrath of the priestly authorities in Bethel and Samaria. It would not have taken long for his words to spread from a city gate or shrine. Amos especially enraged Amaziah, a priest at Bethel, who sent the following message to Jeroboam II.

"Amos is raising a conspiracy against you in the very heart of Israel. The land cannot bear all his words. For this is what Amos is saying:

"'Jeroboam will die by the sword,
and Israel will surely go into exile,
away from their native land.'"
(Amos 7:10–11)

Amaziah ordered Amos out of the country in no uncertain terms. *"Get out, you seer! Go back to the land of Judah. Earn your bread there and do your prophesying there. Don't prophesy anymore at Bethel, because this is the king's sanctuary and the temple of the kingdom"* (7:12–13). Whereupon Amos elaborated on exactly what was going to happen to Israel.

> *Amos answered Amaziah, "I was neither a prophet nor the son of a prophet, but I was a shepherd, and I also took care of sycamore-fig trees. But the LORD took me from tending the flock and said to me, 'Go, prophesy to my people Israel.' Now then, hear the word of the LORD. You say,*
>
> > *"'Do not prophesy against Israel,*
> > *and stop preaching against the descendants of Isaac.'*
>
> *"Therefore this is what the LORD says:*
>
> > *"'Your wife will become a prostitute in the city,*
> > *and your sons and daughters will fall by the sword.*
> > *Your land will be measured and divided up,*
> > *and you yourself will die in a pagan country.*
> > *And Israel will surely go into exile,*
> > *away from their native land'"*
>
> (7:14–17)

The highest religious authority in Israel had rejected the warnings. Amos left for home. Could the people of Israel have escaped the fate that Amos prophesied? Theoretically, yes. The instructions for doing so had been given.

> *This is what the LORD says to Israel:*
> *"Seek me and live;*
> > *do not seek Bethel,*
> *do not go to Gilgal,*
> > *do not journey to Beersheba.*

For Gilgal will surely go into exile,
  and Bethel will be reduced to nothing."
Seek the LORD and live,
  or he will sweep through the tribes of Joseph like a fire;
it will devour them,
  and Bethel will have no one to quench it."
(5:4–6)

However, it was probably known on the skeins of time that it was too late to reverse the spiritual slide and escape the conquest. Assyrian military incursions started in the 730s, and Samaria fell in 722. The kingdom of Israel was no more.

THE PLANTING OF ISRAEL—NEVER TO BE UPROOTED

The ninth and last chapter of the book of Amos looks to the future, both the near and the far. First, the kingdom of Israel will be destroyed:

"Surely the eyes of the Sovereign LORD
  are on the sinful kingdom.
I will destroy it
  from the face of the earth.
Yet I will not totally destroy
  the descendants of Jacob,"
  declares the Lord.
"For I will give the command,
  and I will shake the people of Israel
  among all the nations
as grain is shaken in a sieve,
  and not a pebble will reach the ground.
All the sinners among my people
  will die by the sword,
all those who say,
  'Disaster will not overtake or meet us.'"
(Amos 9:8–10)

57

Immediately following is a prophecy that has traditionally been interpreted as the coming of Jesus, who was a descendant of David, about seven centuries later.

"In that day

> *"I will restore **David's fallen shelter**—*
> *I will repair its broken walls*
> *and restore its ruins—*
> *and will rebuild it as it used to be,*
> *so that they may possess the remnant of Edom*
> *and all the nations that bear my name"*
> *declares the Lord, who will do these things.*
> (9:11–12, emphasis added)

The Christian Covenant would be a new spiritual shelter.

Historically, the Judeans were first restored to their own land after the Babylonian exile when the Persian King Cyrus the Great issued a decree for their return. However, they were vassals of the Persians and then of the Greeks and the Romans. Most were uprooted from the Holy Land after Jerusalem fell to the Romans in 70 CE. The resulting Diaspora of the Jews eventually spread to most countries of the world over two thousand years. Only a small remnant remained in the Holy Land.

Then Amos saw the return of the Jews to their homeland about twenty-six centuries later.

> *"The days are coming," declares the L*ORD,
> *"when the reaper will be overtaken by the plowman*
> *and the planter by the one treading grapes.*
> ***New wine will drip from the mountains***
> ***and flow from all the hills,***
> ***and I will bring my people Israel back***
> ***from exile.***

58

"They will rebuild the ruined cities and live in them.
They will plant vineyards and drink their wine;
they will make gardens and eat their fruit.
I will plant Israel in their own land,
never again to be uprooted
from the land I have given them,"
says the Lord your God.
(9:13–15, emphasis added)

These verses do not point to the return to Jerusalem granted by Cyrus, from which they would be uprooted again. The Jews would establish the modern state of Israel, *never again to be uprooted.* And *new wine* is a symbol of a new religion.

The Zionist movement, the return of the Jews to the Holy Land, started in the mid-nineteenth century and gained momentum during the early twentieth. The modern state of Israel was established in 1948 subsequent to the Balfour Declaration of 1919 that stated: "His Majesty's Government views with favor the establishment in Palestine of a national home for the Jewish people."[12] On November 29, 1947, the United Nations passed Resolution No. 181, which called for the partition of the British-ruled Palestine Mandate into a Jewish state and an Arab state with the city of Jerusalem as a separate entity to be governed by a special international regime.[13] The state of Israel enacted its Law of Return on July 5, 1950, which enabled Jews everywhere to immigrate to the country and be given automatic citizenship. It stated: "Every Jew has the right to come to this country as an oleh [Jewish immigrant]."[14]

Amos and the next prophet, Hosea, might have known each other for a short time while Amos was active in the northern kingdom. Hosea certainly picked up the drumbeat of Amos's righteous anger, as would the prophets to come in Judah. The Mosaic Dispensation had set a divine standard for justice. Without observance of justice as a foundational principle, religious observances were meaningless to God.

Chapter 5

Hosea – Reaping the Whirlwind

But you must return to your God;
maintain love and justice,
and wait for your God always.

THE HEBREWS WERE THE first Middle Eastern people to embrace the one God, to accept monotheism. The gods of other Middle Eastern cultures were mostly understood as capricious beings who needed to be appeased to prevent their harmful actions. They were cajoled for help, and the best a person could expect from them was to simply be left alone. However, the one God of the Hebrews was understood to be involved in their lives, and He had a much different set of attributes—love, beneficence, and forgiveness—despite His often-expressed despair with His people. The prophets presented a dichotomy of God's love and redemption on one hand and disownment and punishment on the other. This is especially clear in the book of Hosea.

The prophet Hosea's ministry stretched several decades, although he seems to have been most active in the mid-730s and the 720s BCE. The call narrative for Hosea places him in the times of several Hebrew kings. *"The word of the LORD that came to Hosea son of Beeri during the reigns of Uzziah, Jotham, Ahaz and Hezekiah, kings of Judah, and during the reign of Jeroboam son of Jehoash king of Israel"* (Hosea 1:1). He lived through

61

the tumultuous last years of violence and instability in the northern kingdom. After the death of long-reigning Jeroboam II in 747, Israel had six kings until the 722 Assyrian conquest of Samaria. Most of these six ascended to the throne through coups and assassinations and suffered the same fates in turn. If Hosea witnessed the conquest in 722, no mention of it survived.

Hosea was the only classical prophet who was a native of the kingdom of Israel, and he probably focused on the cities of Bethel, Gilgal, and Samaria. His use of the name Ephraim for Israel suggests that his origins were in southern Israel in the land of the tribe of Ephraim. A champion for social justice, Hosea preached against the socioeconomic abuses that were at grave odds with the Mosaic teachings. He used the metaphor of an adulterous marriage to symbolize the peoples' unfaithfulness to God.

A MARRIAGE METAPHOR

The first instruction Hosea received was: *"Go, marry a promiscuous woman and have children with her, for like an adulterous wife this land is guilty of unfaithfulness to the LORD"* (Hosea 1:2). The book of Hosea states that he subsequently married a woman named Gomer, and the first three chapters are devoted to the symbol of Israel as an unfaithful wife. The symbology makes it clear that this was not Hosea's actual marriage but was an allegory portraying that the Israelites of God's covenant with Moses had prostituted themselves with idolatry and other sins.

The result was "children" whose names signified the sins of Israel— *Jezreel*, for God would punish the house of Jehu for the massacre at Jezreel;[1] *Lo Ruhamah (Loruhamah)*, "not loved," for God would no longer show love to Israel; and *Lo-Ammi*, "not my people," for the people of Israel were no longer His and He was not their God. When the first son was born, the Lord said to Hosea, *"Call him Jezreel, because I will soon punish the house of Jehu for the massacre at Jezreel, and I will put an end to the kingdom of Israel. In that day I will break Israel's bow in the Valley of Jezreel"* (1:4).

Jezreel was a main northern fortress built by King Ahab in the ninth century and is mentioned more than thirty times in the Hebrew Bible as the setting for various dramatic events during the reigns of the northern kings Ahab, Jehoram, and Jehu. The Valley of Jezreel was an ancient trade route between the Jordan Valley and the coastal plain.

The second child was a daughter. Raw emotions of outrage, distress, and betrayal burst forth, followed by intense sorrow and yearning for reconciliation.

> *Gomer conceived again and gave birth to a daughter. Then the LORD said to Hosea, "Call her Lo-Ruhamah (which means "not loved"), for I will no longer show love to Israel, that I should at all forgive them. Yet I will show love to Judah; and I will save them—not by bow, sword or battle, or by horses and horsemen, but I, the LORD their God, will save them." (1:6–7)*

When a third child, a son, was born, God again chose the name. *Then the LORD said, "Call him Lo-Ammi (which means "not my people"), for you are not my people, and I am not your God"* (1:9).

The Lord has turned His face away from the kingdom of Israel, but a time of redemption was promised. The next two verses promise a most encouraging future:

> *Yet the number of the children of Israel shall be as the sand of the sea, which cannot be measured nor numbered; and it shall come to pass, that in the place where it was said unto them, "Ye are not my people", there it shall be said unto them, "Ye are the sons of the living God." (1:10)*

Israel/Gomer falsely believed that it was her lovers—the gods of idolatrous worship— who gave her food, wool, linen, olive oil, and drink. Therefore, God blocked her path with thorn bushes, walling her in so that she could not find her way to them.

> *"She will chase after her lovers but not catch them;*
> *she will look for them but not find them.*
> *Then she will say, 'I will go back to my husband as at first,*
> *for then I was better off than now.'*

> *She has not acknowledged that I was the one*
> > *who gave her the grain, the new wine and oil,*
> > *who lavished on her the silver and gold—which they used*
> > *for Baal."*

(2:7–8)

After expressing God's pain and anger with Israel, Hosea reveals the divine plan to lure Israel back.

> *"Therefore I am now going to allure her;*
> > *I will lead her into the wilderness*
> > *and speak tenderly to her.*
> *There I will give her back her vineyards,*
> > *and will make the **Valley of Achor** a **door***
> > ***of hope**.*
> *There she will respond as in the days of her youth,*
> > *as in the day she came up out of Egypt."*

(2:14–15, emphasis added)

The Valley of Achor was located halfway between Jerusalem and the north shore of the Dead Sea. Achor translates from Hebrew as "trouble." According to the book of Joshua, an unfortunate fellow named Achan had, against Joshua's orders, kept for himself some of the loot from the defeat of Jericho when it was all to go into the treasury of the Lord. The Israelites' defeat in the next battle indicated that the Lord was unhappy about this. Each tribe, clan, and family were called forth for examination. Achan confessed. Joshua asked, *"Why have you brought this trouble on us? The LORD will bring trouble on you today"* (Joshua 7:25). Achan met his trouble when he was stoned to death.

Hosea's reference to the Valley of Achor was a far-future prophecy. Akka (also called Akko and Acre) was the prison city in Ottoman Palestine to which Bahá'u'lláh, His family, and some of His followers were exiled. David had referred to Akka as *the Strong City* (see Vol. 1, Chapter 12, Psalm 60). Hosea called it a *door of hope*. Bahá'u'lláh quoted the following Islamic tradition, or hadith, in *Epistle to the Son of the Wolf:*

> *The Apostle of God—may the blessings of God and His salutations be upon Him—is reported to have said: "Blessed the man that hath visited 'Akká, and blessed he that hath visited the visitor of 'Akká."*[2]

The *Apostle of God* is a title of Muḥammad and *the visitor* refers to Bahá'u'lláh. 'Abdu'l-Bahá referred to Hosea's *door of hope* as the prison city of Akka.

> *It is recorded in the Torah: And I will give you the valley of Achor for a door of hope. This valley of Achor is the city of 'Akká, and who so hath interpreted this otherwise is of those who know not.*[3]

'Abdu'l-Bahá also remarked on the fulfillment of promises made by the Hebrew prophets.

> *When Bahá'u'lláh arrived at this prison in the Holy Land, discerning souls were awakened to the fact that the prophecies which God had voiced through the tongue of His Prophets two or three thousand years before had been realized and that His promises had been fulfilled, for He had revealed unto certain Prophets and announced unto the Holy Land that the Lord of Hosts would be manifested therein. All these promises were fulfilled,... His enemies intended that this imprisonment should completely destroy and annihilate His Cause, but His incarceration became instead the greatest confirmation and the means of its promotion. The call of God reached the East and the West, and the rays of the Sun of Truth illumined every land. Praise be to God."*[4]

Hosea's *Valley of Achor,* verified above as the city of Akka where Bahá'u'lláh was imprisoned for many years, might also be symbolic of troubled humanity—and this *door of hope* its redemption through Bahá'u'lláh.

CHARGES AGAINST ISRAEL

Hosea's list of charges against Israel has been compared to proceedings in a court of law where an indictment of charges is made. Hosea railed against the sins of Israel in staccato tones. He raged, stormed, and thundered at how Israel had turned against her God and committed innumerable sins:

> *Hear the word of the Lord, you Israelites,*
>> *because the Lord has a charge to bring*
>> *against you who live in the land:*
> *"There is no faithfulness, no love,*
>> *no acknowledgment of God in the land.*
>> *There is only cursing, lying and murder,*
>> *stealing and adultery;*
> *they break all bounds,*
>> *and bloodshed follows bloodshed."*

> *"You stumble day and night,*
>> *and the prophets stumble with you.*
> *So I will destroy your mother—*
>> *my people are destroyed from lack of knowledge."*
> (Hosea 4:1–2, 5)

As in a court of law, a sentence of punishment was given.

> *"Because you have rejected knowledge,*
>> *I also reject you as my priests;*
> *because you have ignored the law of your God,*
>> *I also will ignore your children.*
> *The more priests there were, the more they sinned against me;*
>> *they exchanged their glorious God for something*
>> *disgraceful.*
> *They feed on the sins of my people*
>> *and relish their wickedness.*

And it will be: Like people, like priests.
   I will punish both of them for their ways
   and repay them for their deeds."
(4:5–9)

The sin list was endless—idolatry, temple prostitution, fraud, subversion of the courts, and subjugation of the poor. Punishment would be dire. Hosea was particularly dismayed by the worship of Baal and other gods that the Israelites had adopted from the Canaanites. With biting sarcasm, Hosea ridiculed the Israelites' path to self-destruction through idolatry.

"They set up kings without my consent;
   they choose princes without my approval.
With their silver and gold
   they make idols for themselves
   to their own destruction.
Samaria, throw out your calf-idol!
   My anger burns against them.
How long will they be incapable of purity?
   They are from Israel!
This calf—a metalworker has made it;
   it is not God.
It will be broken in pieces,
   that calf of Samaria."
(8:4–6)

The result was described by Hosea's famous words, *"They sow the wind and reap the whirlwind"* (8:7).

Hosea showed common sense and fairness when he did not blame sacred prostitution on the women, who were often forced into it, but put the blame on the men who patronized the cult prostitutes. God would not punish the daughters because the men themselves consorted with harlots and sacrificed with shrine prostitutes.

How had the people of the kingdom of Israel gone so far off the divine path that had been laid out for them by Moses? One reason was that they were to have been ruled by God through divinely appointed judges and, later, by kings anointed by His prophets. Except for Jeroboam I (931–909), whom the prophet Ahijah told that he was to succeed Solomon, and Jehu (842–814), who was anointed by the prophet Elisha, the kings of the northern kingdom of Israel had not been chosen by God and had ruled without His blessing. *"They set up kings without my consent; they choose princes without my approval"* (8:4).

The leaders were enmeshed in political corruption and the hubris of ignoring the fundamental premise that salvation lay in obedience to God. Instead of returning to the Lord in trust, the kings sought political alliances. *"Ephraim is like a dove, easily deceived and senseless—now calling to Egypt, now turning to Assyria. When they go, I will throw my net over them; I will pull them down like the birds in the sky"* (7:11–12).

And what had God wanted for His people? *"For I desire mercy, not sacrifice, and acknowledgment of God rather than burnt offerings"* (6:6). But the end was near, as Hosea warned.

> *The LORD used a prophet to bring Israel up from Egypt,*
> > *by a prophet he cared for him.*
> *But Ephraim has aroused his bitter anger;*
> > *his Lord will leave on him the guilt of his bloodshed*
> > *and will repay him for his contempt.*
> (12:13–14)

According to Hosea, the nation would fall for many reasons—its selection of rulers without divine approval, its idolatry, and its sins of social injustice. The faithlessness of the people would be the cause of their defeat.

A PROMISE OF FUTURE DISPENSATIONS

Hosea repeatedly exhorted a return to God and His Covenant because He was both the punisher and the forgiver. After emphasizing the punishment of God, Hosea exhorted the people to return to God, Who was the healer and reviver who would restore the people.

> *Come, and let us return unto the* LORD: *for he hath torn, and he will heal us; he hath smitten, and he will bind us up.*
>
> *After* **two days will he revive us: in the third day he will raise us up, and we shall live in his sight.**
>
> *Then shall we know, if we follow on to know the* LORD: *his going forth is prepared as the morning; and he shall come unto us as the rain, as the latter and former rain unto the earth.*
> (Hosea 6:1–3, KJV, emphasis added)

The Bahá'í perspective is that a new revelation from God is like the spring rains that revive the spiritually dead and like the sun that rises to bathe the earth and its inhabitants in light. Hushidar Motlagh, a noted biblical scholar, gave his interpretation of Hosea 6:1–3 and the three-days prophecy:

> A prophecy from Hosea offers the good news of the coming of a "day" when we have the honor of living in the presence of the Lord. He designates the third "day" as the appointed time:
>
> *Come, and let us return to the* LORD; *For He has torn, but He will heal us; He has stricken, but He will bind us up. After* **two** *days He will* **revive us;** *On the* **third day** *He will* **raise us up,** *that we may* **live in His sight.** *Let us know, let us pursue* **the knowledge of the** LORD. *His going forth is established as the morning; He will come to us like the rain, like the latter [new day] and former [previous] rain to the earth* (Hosea 6:1–3, NKJ).

And another translation:

> *Let us set ourselves to know Yahweh [the Promised One]; that he will come is as certain as the dawn; his judgment will rise like the light, he*

will come to us as showers come, like spring rains watering the earth (The Jerusalem Bible).

The "reviving" and the "raising up" are spiritual. The age of the advent of each Redeemer is a new "day," when a new Sun rises and breathes a new life into the spiritually dead. Without the knowledge and the love of God, we are skeletons buried in graves of death and despair.

How many "days" have passed since the prophecy was uttered? Three. The first two pertained to the advent of Jesus and Muhammad. The third pertains to this great day of the Lord.[5]

Returning to the marriage allegory, Hosea was directed by the Lord to reconcile with Gomer after they had been separated because of her promiscuous behavior. He was told by God to show his love to Gomer despite her sins, so he brought her home.

> *And I said unto her, Thou shalt abide for me many days; thou shalt not play the harlot, and thou shalt not be for another man: so will I also be for thee.*
>
> *For the children of Israel shall abide many days without a king, and without a prince, and without a sacrifice, and without an image, and without an ephod, and without teraphim:*
>
> *Afterward shall the children of Israel return, and seek the LORD their God, and David their king; and shall fear the LORD and his goodness in the* **latter days.**
> (3:3–5, KJV, emphasis added)

William Sears, a biblical scholar of renown, asked himself the quintessential question "when?" concerning the *latter days*, also known as the *end times* and the *time of the end*. He came to the following conclusions:

In the book of Hosea, it was promised that:

> "I will give her the vineyards from thence, and the valley of Achor for a door of hope; and she shall sing there as in the days of her youth..." (Hosea 2:15, KJV).

When will this come to pass? It seemed clear to me that it would be *in the last days* when Israel would be forgiven for having turned away from the Messiah in His *first* coming and would have embraced His truth in the time of His *second* coming. On that day, Hosea says:

> "I will have mercy upon her that had not obtained mercy, and I will say to *them which were not my people, Thou art my people*; and they shall say, *Thou art my God*" (2:23, KJV).

Hosea foretells that this will take place at *the time of the end*. First, the valley of Achor will become a place of hope and refuge. Then Israel will return from disbelief and seek their Beloved (David) from the stem of Jesse (seed of Abraham). Hosea says:

> "*Afterward* shall the children of Israel *return*, and seek the Lord their God, and David their king; and shall fear the LORD and his goodness *in the latter days*" (3:5, KJV).

I had already learned that the *"latter days"* and *"the time of the end"* were synonymous. I had also learned that they began in 1844, the year of the birth of Bahá'u'lláh's Faith, and the year of the *return* of the Jews to the Holy Land.[6]

(See Appendix E for the article "End of the World," which discusses the mistranslation of the Greek word *aion*, an error that led to traditional Protestant belief concerning the end of the world.)

Israel fell to the Assyrians in 722 BCE and was no more, despite the efforts of Amos and Hosea. The prophets in Judah emerged next and continued the discourse on disobedience to the Mosaic Covenant. They also continued the tradition of seeing far ahead of their own times.

Chapter 6

Judah on Her Own

*Walk in obedience to all that the L*ORD
your God has commanded you,
so that you may live and prosper and prolong your days
in the land that you will possess.

DEUTERONOMY 5:33

THE TWO IRON AGE kingdoms of Israel and Judah had mostly idol-worshipping, corrupt kings. The few righteous and reformist kings could
not stem the tide of what was to come. Israel had nineteen monarchs
during a little over two hundred years, with average reigns of eleven
years from about 930 to 722 BCE, the date of the Assyrian conquest.
Judah had twenty monarchs over close to three hundred and forty years,
with average reigns of seventeen years from about 930 to 587, the date
of the Babylonian conquest. These numbers indicate that Israel was less
stable than Judah, which had the advantage of the Davidic dynasty.

Judah was only half the size of Israel and had far fewer resources.
It was populated by two tribes, Judah and Benjamin. The Benjaminites
gradually assimilated with the Judahites and lost their identity. Israel was
home to the other ten of the twelve tribes, but Judah had Jerusalem, the
seat of the Davidic house, *whose throne will be established forever* (2 Samuel
7:16). Finkelstein and Silberman commented on the relative weakness of
Judah compared with Israel:

Archaeology shows that the early kings of Judah were not the equals of their northern counterparts in power or administrative ability despite the fact that their reigns and even accession dates are intertwined in the Books of Kings. Israel and Judah were two different worlds.

Despite the long-standing contention that the opulent Solomonic court was the scene of flourishing belles-lettres, religious thought, and history writing, evidence for widespread literacy is utterly lacking in Judah during the time of the united monarchy. Not a single trace of tenth-century Judahite literary activity has been found. Indeed, monumental inscriptions and personal seals—essential signs of a fully developed state—appear in Judah *only two hundred years after Solomon*, in the late eighth century BCE. As mentioned, archaeological surveys indicate that until the eighth century the population of the Judahite highlands was about one-tenth that of the highlands of the northern kingdom of Israel.

It is now clear that Iron Age Judah enjoyed no precocious golden age. David and his son Solomon and the subsequent members of the Davidic dynasty ruled over a marginal, isolated, rural region, with no signs of great wealth or centralized administration.[1]

Mountainous terrain with low rainfall impeded social, economic, and demographic growth. As in Israel, at least eighty percent of the people of Judah lived as nomadic herders or in small villages as agriculturists. However, despite droughts and other depredations of nature, the rural life was remembered, even romanticized, as "the good life." Psalmists and prophets often used rural scenes as metaphors to that effect. The rural life represented independence with a measure of built-in protection and assistance from extended family, the tribe, and the village—not from any king or royal administrative center.

The slowly evolving central governments in Samaria and Jerusalem faced resentment as they spread their tentacles outward. The tax burden fell disproportionately on the poor. The conscription of men for royal works projects and the military disrupted family life, agriculture, and the tending of herds. The past usually looks better when the present is difficult, and it was remembered in the book of Judges that *"In those days Israel had no king; everyone did as they saw fit"* (Jud. 21:25).

Having started as a backwater to Israel, Judah's fortunes changed dramatically in the 720s when refugees fled from Israel to Judah ahead of the invading Assyrian army. This influx was mostly comprised of those who had the money and resources to flee and would contribute greatly to Judah's social and economic development. As is often the case in times of invasion, the urban poor and the rural farmers of Israel would not have had the means to leave and rebuild their lives elsewhere, nor would they have had much reason to do so. The poor were less likely to be deported, and their lives would continue much as before because the Assyrian empire needed their labor for its new province to become profitable. For the poor, one tax collector or military conscription official was as odious as another, regardless of who was in power.

After the division of the united kingdom, the size of Jerusalem expanded from ten or fifteen acres to 150 and the population rose accordingly.[2] Trade increased, towns and industries developed, and a strong middle class of artisans, merchants, civil officials, and entrepreneurs emerged. The seventh century was one of general growth and prosperity until the last Davidic king, Zedekiah (597–596), could not or would not make a firm decision about how to handle the Babylonian invasion despite the explicit, unerring advice he received from the prophet Jeremiah, as we will see.

The two kingdoms, of course, shared the religion of Moses. But as in Israel, few Judahites who lived outside Jerusalem went to the Temple there. It was too far away for most people, especially farmers who could not spare the time away from their crops and animals. In their minds, the nearby high places with altars would serve as well. Finkelstein and Silberman observed the overlay of Mosaic worship over the traditional:

> The existence of high places and other forms of ancestral
> and household god worship was not—as the books of Kings

imply—apostasy from an earlier, purer faith. It was part of
the timeless tradition of the hill country settlers of Judah, who
worshipped YHWH along with a variety of gods and goddesses
known or adapted from the cults of neighboring peoples.
YHWH, in short, was worshipped in a wide variety of ways—
and sometimes pictured as having a heavenly entourage.

This deep-rooted cult was not restricted to the rural districts.
There is ample biblical and archeological information that the
syncretistic cult of YHWH flourished in Jerusalem even in
late monarchic times. The condemnations of various Judahite
prophets make it abundantly clear that YHWH was worshiped
in Jerusalem *together* with other deities, such as Baal, Asherah, the
hosts of heaven, and even the national deities of the neighboring
lands. Jeremiah tells us that the number of deities worshipped in
Judah equaled the number of its cities and that the number of
altars to Baal in Jerusalem equaled the number of bazaar stalls
in the capital (Jeremiah 11:13). Moreover, cult objects dedicated
to Baal, Asherah, and the hosts of heaven were installed in the
Temple of YHWH in Jerusalem.

Thus the great sins of Ahaz and the other evil kings of
Judah should not be seen as exceptional in any way. These rulers
merely allowed the rural traditions to go on unhampered.[3]

Religion was vital to rural people and the gods were all-pervasive in
their lives. The archeologist William Dever noted that feasts and festivals
followed the rhythm of the old Canaanite agriculture calendar. "These
were not at any time specifically 'sacred' celebrations, rather than
secular. There simply was no such distinction in the ancient world, and
certainly not in ancient Israel or Judah. The *whole* of life was permeated
by the presence of the gods. These annual observances were instinctive,
intuitive."[4] Rural life was governed by folk wisdom because the average
person was illiterate and had no access to the Scriptures.

Often the God of Moses was simply added to the pantheon of
deities. This blend was prevalent even in Jerusalem, where Asherah,

a fertility goddess, was honored in the Temple with the installation of an Asherah pole, reputedly as early as the days of Solomon (1 Kings 11:5). This was monolatry, the worship of one god above others but still recognizing the need to worship the others.

Dever reports that three thousand anthropomorphic figurines and cultic objects related to Asherah have been found in the Holy Land, primarily in excavations in Judah and mostly within a domestic context such as a home shrine. He notes, "Here the silence of the biblical texts is deafening. Did the biblical writers deliberately suppress any mention of these 'pagan' artifacts? And does the widespread popularity—precisely in the era of the so-called religious reforms—say anything about their real significance?"[5] The official histories compiled in 1 and 2 Kings and 1 and 2 Chronicles may have been silent, but the prophets were not.

A HOUSE FOR THE LORD

David looked at his lavish palace and wished to build a house for the Lord as His dwelling. His court prophet Nathan had initially acquiesced, but the time was not yet for this enterprise. That night the word of the Lord came to Nathan starting with the question—was David the one to build the house? From there the basic history of the Israelites was recounted, how the Lord had moved with them in a tent and had never asked for a house of cedar. He had taken David from the pasture tending the flocks and appointed him ruler over His people. He had enabled David to conquer his enemies and to prosper. A secure home for the Lord's people, Israel, had been established where the wicked would no longer oppress them. David would be given rest from all his enemies (2 Samuel 7:5–10). The next verses seem to have layers of meaning:

> *"The LORD declares to you that the LORD himself will establish a house for you: When your days are over and you rest with your ancestors, I will raise up your offspring to succeed you, your own flesh and blood, and I will establish his kingdom. He is the one who will build a house for my Name, and I will **establish the throne of his kingdom forever. I will be***

his father, and he will be my son. When he does wrong, I will punish him with a rod wielded by men, with floggings inflicted by human hands. But my love will never be taken away from him, as I took it away from Saul, whom I removed from before you. **Your house and your kingdom will endure forever before me; your throne will be established forever."**

(7:11–16, emphasis added)

David was succeeded by his son, Solomon, who would build the Temple. However, to *establish the throne of his kingdom forever* suggests more than an earthly kingdom. Jesus was of the House of David, and he talked about the eternal Kingdom of God and the promise of life everlasting. No earthly *throne* and *kingdom* endure forever. The earth is littered with the forlorn ruins of formerly great monarchies and civilizations.

The book of 1 Kings describes the building of Solomon's Temple (see Vol. 1, Chapter 11 for details). A promise of forever was seemingly confirmed while the Temple was being built. *"The word of the LORD came to Solomon: 'As for this temple you are building,* **if you follow my decrees, observe my laws and keep all my commands and obey them,** *I will fulfill through you the promise I gave to David your father. And I will live among the Israelites and will not abandon my people Israel'"* (1 Kings 6:11–13, emphasis added). However, there was a most important qualifier contained in this promise—the word **if**. The word **forever** in the Lord's promise to David was embraced wholeheartedly without question, but the **if** condition would be ignored. That would not bode well, as we shall see.

ISAIAH WITH KINGS AHAZ AND HEZEKIAH

The descendants of Solomon reflected poorly on their royal ancestors, but they also reflected their times. Rehoboam continued his father Solomon's support of Asherah worship, thus triggering the "if" warning in the Lord's promise to his father. Five years into Rehoboam's rule, the Egyptian pharaoh Shishak attacked Jerusalem and carried off the treasures of the Temple and the royal palace. The compilers of 1 Kings saw divine retribution at work and gave Rehoboam a scorching epitaph.

Judah did evil in the eyes of the LORD. *By the sins they committed they stirred up his jealous anger more than those who were before them had done. They also set up for themselves high places, sacred stones and Asherah poles on every high hill and under every spreading tree. There were even male shrine prostitutes in the land; the people engaged in all the detestable practices of the nations the Lord had driven out before the Israelites.*
(1 Kings 14:22–24)

This was not an auspicious start for the kingdom of Judah.

Over a century and a half later, Ahaz (Jehoahaz II, 732–716) received the prophet Isaiah's counsel about handling threats from the Assyrians. Ahaz had refused to join three neighboring kings—Pekah of Israel, Rezin of Damascus, and the king of Gaza and Ashkelon to the west—to plot conspiracy against Assyria. These three kings sought revenge by putting Jerusalem under siege with the intent to oust Ahaz and enthrone a king of their own choosing. Panic ensued in Jerusalem. But Isaiah counseled Ahaz to be calm, to not lose heart over these *"two smoldering stubs of firewood"* (Isaiah 7:4) because the Lord had told him as follows:

> *"It will not take place,*
> > *it will not happen,*
> *for the head of Aram is Damascus,*
> > *and the head of Damascus is only Rezin.*
> *Within sixty-five years Ephraim*
> > *will be too shattered to be a people.*
> *The head of Ephraim is Samaria,*
> > *and the head of Samaria is only Remaliah's son.*
> *If you do not stand firm in your faith,*
> > *you will not stand at all."*
> (7:1–9)

However, sixty-five years was a bit long to wait for a solution to an immediate problem. Could faith in God be a realistic government policy? Could a king convince his advisers and military officers to be patient when under threat? What a quandary for Ahaz. Isaiah told him that he was to ask the Lord for a sign, but Ahaz vacillated and refused to ask, giving his reason, or excuse, as not wanting to put the Lord to the test. Isaiah was exasperated.

> *"Hear now, you house of David! Is it not enough to try the patience of humans? Will you try the patience of my God also? Therefore the* LORD *himself will give you a sign:* **The virgin will conceive and give birth to a son, and will call him Immanuel.** *He will be eating curds and honey when he knows enough to reject the wrong and choose the right, for before the boy knows enough to reject the wrong and choose the right, the land of the two kings you dread will be laid waste. The* LORD *will bring on you and on your people on the house of your father a time unlike any since Ephraim broke away from Judah—he will bring the king of Assyria."* (7:13–17, emphasis added)

The above seems to contain an example of a bookended far-future prophecy, that of the virgin birth of Jesus, preceded and succeeded by Isaiah's words to Ahaz.

Ahaz disregarded Isaiah and instead wrote to the Assyrian emperor Tiglath-pileser (745–727) as *"your servant and vassal"* (2 Kings 16:7) and asked for help against the kings of Damascus and Israel. To sweeten the deal, Ahaz sent gold and silver from Judah's treasury. But the Assyrian armies were already on the march and had defeated Damascus and taken over northern Israel. Had Ahaz simply waited out the situation, the armies of the three kings would have withdrawn from the siege of Jerusalem to face the Assyrians. As a neutral, uninvolved kingdom, Judah probably would not have been invaded. Instead, Ahaz brought his kingdom into voluntary vassalage. This foolish decision, which was made against Isaiah's advice, brought a steady stream of Assyrian officials into Judah with their various idolatrous ideologies that reinforced an already strong current of idolatry in Judean religious life.

Ahaz had not finished weakening Judah. When he went to Damascus to meet and pay homage to Tiglath-pileser, he saw a pagan altar that he liked. He had this altar replicated in the Jerusalem Temple and Ahaz offered his sacrifices on it. He gave instructions that this new altar was now the one to be used for all sacrifices and the bronze altar that had been used since the days of Solomon was to be put aside. Ahaz didn't stop there:

> *King Ahaz cut off the side panels and removed the basins from the movable stands. He removed the Sea from the bronze bulls that supported it and set it on a stone base. He took away the Sabbath canopy that had been built at the temple and removed the royal entryway outside the temple of the LORD, in deference to the king of Assyria."* [6]
> (2 Kings 16:17–18)

Ahaz reigned sixteen years and was severely castigated in his remembrance:

> *Unlike David his father, he did not do what was right in the eyes of the LORD his God. He followed the ways of the kings of Israel and even sacrificed his son in the fire, engaging in the detestable practices of the nations the LORD had driven out before the Israelites. He offered sacrifices and burned incense at the high places, on the hilltops and under every spreading tree.*
> (16:2–4)

Hezekiah (715–686), vassal king and son of Ahaz, was made of sterner stuff. He must have pondered long and hard about how the kingdom had fallen so low and perhaps took to heart the warnings Isaiah had given to his father. He recognized idolatry as the causative agent of the fall of Israel and the humiliation of Judah's subservience to Assyria. He started a sweeping religious reformation by assembling the Levite priests and ordering them to purify the Jerusalem Temple by emptying it of everything that was unclean, that is, idolatrous, and then reconsecrating it. It is written that Hezekiah destroyed the pagan high places, broke the Asherah pillars, and removed cultic images wherever he found them.

Hezekiah sought to establish not only the exclusive worship of God but also to concentrate such worship in the Jerusalem Temple, although the temples in administrative centers throughout Judah were not closed. According to the book of 2 Kings, tithing was reinstated, the priests served as they should, and the country prospered to the extent that storerooms were built in the Temple. *"Hezekiah trusted in the LORD, the God of Israel. There was no one like him among all the kings of Judah, either before him or after him. He held fast to the LORD and did not stop following him; he kept the commands the LORD had given Moses"* (18:5–6).

Unfortunately, Hezekiah made a disastrous decision to rebel against Assyria through an alliance with Egypt, which triggered warnings from Isaiah, who had previously strongly advised him against this path but to trust in God. It is speculated that, in Hezekiah's mind, rebellion was a supreme act of faith that God would assure military victory for the newly reformed and purified Judah. The new Assyrian king, Sennacherib (705–681), did not share this sentiment. In about 701 BC, Sennacherib invaded Judah with a vengeance, scourging the country with a savage campaign of economic destruction and deportations. Archeological investigations indicate that forty-six cities, forts, and villages were conquered. Urban centers and the countryside alike were devastated. As usual in such situations, the rural folk suffered the most. The Hebrew Bible gives this disaster only one sentence: *"In the fourteenth year of King Hezekiah's reign, Sennacherib king of Assyria attacked all the fortified cities of Judah and captured them"* (18:13). Whether from embarrassment or denial, this scant attention to the ruination of the country avoided recognizing the suffering of Judah's population that lived outside Jerusalem. The Shephelah, the Judean foothills in western Judah, never recovered and the deportations left it sparsely inhabited.

Sennacherib then put Jerusalem under siege. The Siloam tunnel, also known as Hezekiah's tunnel, was built quickly in 701 to bring water into Jerusalem from the Gihon Spring, which was protected by a massive tower included in the city's defensive wall system. *"It was Hezekiah who blocked the upper outlet of the Gihon spring and channeled the water down to the west side of the City of David"* (2 Chron. 32:30). The tunnel was an engineering marvel built by two teams of workers, one starting from inside Jerusalem and the other from the Gihon Spring outside the city walls. They met in the middle. The meeting point was commemorated with the Siloam Inscription written on the rock wall. The inscription was discovered in 1880 CE and removed from the rock, but it was damaged in the process. It is now displayed in the Istanbul Archaeological Museum.[7]

Sennacherib tried to infuse doubt into Hezekiah's mind by sending him a letter that ridiculed his faith in God for deliverance.

> *"Do not let the god you depend on deceive you when he says, 'Jerusalem will not be given into the hands of the king of Assyria.' Surely you have heard what the kings of Assyria have done to all the countries, destroying them completely. And will you be delivered? Did the gods of the nations that were destroyed by my predecessors deliver them—the gods of Gozan, Harran, Rezeph and the people of Eden who were in Tel Assar?"* (2 Kings 19:10–11)

Now comes a fascinating account of how, finally, Hezekiah turned to God in faith. He took the letter into the Temple and spread it before God in prayer for deliverance. The divine response came through Isaiah, who sent it to Hezekiah in a letter. The words of God told of a reprieve.

> *"Therefore this is what the LORD says concerning the king of Assyria:*
>
> > *'He will not enter this city*
> >   *or shoot an arrow here.*
> > *He will not come before it with shield*
> >   *or build a siege ramp against it.*
> > *By the way that he came he will return;*
> >   *he will not enter this city,*
> >   *declares the LORD.*
> > *I will defend this city and save it,*
> >   *for my sake and for the sake of David my servant.'"*
> (19:32–34)

Tradition states that the besieging soldiers were put to death overnight by an angel of the Lord (19:35). It's been speculated that dysentery, the scourge of armies throughout history, spread through the camp. Perhaps Sennacherib received disturbing news from home about an insurrection of the Babylonians and Chaldeans and withdrew from the siege to return to Nineveh.

The stage was set for Isaiah's ministry and that of Micah and other independent prophets. Isaiah would be a towering figure in the next phase of the Hebrew prophets, who provided more drama than any written by the Greeks or Shakespeare. Isaiah would deal with obtuse denial in the face of stark reality. He would chastise Judah for her sins and utter awesome prophecies. Isaiah would be the most "political" of the prophets, but there was a lot more on his mind than geopolitics. Isaiah's words would reverberate from his time to ours.

Chapter 7

Isaiah – The Day of the Lord of Hosts

Come now, and let us reason together, saith the LORD:
though your sins be as scarlet, they shall be as white as snow;
though they be red like crimson, they shall be as wool.

ISAIAH 1:18, KJV

ISAIAH IS CONSIDERED BY most biblical scholars to be the greatest of the Hebrew prophets and he is the most quoted in the New Testament. He had an unusually long ministry that reportedly started in the last year of the reign of Uzziah, which would have been about 739 BCE, and lasted through three additional Judean kings, traditionally until 687, the last year of the reign of Hezekiah. *"The vision concerning Judah and Jerusalem that Isaiah son of Amoz saw during the reigns of Uzziah, Aha, Ahaz and Hezekiah, kings of Judah"* (Isaiah 1:1). Even though Isaiah had a long period of activity, little is known about him as a person except that he was obviously well educated and was probably a member of the aristocracy since he had access to the court. His book indicates that he was married to a woman he referred to as "the prophetess" and had at least two sons.

Isaiah lived in complex, turbulent times, both politically and religiously, during the decline and fall of the northern kingdom. His book states that he counseled Ahaz during the Assyrian threats of the late

730s, and he also counseled Hezekiah during the Assyrian depredations of Judah and the siege of Jerusalem. He was closer to the kings of Judah than any other prophet, except possibly for Jeremiah, who had intense interactions and altercations with Jehoiakim and also advised and warned Zedekiah personally about the Babylonian threat.

One can feel Isaiah's pain and anguish acutely as he transmits the words of God. His outrage at the victimization of the lower classes is barely contained. Isaiah fights a lonely battle against the low moral standards of his day that desecrated the Mosaic Covenant.

The book of Isaiah is the largest extant trove of Hebrew prophecy. It was preserved first by Isaiah's followers and then probably by a school of scribes and scholars that perpetuated his legacy. Biblical scholars mostly agree that this large book contains distinct works of at least three men from three separate periods. Isaiah himself could only have authored Chapters 1 to 39, called First Isaiah, Proto-Isaiah, and the historical Isaiah. Chapters 40 to 55, called Second Isaiah and Deutero-Isaiah, were written by a person living in Babylonia during late exilic times. Chapters 56 to 66, called Third Isaiah and Trito-Isaiah, were written by an individual living in postexilic Jerusalem. The identities of Second and Third Isaiah are not known.

It is not known why these three works were put together under one name, but the most probable reason is that Second and Third Isaiah were written by adherents of a school inspired by First Isaiah, who is called Isaiah in this chapter and the following one. A comprehensive study of the prophet Isaiah would be encyclopedic. Therefore, only some of the best-known sections of Isaiah are discussed below and in summary form.

THE CALL NARRATIVE

The call to prophethood came to Isaiah in a vision of the Lord in His divine court with seraphim calling to one another.

In the year that King Uzziah died, I saw the LORD, high and exalted, seated on a throne; and the train of his robe filled the temple. Above him were

*seraphim, each with six wings: With two wings they covered their faces,
with two they covered their feet, and with two they were flying. And they were
calling to one another:*

> *"Holy, holy, holy is the LORD Almighty;*
> *the whole earth is full of his glory."*

*At the sound of their voices the doorposts and thresholds shook and the temple
was filled with smoke.*

*"Woe to me!" I cried. "I am ruined! For I am a man of unclean
lips, and I live among a people of unclean lips, and my eyes have seen the
King, the LORD Almighty."*

*Then one of the seraphim flew to me with a live coal in his hand, which
he had taken with tongs from the altar. With it he touched my mouth and
said, "See, this has touched your lips; your guilt is taken away and your sin
atoned for."*

*Then I heard the voice of the Lord saying, "Whom shall I send? And
who will go for us?"*

And I said, "Here am I. Send me!"
(Isaiah 6:1–8)

Having accepted the call, Isaiah received his first instruction from
the Lord.

He said, "Go and tell this people:

> *"'Be ever hearing, but never understanding;*
> *be ever seeing but never perceiving.'*
> *Make the heart of this people calloused;*
> *make their ears dull*
> *and close their eyes.*
> *Otherwise they might see with their eyes*
> *hear with their ears,*

> *understand with their hearts,*
> *and turn and be healed.''*
> (6:9–10).

The perplexity of this charge has long engaged biblical scholars. Surely Isaiah was not being told to enhance the peoples' blindness, deafness, and closed hearts, but that his ministry would make evident these human shortcomings. Moses shared similar thoughts when He summoned the Israelites and said to them: *"Your eyes have seen all that the LORD did in Egypt to Pharaoh, to all his officials and to all his land. With your own eyes you saw those great trials, those signs and great wonders. But to this day the LORD has not given you a mind that understands or eyes that see or ears that hear"* (Deut. 29:2–4). Isaiah was given an alert of the heartbreak in preaching to a people who would react with increased denial, who would not see and would not hear. A stunned Isaiah asked the heartrending question, *"For how long, LORD?"* (6:11). The answer was not encouraging.

> *"Until the cities lie ruined*
> *and without inhabitant,*
> *until the houses are left deserted*
> *and the fields ruined and ravaged,*
> *until the LORD has sent everyone far away*
> *and the land is utterly forsaken.*
> *And though a tenth remains in the land,*
> *it will again be laid waste.*
> *But as the terebinth and oak*
> *leave stumps when they are cut down,*
> *so the holy seed will be the stump in the land.''*
> (6:11–13).

It seems that Isaiah was shown both the looming destruction of the northern kingdom of Israel by the Assyrians culminating in 722 BCE and the many subsequent Assyrian incursions into the southern kingdom of Judah that would lead to her vassalage and then defeat by the Babylonians that culminated in 586. Was Isaiah's mission to be more valuable in the future than in his own time? These verses were certainly a commentary on human obtuseness.

Jesus addressed the theme of closed eyes, ears, and hearts when He was asked by His disciples why He spoke in parables.

He replied, "Because the knowledge of the secrets of the kingdom of heaven has been given to you, but not to them. Whoever has will be given more, and they will have an abundance. Whoever does not have, even what they have will be taken from them. This is why I speak to them in parables:

> *"Though seeing, they do not see;*
>> *though hearing, they do not hear or understand.*
> *In them is fulfilled the prophecy of Isaiah:*

> *"'You will be ever hearing but never understanding;*
>> *you will be ever seeing but never perceiving.*
> *For this people's heart has become calloused;*
>> *they hardly hear with their ears,*
>> *and they have closed their eyes.*
> *Otherwise they might see with their eyes,*
>> *hear with their ears,*
>> *understand with their hearts*
> *and turn, and I would heal them.'"*
(Matt. 13:11–15)

The deeper meaning from Isaiah and Jesus was the refusal, not the inability, of most people to see and hear new truths, to release the hold of religious tradition. Jesus congratulated His disciples for being willing to see and hear. *"For truly I tell you, many prophets and righteous people longed to see what you see but did not see it, and to hear what you hear but did not hear it"* (Matt: 13:17).

WOES AND WARNINGS

Hosea, Micah, and Isaiah were contemporaries for many years, even decades. One wonders if they ever met! Their bitter condemnation of the sins of the leaders in Israel and Judah, of their arrogance and hypocrisy, was similar but with varying degrees of hope as to whether repentance could forestall the calamities that they prophesied. Isaiah was the most forthright about the conquests of both Israel and Judah, whether sooner or later, although He still made every effort to bring Judah to repentance and to renew its commitment to the laws of Moses.

Isaiah starts with a poignant depiction of God's pain caused by the disobedience and rebelliousness of His people.

> *Hear me, you heavens! Listen, earth!*
> > *For the LORD has spoken:*
> *"I reared children and brought them up,*
> > *but they have rebelled against me.*
> *The ox knows its master,*
> > *the donkey its owner's manger,*
> *but Israel does not know,*
> > *my people do not understand."*

(Isaiah 1:2–3)

Isaiah's condemnations of the Israelites' apostasy from the Mosaic teachings are endless, revealing the pleadings of the Lord that they return to the ways of the righteous.

> *Wash you, make you clean; put away the evil of your doings from before mine eyes; cease to do evil;*
> > *Learn to do well; seek judgment, relieve the oppressed, judge the fatherless, plead for the widow.*
> > *Come now, and let us reason together, saith the LORD: though your sins be as scarlet, they shall be as white as snow; though they be red like crimson, they shall be as wool.*
> > *If ye be willing and obedient, ye shall eat the good of the land:*

But if ye refuse and rebel, ye shall be devoured with the sword: for the mouth of the Lord hath spoken it.
(1:16–20, KJV)

Isaiah had a unique manner of itemizing a sin and its punishment in the same breath by issuing a series of "woes" that should have curdled the blood of all who heard them, as follows:

"Woe to the wicked! Disaster is upon them! They will be paid back for what their hands have done" (Isaiah 3:11).

"Woe to you who add house to house and join field to field till no space is left and you live alone in the land" (5:8).

"Woe to those who draw sin along with cords of deceit, and wickedness as with cart ropes" (5:18).

"Woe to those who call evil good and good evil, who put darkness for light and light for darkness, who put bitter for sweet and sweet for bitter. Woe to those who are wise in their own eyes and clever in their own sight. Woe to those who are heroes at drinking wine and champions at mixing drinks, who acquit the guilty for a bribe, but deny justice to the innocent" (5:20–22).

"Woe to those who make unjust laws, to those who issue oppressive decrees, to deprive the poor of their rights and withhold justice from the oppressed of my people, making widows their prey and robbing the fatherless" (10:1–2).

"Woe to those who go to great depths to hide their plans from the LORD, who do their work in darkness and think, 'Who sees us? Who will know?'" (29:15).

If Isaiah's speech was like his written word, he must have been a powerful and mesmerizing speaker. Listeners must have felt like they were dodging verbal spears. Maybe a few spears hit receptive listeners.

He would not have been a soft sounding board for casual arguments. Isaiah saw Judah's ravaging by the Assyrians, which happened during the reign of Hezekiah when the Assyrian armies scourged the country-side and devastated towns and cities. Isaiah's warnings were explicit.

The LORD spoke to me again:

> *"Because this people has rejected*
> > *the gently flowing waters of Shiloah*
> *and rejoices over Rezin*
> > *and the son of Remaliah,*
> *therefore the LORD is about to bring against them*
> > *the mighty floodwaters of the Euphrates—*
> > *the king of Assyria with all his pomp.*
> *It will overflow all its channels,*
> > *run over all its banks*
> > *and sweep on into Judah, swirling over it,*
> > *passing through it and reaching up to the neck.*
> *Its outspread wings will cover the breadth of your land,*
> > *Immanuel!"*
>
> (8:5–8)

Isaiah saw a stark future for Judah after the conquest of Israel. There was only one ray of hope, the promise that God had made for the Davidic kingdom, but its understanding had been perverted. The message given to Solomon had been embraced as false hope because the qualifier "if" had been ignored (see above). The Davidic kings must trust in God rather than in foreign alliances, but they did not. Isaiah had another woe that addressed this lack of faith.

> *Woe to those who go down to Egypt for help,*
> > *who rely on horses,*
> *who trust in the multitude of their chariots*
> > *and in the great strength of their horsemen,*

but do not look to the Holy One of Israel,
*or seek help from the L*ORD.
(31:1)

Ahaz (731–715) and Hezekiah (715–698) both formed alliances with Egypt against Assyria after Isaiah had exhaustively counseled them not to substitute foreign alliances for trust in God. Yet in the "real world," meaning the material world of power and authority, kings had to answer to the court nobility, military commanders, and other voices who clamored for the traditional manner of meeting threat with threat, force with force.

Isaiah warned that although lack of trust in God would doom Judah, there would be positive futures for descendants of the survivors. There would be redemption in the Restoration, the return to Jerusalem in the late sixth century. After that, a new Dispensation would be brought by Jesus. And there would be *the last days.*

A FAR FUTURE

The glimpses Isaiah received of the far future are gentle, soothing, and hopeful:

> *The word that Isaiah the son of Amoz saw concerning Judah and Jerusalem.*
>
> *And it shall come to pass in **the last days**, that the mountain of the **L*ORD*'s house** shall be established in the **top of the mountains**, and shall be exalted above the hills; and **all nations shall flow unto it.***
>
> *And many people shall go and say, Come ye, and **let us go up to the mountain of the L*ORD**, *to the house of the God of Jacob; and he will teach us of his ways, and we will walk in his paths: for out of **Zion** shall go forth the **law**, and the **word of the L*ORD *from Jerusalem**.*
>
> *And he shall judge among the nations, and shall rebuke many people: and they shall beat their **swords into plowshares**, and their **spears into pruning hooks**: nation shall not lift up sword against nation, neither shall they learn war any more.*

*O house of Jacob, come ye, and let us walk in **the light of the LORD**.*
(Isaiah 2:1–5, KJV, emphasis added)

As discussed previously, the terms "time of the end," the "end times," and the "last days" refer to the end of the Prophetic Cycle that started with Adam and ended with Muḥammad, and the beginning of the Cycle of Fulfillment, the Bahá'í Cycle that started in 1844 with the Dispensation of the Báb and then of Bahá'u'lláh.

Shoghi Effendi commented on Isaiah 2:4 and the inevitable maturity of humanity when he wrote as follows:

> No less enthralling is the vision of Isaiah, the greatest of the Hebrew Prophets, predicting, as far back as twenty-five hundred years ago, the destiny which mankind must, at its stage of maturity, achieve: "And He (the Lord) shall judge among the nations, and shall rebuke many people: and they shall beat their swords into plowshares, and their spears into pruninghooks: nation shall not lift up sword against nation, neither shall they learn war anymore."[1]

The biblical scholar Hushidar Motlagh offered his understanding of the symbols Isaiah used as follows:

> The prophecy conveys both literal and symbolic meanings. The literal meaning is that the Lord's House will be built on mountains. The symbolic meaning is that the mountain (the institution) of the House of Justice stands on top of all mountains (institutions). As we noted earlier, according to the Christian scholar, George Lamsa, "the mountain of the Lord means 'the Kingdom of the Lord.'"
>
> "The light of the Lord" literally means Bahá'u'lláh. The same prophecy also appears with slight variations in Micah 4:2. Instead of "Many people shall go and say," it declares "Many nations shall come and say…"

94

"The House" also symbolizes God's Plan for humankind. Every Messenger and Redeemer has offered to build that house—one of justice and order—on our planet, but people have refused to accept it.

"The house" may also apply to Bahá'í local and national institutions. They too are called Houses of Justice. Thousands of them exist today. For the present, they are called Local or National Spiritual Assemblies.

Once again, the Spirit of Christ has come to build His house, based on the divine Plan.[2]

Shrines and altars were built on hilltops and mountaintops, commonly called the high places. However, Isaiah used the singular for mountain—*let us go up to the mountain of the* **LORD**—which Bahá'ís understand to mean Mount Carmel. Members of National Spiritual Assemblies from all over the world have been coming as delegates from almost every country and territory to the International Bahá'í Conventions held on Mount Carmel every five years to cast their ballots for members of the Universal House of Justice. These Conventions are the most diverse gatherings of humanity ever held on earth. In addition, thousands of Bahá'í pilgrims, visitors, and tourists come each year to the Shrine of the Báb and the gardens and offices of the Bahá'í World Center on Mount Carmel. The peace brought by beating *swords into plowshares* and *spears into pruning hooks* is the inevitable peace, foretold by Bahá'u'lláh, that mankind must, and will, achieve in its maturity.

The term *Zion* originally referred to a Jebusite fortress located on the crest of a hill in the southeast corner of Jerusalem. After David moved the Ark of the Covenant into the Temple, the Temple became known as Zion and symbolized the presence of God. Zion gradually lost its specific geographic designation and came to mean the Temple area and even the entire city of Jerusalem. *"God is renowned in Judah; in Israel his name is great. His tent is in Salem, his dwelling place in Zion"* (Ps. 76:1–2).

After Jerusalem and the Temple were destroyed by the Babylonians in the early sixth century BCE, prophetic hope for the future was often expressed in terms of the restoration of Zion, and sometimes Zion referred to the people. Jerusalem and the Temple were rebuilt in the fifth century, but the symbolic meaning of Zion evolved to mean the Holy Land in general and its people, and then Mount Carmel in particular. Jerusalem denoted the renewed word of God that would issue from Zion. Bahá'u'lláh elaborated on this theme.

> *The time foreordained unto the peoples and kindreds of the earth is now come. The promises of God, as recorded in the holy Scriptures, have all been fulfilled. Out of Zion hath gone forth the Law of God, and Jerusalem, and the hills and land thereof, are filled with the glory of His Revelation. Happy is the man that pondereth in his heart that which hath been revealed in the Books of God, the Help in Peril, the Self-Subsisting.*[3]

Bahá'u'lláh wrote the *Kitáb-i-Aqdas*, the Book of Laws, while He was a prisoner in Akka. Today the laws of Bahá'u'lláh are promulgated from the Universal House of Justice, whose Seat is on Mount Carmel. 'Abdu'l-Bahá clarified the symbolism of the holy city, Jerusalem.

> *We have explained before that what the Sacred Scriptures most often mean by the Holy City or divine Jerusalem is the religion of God, which has at times been likened to a bride, or called "Jerusalem", or depicted as the new heaven and the new earth.*
>
> *Likewise, the religion of God is described as the Holy City or the New Jerusalem. Clearly, the New Jerusalem which descends from heaven is not a city of stone and lime, of brick and mortar, but is rather the religion of God which descends from heaven and is described as new. For it is obvious that the Jerusalem which is built of stone and mortar does not descend from heaven and is not renewed, but that what is renewed is the religion of God.*[4]

Zion and Jerusalem are often used symbolically in the Hebrew Scriptures.

96

THE DAY OF THE LORD

Isaiah condemned the peoples' superstitions, their practice of divination and pagan customs, idolatry, and militarism that would bring them low. However, Isaiah often sought to give comfort through his sight into the far future:

> *Enter into the rock, and hide thee in the dust, for fear of the LORD, and for the glory of his majesty.*
>
> *The lofty looks of man shall be humbled, and the haughtiness of men shall be bowed down, **and the LORD alone shall be exalted in that day.***
>
> *For the day of the LORD of hosts shall be upon every one that is proud and lofty, and upon every one that is lifted up; and he shall be brought low...*
> (Isaiah 2:10–12, KJV, emphasis added)

Bahá'u'lláh wrote that Isaiah was proclaiming the day of God in these verses, a day glorified in all the holy scriptures, by which is meant the day of Bahá'u'lláh's Cause:

> *In the Book of Isaiah it is written: "Enter into the rock, and hide thee in the dust, for fear of the Lord, and for the glory of His majesty." No man that meditateth upon this verse can fail to recognize the greatness of this Cause, or doubt the exalted character of this Day—the Day of God Himself. This same verse is followed by these words: **"And the LORD alone shall be exalted in that Day."** This is the Day which the Pen of the Most High hath glorified in all the holy Scriptures. There is no verse in them that doth not declare the glory of His holy Name, and no Book that doth not testify unto the loftiness of this most exalted theme. Were We to make mention of all that hath been revealed in these heavenly Books and holy Scriptures concerning this Revelation, this Tablet would assume impossible dimensions. It is incumbent in this Day, upon every man to place his whole trust in the manifold bounties of God, and arise to disseminate, with the utmost wisdom, the verities of His Cause. Then, and only then, will the whole earth be enveloped with the morning light of His Revelation*[5] (emphasis added).

Isaiah moved like a pendulum between pronouncing God's judgment and devastation and then speaking of God's mercy and redemption. He didn't mince words when he proclaimed divine judgment on Judah and Jerusalem. *"Jerusalem staggers, Judah is falling; their words and deeds are against the LORD, defying his glorious presence. Woe to them! They have brought disaster upon themselves"* (3:8–9). Isaiah warned that the social structure would collapse and oppression would ensue, *man against man, neighbor against neighbor* (3:3). Like Hosea, Isaiah used the metaphor of a courtroom where the Lord takes His place and rises to enter judgment against the elders and leaders of the people.

> *"It is you who have ruined my vineyard;*
> *the plunder from the poor is in your houses.*
> *What do you mean by crushing my people*
> *and grinding the faces of the poor?"*
> *declares the Lord, the LORD Almighty.*
> (3:14–15)

Isaiah's pendulum could swing to blame and judgment upon the upper class for crushing the poor, and then reverse direction to a day of beauty and glory in a drastic time shift into the far future.

> *In that day shall **the branch of the LORD** be beautiful and glorious, and the fruit of the earth shall be excellent and comely for them that are escaped of Israel.*
>
> *And it shall come to pass, that **he that is left in Zion, and he that remaineth in Jerusalem,** shall be called holy, even every one that is written among the living in Jerusalem:*
>
> *When the LORD shall have washed away the filth of the daughters of Zion, and shall have purged the blood of Jerusalem from the midst thereof by the spirit of judgment, and by the spirit of burning.*
>
> *And the LORD will create upon every dwelling place of mount Zion, and upon her assemblies, **a cloud and smoke by day, and the shining of a flaming fire by night**: for upon all the glory shall be a **defence**.*

*And there shall be a **tabernacle** for a shadow in the day time from*
the heat, and for a place of refuge, and for a covert from storm and from rain.
(Isaiah 4:2–6, KJV, emphasis added)

The above strongly suggests that Isaiah was speaking of the Day of
the Lord of our time, Bahá'u'lláh. Abdu'l-Bahá was called by Bahá'u'lláh
the Branch and also the Most Mighty Branch.[6] As reviewed above, Zion
can symbolize Mount Carmel. One of the symbolic meanings of Jerusalem is the new Word of God.

The *cloud of smoke by day and a glow of flaming fire by night* brings to
mind Exodus 13:21: *"By day the Lord went ahead of them in a pillar of cloud to*
guide them on their way and by night in a pillar of fire to give them light, so that
they could travel by day or night." As the Lord guided the ancient Israelites
on their spiritual journey and has guided peoples throughout the ages,
He is still guiding humanity on its spiritual journey by day and night.
The *Tabernacle* is reminiscent of the early Israelites believing that God
accompanied the tablets of the Ten Commandments in the ark of the
covenant as it was carried on the journey and subsequently put in a tent.
The tent that was erected on Mount Carmel for Bahá'u'lláh during His
visits there was called the Tabernacle of Glory. The *Tabernacle* could also
be a metaphor for the Covenant of Bahá'u'lláh, which offers protection
and refuge for all who seek it.

Isaiah also alluded many times to the mysticism of Mount Carmel
and to its future significance for the Bahá'í Faith.

> *The desert and the parched land will be glad;*
>   *the wilderness will rejoice and blossom.*
> *Like the crocus, it will burst into bloom;*
>   *it will rejoice greatly and shout for joy.*
> *The glory of Lebanon will be given to it,*
>   *the splendor of Carmel and Sharon;*
> *they will see **the glory of the LORD**,*
>   *the splendor of our God.*
> (35:1–2, emphasis added)

Modern Israel is renowned for planting trees and flowers to transform the barren areas of Ottoman Palestine and the British Mandate, and for draining the swamps to claim agricultural land. The early Bahá'ís planted shrubs and flowers on Mount Carmel, and Shoghi Effendi planned extensive gardens for Mount Carmel and made substantial progress in their development that is continued to this day. The beautiful gardens of the Bahá'í World Centre reflect how the *glory of the Lord*, Bahá'u'lláh, would illuminate Carmel, as Bahá'u'lláh.

> *Call out to Zion, O Carmel, and announce the joyful tidings: He that was hidden from mortal eyes is come! His all-conquering sovereignty is manifest; His all-encompassing splendour is revealed. Beware lest thou hesitate or halt. Hasten forth and circumambulate the City of God that hath descended from heaven, the celestial Kaaba round which have circled in adoration the favoured of God, the pure in heart, and the company of the most exalted angels.*[7]

The modern state of Israel blossoms on the physical level while divine blessings of the Glory of the Lord emanate from the global headquarters of the Bahá'í Faith on Mount Carmel, where His Writings are preserved and the global administrative work of His Faith is conducted. On the slopes of the holy mountain are the Shrine of the Báb and the Seat of the Universal House of Justice, as well as other edifices. The beautiful gardens at the Bahá'í World Centre, and the nineteen garden terraces built from street level to the top of Mount Carmel, attract visitors from around the world.

THE NAMES OF BAHÁ'U'LLÁH

Shoghi Effendi listed several of the titles and references to Bahá'u'lláh that Isaiah used. All but one of them, as shown below in quotation marks, are found in First Isaiah. The other one, *"will come with strong hand,"* is found in Second Isaiah.

To Him Isaiah, the greatest of the Jewish prophets, had alluded as the *"Glory of the Lord,"* the *"Everlasting Father,"* the

"Prince of Peace," the *"Wonderful,"* the *"Counsellor,"* the *"Rod come forth out of the stem of Jesse"* and the *"Branch grown out of His roots,"* Who *"shall be established upon the throne of David,"* Who *"will come with strong hand,"* Who *"shall judge among the nations,"* Who *"shall smite the earth with the rod of His mouth, and with the breath of His lips slay the wicked,"* and Who *"shall assemble the outcasts of Israel, and gather together the dispersed of Judah from the four corners of the earth."* [8]

*O Pope! Rend the veils asunder. He Who is the **Lord of Lords** is come overshadowed with clouds, and the decree hath been fulfilled by God, the Almighty, the Unrestrained. He, verily, hath again come down from Heaven even as He came down from it the first time. Beware that thou dispute not with Him even as the Pharisees disputed with Him [Jesus] without a clear token or proof.* [9] (emphasis added)

*O followers of the Son! We have once again sent John unto you, and He, verily, hath cried out in the wilderness of the Bayán: O peoples of the world! Cleanse your eyes! The Day whereon ye can behold the Promised One and attain unto Him hath drawn nigh! O followers of the Gospel! Prepare the way! The Day of the advent of the **Glorious Lord** is at hand! Make ready to enter the Kingdom. Thus hath it been ordained by God, He Who causeth the dawn to break.* [10] (emphasis added)

*The **King of Glory** proclaimeth from the tabernacle of majesty and grandeur His call, saying: O people of the Gospel! They who were not in the Kingdom have now entered it, whilst We behold you, in this day, tarrying at the gate.* [11] (emphasis added)

(See Appendix F for additional information on the titles of Bahá'u'lláh.)

"OUR GREEN ISLAND"

Isaiah may have foreseen how Bahá'u'lláh, in His later years, would enjoy a garden on a beautiful island.

*Look upon Zion, the city of our solemnities: thine eyes shall see Jerusalem a quiet habitation, a **tabernacle** that shall not be taken down; not one of the **stakes** thereof shall ever be removed, neither shall any of the **cords** thereof be broken.*

*But there the glorious LORD will be unto us a place of broad rivers and streams; wherein shall go no galley with oars, neither shall **gallant ship** pass thereby.*

(Isaiah 33:20–21, KJV, emphasis added)

We've discussed the meaning of the *tabernacle.* The *stakes* and *cords* that secure the tabernacle suggest the many aspects of the Covenant of Bahá'u'lláh that prevent schisms over questions of successorship as head of the Bahá'í Faith, interpretations of the Bahá'í Scriptures, and the authority of the Universal House of Justice as infallible in its decisions arrived at as a consultative body under the care and guidance of Bahá'u'lláh.

Bahá'u'lláh had been initially imprisoned in Akka under severe restrictions, but gradually these were lessened and He became freer in His movements. In 1875, 'Abdu'l-Bahá rented an island near Akka that was formed by two canals diverted from the Na'mayn River to power flour mills. These canals could not accommodate a *gallant ship.* He and the early Bahá'ís created an exquisite garden for Bahá'u'lláh on this island. Bahá'u'lláh wrote about this island of retreat for Him as follows:

One day of days We repaired unto Our Green Island. Upon Our arrival, We beheld its streams flowing, and its trees luxuriant, and the sunlight playing in their midst. Turning Our face to the right, We beheld what the pen is powerless to describe; nor can it set forth that which the eye of the Lord of Mankind witnessed in that most sanctified, that most sublime, that blest, and most exalted Spot. Turning, then, to the left We gazed on one of the Beauties of the Most Sublime Paradise, standing on a pillar of light, and calling aloud saying: "O inmates of earth and heaven! Behold ye My beauty, and My radiance, and My revelation, and My effulgence. By God, the True

One! I am Trustworthiness and the revelation thereof, and the beauty thereof.
I will recompense whosoever will cleave unto Me, and recognize My rank
and station, and hold fast unto My hem. "[12]

In time, this Green Island came to be known as the Riḍván Garden,
in commemoration of the original Garden of Riḍván in Baghdad
to which Bahá'u'lláh retreated for a few days with His companions
before embarking on the next phase of His exile to Constantinople. It
was in the Garden of Riḍván that Bahá'u'lláh announced His identity
and ministry.

Taherzadeh related how a Bahá'í pilgrim named Haji Yahuda,
a Persian Jewish convert, met Bahá'u'lláh on the Green Island about
1890.

As soon as he was ushered into His presence, the scene of water
flowing from the fountain near Bahá'u'lláh's feet as He sat on the bench
surrounded by the two streams, vividly brought to his mind the vision of
the Prophets of Israel as recorded in the Old Testament:

There is a river, the streams whereof shall make glad the city of God, the
holy place of the tabernacles of the most High. God is in the midst of her;
she shall not be moved: God shall help her, and that right early.
(Psalm 46:4–5, KJV)

But there the glorious LORD will be unto us a place of broad rivers and
streams; wherein shall go no galley with oars, neither shall gallant ship
pass thereby.
(Isaiah 33:21, KJV)

He was overwhelmed by this vision so suddenly and vividly
revealed to him. It came upon him like a thunderbolt and he
was carried away into a different world. His whole being was
stirred to its depths as he saw himself standing with awe and
wonder in the presence of the Lord of the Old Testament. His
instant urge was to prostrate himself at the feet of Bahá'u'lláh,

and this he did. The effect of this first meeting, and of hearing the utterances of Bahá'u'lláh on that occasion, was to create a fire of love and adoration which continued to burn within his heart till the end of his life. He was transformed into a new creation and was exultant with joy as he left the Holy Land.[13]

Upon his return to Persia, Haji Yahuda became one of the foremost teachers of the Bahá'í Faith. He brought many of his fellow Jews under the banner of Bahá'u'lláh while enduring hardships as a Bahá'í teacher in an Islamic land.

Chapter 8

Isaiah – A Child, a Rod, and a Branch

Spiritual discoveries are of two kinds: One, which is commonly
referred to among other peoples, is mere
imagination, while the other
is true spiritual visions such as the revelations of Isaiah,
of Jeremiah, and of John.

'Abdu'l-Bahá

THE PROPHET ISAIAH CASTIGATED the kings, priests, and people for their sins; counseled kings, often to no avail; and gave prophecies that were sometimes straightforward but oftentimes complex with deep theological perplexities. This chapter will examine the prophecies found in Isaiah 9:6–7 and 11:1–12. There is much to ponder in the themes of the child and the governance that will fall on his shoulders; the Prince of Peace; the throne of David; the rod out of the stem of Jesse; the Branch; the wolf and the lamb; the knowledge of the Lord as the waters cover the sea; and the gathering of the Jewish people in the Holy Land from all over the world. Some of the verses find fulfillment in Jesus's ministry, while others do not. It was not until recently in religious history, with the benefit of hindsight, that it became apparent that some of Isaiah's prophecies were fulfilled by the Bahá'í Dispensation.

A CHILD IS BORN

The phrase *"For unto us a child is born"* introduces one of the best known, most quoted, passages from Isaiah. They are commemorated in George Frederick Handel's oratorio masterpiece *Messiah*.

Responding to the failure of Ahaz and his court to trust in the Lord when under military threat, and to Ahaz seeking protection by voluntarily putting Judah under vassalage to Assyria, Isaiah warned that the times would be desperate. *"Prepare for battle, and be shattered!"* (Isaiah 7:9) because *"the LORD is about to bring against them the mighty floodwaters of the Euphrates— the king of Assyria with all his pomp"* (8:7). The people of Jerusalem *"will fall and be broken, they will be snared and captured"* (8:15). Isaiah warned against consulting mediums and spiritists instead of turning to God. *"Consult God's instruction and the testimony of warning. If anyone does not speak according to this word, they have no light of dawn"* (8:20). The famished would roam through the land and curse their king and God. *"Then they will look toward the earth and see only distress and darkness and fearful gloom, and they will be thrust into utter darkness"* (8:22). Surprisingly, Isaiah gave hope as he turned deftly to another time.

The gloom will not be forever because in the future God *"will honor the Galilee of the nations, by Way of the Sea, beyond the Jordan"* (9:1). There will be jubilation because people will see a great light and their yoke of a burden will be shattered. War will be no more. *"Every warrior's boot used in battle and every garment rolled in blood will be destined for burning, will be fuel for the fire"* (9:5). Why will this be? When will this be? What will have happened to bring an end to war?

> For unto us **a child is born**, unto us a son is given: and **the government shall be upon his shoulder**: and his name shall be called *Wonderful*, **Counsellor**, *The mighty God*, **The everlasting Father**, **The Prince of Peace**.
>
> *Of the increase of his* **government** *and peace there shall be no end, upon the* **throne of David**, *and upon his kingdom, to order it, and to establish it with judgment and with justice from henceforth even forever. The zeal of the* **LORD of hosts** *will perform this.*
>
> (Isaiah 9:6–7, KJV, emphasis added)

We now come to the interesting concept of partial fulfillment and greater fulfillment of biblical prophecy. The verses of Isaiah 9:6–7 were partially fulfilled through Jesus, who was a descendant of David and sat on the spiritual *throne of David*. 'Abdu'l-Bahá said in an address given during His tour in the United States in 1912: *"He was seated upon the* **throne of David***, but His sovereignty was neither Napoleonic sovereignty nor the vanishing dominion of a Pharaoh. The Christ Kingdom was everlasting, eternal in the heaven of the divine Will"*[2] (see Appendix G for excerpts from the talk).

Jesus denounced any claim to temporal authority when He said, *"My kingdom is not of this world"* (John 18:36). His name was not *the everlasting Father.* He referred to Himself as the Son. Rather than being known as *Counsellor,* Jesus was often called Rabbi, or teacher. Jesus made no claim to be the *Prince of Peace*, saying instead, *"Do not suppose that I have come to bring peace to the earth. I did not come to bring peace, but a sword"* (Matt. 10:34).

There is a fulfillment of the above two verses through Bahá'u'lláh for many reasons. Consider the phrase *the zeal of the* LORD *of hosts* (9:7, 37:32), which was twice spoken by Isaiah. Just before assuring Hezekiah that Jerusalem would not be defeated by the Assyrians at its gate, that they would not launch a single arrow, Isaiah seemed to see the far future in the same respect as had Hosea:

"This will be the sign for you, Hezekiah:

> *"**This year** you will eat what grows by itself,*
>> *and the **second year** what springs from that.*
> *But in the **third year** sow and reap,*
>> *plant vineyards and eat their fruit.*
> *Once more a remnant of the kingdom of Judah*
>> *will take root below and bear fruit above.*
> *For out of Jerusalem will come a remnant,*
>> *and out of **Mount Zion** a band of survivors.*

"The zeal of the LORD *Almighty will accomplish this."*
(2 Kings 19:29, 31, emphasis added)

Hosea used the metaphors of the first year, the second year, and the third year to designate the three Dispensations to come—Christianity, Islam, and the Bahá'í Faith. The same could be true in the above verses of Isaiah. The fullness of the fruits of the third year, after subsisting on what had come before, suggests the completeness of the Revelation of Bahá'u'lláh for a new cycle. The *Lord of Hosts* is one of the titles of Bahá'u'lláh.

'Abdu'l-Bahá referred to Isaiah 9:7 and the *Lord of Hosts* when He wrote about Bahá'u'lláh's arrival to the prison in Akka.

> *"When Bahá'u'lláh arrived at this prison in the Holy Land, discerning souls were awakened to the fact that the prophecies which God had voiced through the tongue of His Prophets two or three thousand years before had been realized and that His promises had been fulfilled, for He had revealed unto certain prophets and announced unto the Holy Land that the **Lord of Hosts** would be manifested therein."*[3] (emphasis added)

Bahá'u'lláh wrote a tablet to Pope Pius IX in which first He touched upon the missions of John the Baptist and Jesus. Then He focused on *these Days* of cleansing *with the water of life at the hands of His providence* and identified Himself as the *Father* and the *Comforter* as follows:

> *We sent forth him who was named John to baptize you with water, that your bodies might be cleansed for the appearance of the Messiah. He, in turn, purified you with the fire of love and the water of the spirit in anticipation of these Days whereon the All-Merciful hath purposed to cleanse you with the water of life at the hands of His loving providence. This is the **Father** foretold by Isaiah, and the **Comforter** concerning Whom the Spirit [Jesus] had covenanted with you. Open your eyes, O concourse of bishops, that ye may behold your Lord seated upon the Throne of might and glory.*[4] (emphasis added)

'Abdu'l-Bahá referred to Bahá'u'lláh as the *Prince of Peace* when He wrote about the eventuality and inevitability of universal peace:

*The **Sun of Truth** hath risen above the horizon of this world and cast down its bounty of guidance. Eternal grace is never interrupted, and a fruit of that everlasting grace is universal peace. Rest thou assured that in this era of the spirit, the Kingdom of Peace will raise up its tabernacle on the summits of the world, and the commandments of the **Prince of Peace** will so dominate the arteries and nerves of every people as to draw into His sheltering shade all the nations on earth. From springs of love and truth and unity will the true Shepherd give His sheep to drink.*[5] (emphasis added)

'Abdu'l-Bahá reiterated that Bahá'u'lláh was the *Sun of Truth* when He wrote: *"This is my firm, my unshakable conviction, the essence of my unconcealed and explicit belief—a conviction and belief which the denizens of the Abhá Kingdom fully share: The Blessed Beauty is the Sun of Truth, and His light the light of truth. The Báb is likewise the Sun of Truth, and His light the light of truth."*[6]

The Sun of Truth and the Spirit of Truth seem to be interchangeable phrases, subject to the vagaries of translation. The Gospel of John states how Jesus had warned His disciples that He must soon go away so that the Spirit of Truth could come. Jesus explained to His grief-stricken disciples that it was for their good that He was leaving because the Spirit of Truth would guide them unto all truth.

*And I will pray the Father, and he shall give you another **Comforter**, that he may abide with you for ever;*

*Even the **Spirit of truth**; whom the world cannot receive, because it seeth him not, neither knoweth him: but ye know him; for he dwelleth with you, and shall be in you.* (John 14:16–17, KJV, emphasis added)

In addition,

I have yet many things to say unto you, but ye cannot bear them now. Howbeit when he, the Spirit of truth, is come, he will guide you into all truth: for he shall not speak of himself; but whatsoever he shall hear, that shall he speak: and he will shew you things to come.

(John 16:12–13)

One traditional interpretation is that Jesus was speaking of the coming of the Holy Spirit, which in Christianity is the third Person of the Trinity—the spirit of God. Bahá'u'lláh identified Himself as the *Spirit of Truth* when He wrote in the *Lawḥ-i-Aqdas* (Tablet to the Christians):

> *"Announce thou unto the priests: Lo! He Who is the Ruler is come. Step out from behind the veil in the name of thy Lord, He Who layeth low the necks of all men. Proclaim then unto all mankind the glad tidings of this mighty, this glorious Revelation. Verily, He Who is **the Spirit of Truth** is come to guide you unto all truth. **He speaketh not as prompted by His own self, but as bidden by Him Who is the All-Knowing, the All-Wise.**"*[7] (emphasis added)

Note the similarity of meaning with Jesus's statement—*"He will not speak on his own; he will speak only what he hears"*—with what Bahá'u'lláh wrote of Himself—*"He speaketh not as prompted by His own self, but as bidden by Him Who is the All-Knowing, the All-Wise."*

It appears that Isaiah shifted into a future twenty-five hundred years ahead of his time and even beyond. William Sears studied possible meanings of Isaiah 9:6–7 and noted:

1. The *government was upon the shoulder* of Bahá'u'lláh. His Writings established local, national, and international institutions to preserve His faith, and to protect the human rights of mankind.

2. His name *could* be called *the Counsellor,* for his laws established the principle of "consultation" for each of these governing institutions.

3. As Christ was called the Son, in like manner, I found that Bahá'u'lláh was called *the Father.* His mission was that of a Father: to gather together the human family into one household, the planet. To unite the nations, races, and religions was the purpose of his coming, Bahá'u'lláh declared. He was the Father of all religions, races, and peoples, with complete equality.

4. Unlike Christ, Bahá'u'lláh's mission *was* to bring peace. His whole purpose was to establish universal peace. He was a *Prince of Peace*.

5. There was indeed an *increase in the kingdom* of Bahá'u'lláh. It has spread from the day of its birth ... to all parts of the world.[8]

A ROD AND A BRANCH

Isaiah addressed the subjects of the *rod* and the *Branch* and foretold in a scant twelve verses events starting in the nineteenth century CE and reaching many hundreds of years beyond.

And there shall come forth **a rod out of the stem of Jesse**, *and* **a Branch** *shall grow out of his roots:*

And the spirit of the Lord *shall rest upon him, the spirit of wisdom and understanding, the spirit of counsel and might, the spirit of knowledge and of the fear of the* Lord;

And shall make him of quick understanding in the fear of the Lord: *and he shall not judge after the sight of his eyes, neither reprove after the hearing of his ears:*

But with righteousness shall he judge the poor, and reprove with equity for the meek of the earth: and he shall smite the earth: with the rod of his mouth, and with the breath of his lips shall he slay the wicked.

And righteousness shall be the girdle of his loins, and faithfulness the girdle of his reins.

The **wolf also shall dwell with the lamb, and the leopard shall lie down with the kid; and the calf and the young lion** *and the fatling together; and* **a little child shall lead them.**

And the cow and the bear shall feed; their young ones shall lie down together: and the lion shall eat straw like the ox.

And the **sucking child shall play on the hole of the asp,** *and the weaned child shall put his hand on the cockatrice' den.*

They shall not hurt nor destroy in all my holy mountain: for the earth shall be full of the knowledge of the Lord, **as the waters cover the sea.**

*And in that day there shall be a root of Jesse, which shall stand for an **ensign*** of the people; to it shall the Gentiles seek: and his rest shall be glorious.*

And it shall come to pass in that day, that the LORD shall set his hand again the second time to recover the remnant of his people, which shall be left, from Assyria, and from Egypt, and from Pathros, and from Cush, and from Elam, and from Shinar, and from Hamath, and from the islands of the sea.

*And he shall set up **an ensign for the nations**, and **shall assemble the outcasts of Israel, and gather together the dispersed of Judah from the four corners of the earth*** (Isaiah 11:1–12, KJV, emphasis added).

*The NIV version uses the word banner instead of ensign.

'Abdu'l-Bahá gave a lengthy discourse on these verses. His words are too succinct, and his train of thought too precise, to be summarized or excerpted. Therefore, His commentary is presented in full:

*This **"rod out of the stem of Jesse"** might seem to apply to Christ, for Joseph was a descendant of Jesse, the father of David. However, since Christ had come into being through the Divine Spirit, He called Himself the Son of God. Had this not been the case, this passage could have indeed applied to Him. Moreover, the events that are said to occur in the days of that rod, if they be interpreted figuratively, came to pass only in part, and if they be taken literally, failed absolutely and entirely to take place in the days of Christ.*

*For instance, we might say **that the leopard and the kid, the lion and the calf, the sucking child and the asp,** represent the various nations, the hostile peoples and contending kindreds of the earth who in their opposition and enmity were even as the **wolf and the lamb,** and who through the breezes of the messianic Spirit came to be endowed with the spirit of unity and fellowship, were quickened to life, and associated intimately one with another. But the condition referred to in the statement **"they shall not hurt nor destroy in all My holy mountain:***

for the earth shall be full of the knowledge of the LORD, as the waters cover the sea," did not materialize in the Dispensation of Christ. For to this day there are various hostile and contending nations in the world: few acknowledge the God of Israel, and most are deprived of the knowledge of God. Likewise, universal peace was not established with the advent of Christ; that is, peace and well-being were not realized among the hostile and contending nations, disputes and conflicts were not resolved, and harmony and sincerity were not attained. Thus, even to this day intense enmity, hatred and conflict prevail among the Christian peoples themselves.

But these verses apply word for word to Bahá'u'lláh. Moreover, in this wondrous Dispensation the earth will become another earth and the world of humanity will be arrayed with perfect composure and adornment. Strife, contention and bloodshed will give way to peace, sincerity, and harmony. Among the nations, peoples, kindreds and governments, love and amity will prevail, and cooperation and close connection will be firmly established. Ultimately, war will be entirely banned, and when the laws of the Most Holy Book are enacted, arguments and disputes will, with perfect justice, be settled before a universal tribunal of governments and peoples, and any difficulties which may arise will be resolved. The five continents of the world will become as one, its diverse nations will become one nation, the earth will become one homeland, and the human race will become one people. Countries will be so intimately connected, and peoples and nations so commingled and united, that the human race will become as one family and one kindred. The light of heavenly love will shine, and the gloomy darkness of hatred and enmity will be dispelled as far as possible. Universal peace will raise its pavilion in the midmost heart of creation and the blessed Tree of Life will so grow and flourish as to stretch its sheltering shade over the East and the West. Strong and weak, rich and poor, contending kindreds and hostile nations—which are like **the wolf and the lamb, the leopard and kid, the lion and the calf**—will treat one another with the utmost love, unity, justice and equity. The earth will be filled with knowledge and learning, with the realities and mysteries of creation, and with the knowledge of God.

Now, in this glorious age, which is the century of Bahá'u'lláh, consider how far knowledge and learning have progressed, how fully the mysteries of *creation have been unveiled, and how many great undertakings have been embarked upon and are multiplying day by day! Soon will material knowledge and learning, as well as spiritual knowledge, make such progress and display such wonders as to dazzle every eye and to disclose the full meaning of the verse of Isaiah:* **"for the earth shall be full of the knowledge of the Lord."**

Consider likewise that in the short span of time since the advent of Bahá'u'lláh, people of all nations, kindreds and races have entered beneath the shadow of this Cause. Christians, Jews, Zoroastrians, Hindus, Buddhists and Persians all consort together with perfect love and fellowship, as if for a thousand years they had belonged to the same kindred and family; indeed, as if they were father and son, mother and daughter, sister and brother. This is one of the meanings of the fellowship between **the wolf and the lamb, the leopard and the kid, and the lion and the calf.**

One of the great events which is to occur in the Day of the manifestation of that Incomparable **Branch** *is the hoisting of the Standard of God among* **all nations**. *By this is meant that all nations and kindreds will be gathered together under the shadow of this* **Divine Banner [ensign],** *which is none other than the Lordly* **Branch** *itself, and will become a single nation. Religious and sectarian antagonism, the hostility of races and peoples, and differences among nations, will be eliminated. All men will adhere to one religion, will have one common faith, will be blended into one race, and become a single people. All will dwell in one common homeland, which is the planet itself. Universal peace and concord will be established among all nations. That Incomparable* **Branch** *will gather together all Israel, that is, in His Dispensation Israel will be gathered in the Holy Land, and* **the Jewish people who are now scattered in the East and the West, the North and the South, will be assembled together.**

Now observe that these events did not take place in the Christian Dispensation, for the nations did not enlist under that single banner— that divine **Branch**—*but in this Dispensation of the* **Lord of Hosts** *all nations and peoples will enter beneath His shadow. Likewise Israel,* *which had been scattered throughout the world, was not gathered together in the Holy Land in the course of the Christian Dispensation, but in the beginning of the Dispensation of Bahá'u'lláh this divine promise, which has been clearly stated in all the Books of the Prophets, has begun to materialize. Observe how from all corners of the world Jewish peoples are coming to the Holy Land, acquiring villages and lands to inhabit, and increasing day by day to such an extent that all Palestine is becoming their home.*[9] (emphasis added)

In Isaiah 11:1–12, the *Branch* is Bahá'u'lláh, Who was descended from Abraham and David. 'Abdu'l-Bahá was surnamed the Most Mighty Branch by Bahá'u'lláh. Has this era of universal peace been arbitrarily delayed for millennia? No, it has been delayed until mankind achieves sufficient maturity to accept global peace as the will of God and then commit to accomplishing it. In the days of previous Prophets of God, most of humanity was unaware of people living beyond their small geographic areas. Individuals who listened to Jesus knew about Rome, but they knew nothing about the tribes and cultural groups living in Europe, the Americas, and the Far East. The Arabs of Muḥammad's time only knew about the other Arab tribes with whom they were usually skirmishing. Only when knowledge of the earth as a vast globe with many continents, kingdoms, and cities took root, and universal literacy began to take hold, could people grasp the concept of human connectedness. The internet and interactive communication programs like Zoom and Google Meet have connected an increasing number of people globally in forums where they can experience their shared humanity.

More attention is deserved for the sentence *"They shall not hurt nor destroy in all my holy mountain: for the earth shall be full of the knowledge of the LORD, as the waters cover the sea."* The sea, or ocean, is used many times as a symbol for the Revelation of Bahá'u'lláh.

*PRAISE and glory beseem the Lord of Names and the Creator of the heavens, He, **the waves of Whose ocean of Revelation** surge before the eyes of the peoples of the world.*[10] (emphasis added)

*The Great Being saith: The Tongue of Wisdom proclaimeth: He that hath Me not is bereft of all things. Turn ye away from all that is on earth and seek none else but Me. I am the Sun of Wisdom and **the Ocean of Knowledge**. I cheer the faint and revive the dead. I am the guiding Light that illumineth the way. I am the royal Falcon on the arm of the Almighty. I unfold the drooping wings of every broken bird and start it on its flight.*[11] (emphasis added)

*The Mother Book is made manifest, summoning mankind unto God, the Lord of the worlds, while the seas proclaim: The **Most Great Ocean** hath appeared, from whose waves one can hear the thundering cry: "Verily, no God is there but Me, the Peerless, the All-Knowing."*[12] (emphasis added)

A LITTLE CHILD SHALL LEAD THEM

In 1897, 'Abdu'l-Bahá gave extraordinary information concerning *"a little child shall lead them"* (Isaiah 11:6). 'Abdu'l-Bahá had received a letter asking whether this verse meant a real child who was then alive, and He responded by writing to the inquirer as follows:

Verily, that child is born and is alive and from him will appear wondrous things that thou wilt hear of in the future. Thou shalt behold him endowed with the most perfect appearance, supreme capacity, absolute perfection, consummate power and unsurpassed might. His face will shine with a radiance that illumines all the horizons of the world; therefore, forget this not as long as thou dost live inasmuch as ages and centuries will bear traces of him.[13]

That child was Shoghi Effendi, designated Guardian of the Bahá'í Faith by 'Abdu'l-Bahá. He was the first grandson of 'Abdu'l-Bahá, born to his oldest daughter. All of 'Abdu'l-Bahá's three sons had died during childhood, including one named Husayn who was described as a beautiful and dignified little boy who especially loved being with his grandfather, Bahá'u'lláh. At 'Abdu'l-Bahá's request, this first grandson was named Shoghi, which meant one who yearns. 'Abdu'l-Bahá also insisted that he be addressed from a young age with the title Effendi, which meant sir.

A further and fascinating reference, from a non-Bahá'í source, is found in the reminiscences of Dr. J. Fallscheer, a female German doctor who lived in Haifa and served the women in the household of 'Abdu'l-Bahá. During a visit with 'Abdu'l-Bahá, Dr. Fallscheer witnessed the child Shoghi Effendi taking a dignified, respectful leave of his grandfather. 'Abdu'l-Bahá asked her, "How do you like my future Elisha?"[14] She replied, "Master, if I may speak openly, I must say that in his boy's face are the dark eyes of a sufferer, one who will suffer a great deal!"[15] After a thoughtful silence, 'Abdu'l-Bahá replied:

"My grandson does not have the eyes of a trailblazer, a fighter or a victor, but in his eyes one sees deep loyalty, perseverance and conscientiousness. And do you know why, my daughter, he will fall heir to the heavy inheritance of being my Vazir (Minister, occupant of a high post)?" Without waiting for my reply, looking more at His dear sister than at me, as if He had forgotten my presence, He went on: "'Bahá'u'lláh, the Great Perfection—blessed be His words—in the past, the present and forever—chose this insignificant one to be His successor, not because I was the first born, but because His inner eye had already discerned on my brow the seal of God.

"Before His ascension into eternal Light the blessed Manifestation reminded me that I too—irrespective of primogeniture or age—must observe among my sons and grandsons whom God would indicate for His office. My sons passed to eternity in their tenderest years, in my line, among my relatives, only little Shoghi has the shadow of a great calling in the depths of his eyes."[16]

Shoghi Effendi was the grandson of 'Abdu'l-Bahá and great-grandson of Bahá'u'lláh. 'Abdu'l-Bahá had taken the title of servant, and Shoghi Effendi took the modest title of Guardian when his grandfather's Will and Testament appointed him head of the Bahá'í Faith. He labored steadfastly in this position for thirty-six years until his passing in 1957 (see Appendix H for an overview of Shoghi Effendi's life and accomplishments).

Chapter 9

Micah – He Watched in Hope for the Lord

And what does the LORD require of you?
To act justly and to love mercy and to
walk humbly with your God.

MICAH 6:8

AS WITH THE BOOKS of Amos, Hosea, and Isaiah, the book of Micah starts with naming the kings of the relevant ministry, thus identifying the years Micah was active. *"The word of the Lord that came to Micah of More-sheth during the reigns of Jotham, Ahaz and Hezekiah, kings of Judah—the vision he saw concerning Samaria and Jerusalem"* (Micah 1:1). These kings reigned from the 730s to the 690s BCE. If that timeframe is accurate, Micah was active from before the conquest of Israel by the Assyrians in 722 and witnessed the devastation of rural Judah wrought by Sennacherib's invasion in 701 that defeated 46 fortified towns.

The focus of prophetic activity shifted with Isaiah and Micah from Israel to Judah, although each prophet issued warnings to both nations. As with Amos and Hosea, a living prophetic tradition developed from the work of these two prophets after their passing. Groups of followers, perhaps coalescing into schools, safeguarded their written legacies, and possibly supplemented them, perhaps to a larger extent than happened with the books of Amos and Hosea. Literacy would have been highest in

Jerusalem and the surrounding area, and the spirit of Isaiah and Micah lived on in the scrolls that preserved their words.

Micah lived in Moresheth-Gath, a tiny village in the Judean foot-hills twenty miles southwest of Jerusalem and four miles northeast of Lachish, the second-largest city in Judah. There is little biographical information about Micah, but his familiarity with public affairs and insti-tutional abuses suggests that he may have traveled in elite circles and had access to the royal court in Jerusalem. There is speculation that he had served as a government official in Moresheth-Gath, but later he seems to have considered himself a Jerusalemite. However, his rural roots gave him intimate knowledge of the suffering of the peasantry and rural poor. Micah has been referred to as "the Amos of the southern kingdom" because of his vehement defense of justice and his excoriation of the wealthy who oppressed the lower classes. Micah has also been called "the prophet of the poor" because of his defense of those who had fallen from independent farming into sharecropping or debt slavery after being cheated out of their land by rich landowners and then denied justice by corrupt judges.

No typical call narrative is recorded for Micah, but he described his mission in no uncertain terms when he said, *"But as for me, I am filled with power, with the Spirit of the Lord, and with justice and might, to declare to Jacob his transgression, to Israel his sin"* (3:8). His book portrays a resolute man who was fueled by faith and patience.

The Hebrew Bible does not mention whether Amos, Hosea, Isaiah, or Micah communicated with each other even though they must have been aware of each other's work. If only a corpus of letters between them, if it ever existed, had survived as Paul's did! As prophets, though, they would have had no need to collaborate with each other, only possibly to commiserate. Called individually by God to serve as His voice, neither persuasion nor dissuasion would have altered their discourses.

Since these four prophets were all well-educated, it's likely that they initially took responsibility for securing their legacies. But over the years and centuries, scribes and editors made whatever changes they thought reasonable such as rearranging material and, quite possibly, adding more from other sources. They undoubtedly labored in good faith as they endeavored to encapsulate vocations of divinely inspired labor into cohesive literary works. Despite possible alterations and additions, the unique voice of each prophet is clearly discernible.

Micah spoke in bold, uncompromising terms. He delivered a particularly harsh warning for both Israel and Judah before Assyria conquered the northern kingdom and marauded through the southern kingdom:

> *Look! The LORD is coming from his dwelling place;*
> > *he comes down and treads on the heights of the earth.*
> *The mountains melt beneath him*
> > *and the valleys split apart,*
> *like wax before the fire,*
> > *like water rushing down a slope.*
> *All this is because of Jacob's transgression,*
> > *because of the sins of the people of Israel.*
> *What is Jacob's transgression?*
> > *Is it not Samaria?*
> *What is Judah's high place?*
> > *Is it not Jerusalem?*
> *"Therefore I will make Samaria a heap of rubble,*
> > *a place for planting vineyards.*
> *I will pour her stones into the valley*
> > *and lay bare her foundations.*
> *All her idols will be broken to pieces;*
> > *all her temple gifts will be burned with fire;*
> > *I will destroy all her images.*
> *Since she gathered her gifts from the wages of prostitutes,*
> > *as the wages of prostitutes they will again be used."*
> (1:3–7)

A prophet could not have spoken in a more ominous fashion. The people had broken their covenant with God, a covenant that had been extended in love, trust, and commitment. Instead of remaining faithful to the one God and striving to live by the spiritual codes that expanded upon the Ten Commandments,[1] the people had fallen into idolatrous worship and social corruption. There was a pervasive belief throughout the Middle East that the fertility of women, the earth, and farm animals was renewed each year through the sexual union of the gods and goddesses of fertility. It was believed that deific sex for fecundity was assisted by sacred prostitution. The *wages of prostitutes* supported the cultic shrines and even the Jerusalem Temple.

Like his prophet compatriots, Micah raged in the name of the Lord at the moral rot of Israelite society.

> *Shall I acquit someone with dishonest scales, with a bag of false weights?*
> *Your rich people are violent; your inhabitants are liars and their tongues speak deceitfully.*
> (6:11–12)

> *The faithful have been swept from the land; not one upright person remains.*
> *Everyone lies in wait to shed blood; they hunt each other with nets.* (7:2)

Especially egregious to Micah were the land grabs that swindled the small farmers of their inherited land.

> *Woe to those who plan iniquity,*
>   *to those who plot evil on their beds!*
> *At morning's light they carry it out*
>   *because it is in their power to do it.*
> *They covet fields and seize them,*
>   *and houses, and take them.*
> *They defraud people of their homes,*
>   *they rob them of their inheritance.*
> (2:1–2)

Hebrew scripture stated that God had given the land to the Israelites. "*See, the* LORD *your God has given you the land*" (Deut. 1:21). Life on the land was an essential part of the covenantal community and, in an agrarian economy, an individual's life depended on his land. Therefore, land rights and inheritances were safeguarded by Deuteronomic law. For example, *"Do not move your neighbor's boundary stone set up by your predecessors in the inheritance you receive in the land the* LORD *your God is giving you to possess"* (Deut. 19:14). The loss of one's land meant being reduced to the status of a day laborer or even a slave. How long would God tolerate this?

Micah caustically condemned the rulers and leaders. He harshly castigated them for the degenerate state of Israelite society and the practice of its religion. His denunciation could not have been more stinging.

> *Both hands are skilled in doing evil;*
> *the ruler demands gifts,*
> *the judge accepts bribes,*
> *the powerful dictate what they desire—*
> *they all conspire together.*
> (Micah 7:3)

Micah even used cannibalistic imagery to describe the rapaciousness of his society's rulers.

> *Then I said,*
>
> *"Listen, you leaders of Jacob,*
> *you rulers of Israel.*
> *Should you not embrace justice,*
> *you who hate good and love evil;*
> *who tear the skin from my people*
> *and the flesh from their bones;*
> *who eat my people's flesh,*
> *strip off their skin*
> *and break their bones in pieces;*
> *who chop them up like meat for the pan,*
> *like flesh for the pot?*

Then they will cry out to the LORD,
but he will not answer them.
At that time he will hide his face from them
because of the evil they have done."
(3:1–4)

Micah warned that disaster would befall individuals and the nation, and specifically Jerusalem, whose name Isaiah had subtly avoided in his warnings. Micah waded in. The prevalent belief was that Jerusalem was invincible and inviolable because it was the seat of the Davidic kings. Had not Nathan conveyed the words of God to David that his kingdom and the Davidic throne would endure forever? Had not the Ark of the Covenant been placed in the Temple by Solomon, thus making Mount Zion (Jerusalem) protected as God's chosen mountain? Micah thought differently.

For Samaria's plague is incurable;
it has spread to Judah.
It has reached the very gate of my people,
even to Jerusalem itself.

Those who live in Maroth writhe in pain,
waiting for relief,
because disaster has come from the LORD,
even to the gate of Jerusalem.
(1:9, 12)

(A footnote states: "Maroth sounds like the Hebrew word for *bitter.*")

Therefore because of you,
Zion will be plowed like a field,
Jerusalem will become a heap of rubble,
the temple hill a mound overgrown with thickets.
(3:12)

Put mildly, Micah's warnings and prophecies conflicted with the conventional wisdom of the day. The false prophets of the court and Temple sorely provoked Micah's ire by clinging to the tradition that the Davidic kingdom would last forever, conveniently ignoring the qualifier *if* given to Solomon. *"As for this temple you are building,* ***if*** *you follow my decrees, observe my laws and keep all my commands and obey them, I will fulfill through you the promise I gave to David your father"* (1 Kings 6:12, emphasis added). Micah's opinion dripped with scathing sarcasm when he countered the attitude that God could be held to a contract that the people themselves had broken, or that He could be manipulated with the form and ritual of worship:

> *"Do not prophesy," their prophets say.*
> *"Do not prophesy about these things;*
> *disgrace will not overtake us."*
>
> *If a liar and deceiver comes and says,*
> *"I will prophesy for you plenty of wine and beer,"*
> *that would be just the prophet for this people!*
> (Micah 2:6, 11)

The false prophets, protecting their livelihoods at the court or temple, reinforced the pervasive belief that because the Israelites were the chosen people and had a covenant with God, Who was the all-merciful, all manner of sin would be forgiven. Reminiscent of Amos, Micah countered this thinking by asking a rhetorical question: What would please the Lord? Herds of thousands? Rivers of olive oil? Child sacrifice? The answer was remarkably simple:

> *Will the LORD be pleased with thousands of rams,*
> *with ten thousand rivers of olive oil?*
> *Shall I offer my firstborn for my transgression,*
> *the fruit of my body for the sin of my soul?*
> *He has shown you, O mortal, what is good.*
> *And what does the LORD require of you?*

> *To act justly and to love mercy*
>> *and to walk humbly with your God.*
> (6:7–8)

THE STAR OF BETHLEHEM

Israel finally fell to the Assyrians in 722 BCE. Judah did not, but the lands of Judah were ravished by the armies of Sennacherib off and on. Jerusalem was spared the devastation and Judah lived to fight another day, but the earthly Davidic kingdom was doomed. How does a prophet comfort his people when he knows what is coming? The postexilic return to Jerusalem would provide only short-term solace because it would be followed by successive imperial domination by the Persians, Greeks, Romans, Byzantines, Islamic caliphates, Ottoman Turks, and the British Mandate. When would Israel be truly redeemed? Micah hinted that redemption would occur over more than twenty-five hundred years in slow lockstep with progressive revelation. The first redeemer would be Jesus.

Bethlehem may be the most famous small town in the world because, according to Matthew 2:1–12 and Luke 2:4–20, Jesus was born there. Micah foresaw the birth of the Jewish Messiah in Bethlehem.

> *Marshal your troops now, city of troops,*
>> *for a siege is laid against us.*
> *They will strike Israel's ruler*
>> *on the cheek with a rod.*

> *"But you, Bethlehem Ephrathah,*
>> *though you are small among the clans of Judah,*
> *out of you will come for me*
>> *one who will be ruler over Israel,*
> *whose origins are from of old,*
>> *from ancient times."*

> *Therefore Israel will be abandoned*
>> *until the time when she who is in labor bears a son,*

and the rest of his brothers return
  to join the Israelites.

He will stand and shepherd his flock
  in the strength of the LORD,
  in the majesty of the name of the LORD his God.
And they will live securely, for then his greatness
  will reach to the ends of the earth.
(Micah 5:1–4)

Jesus was struck on the cheek at his interrogation by the high priest, Caiaphas. *"When Jesus said this, one of the officials nearby slapped him in the face. 'Is this the way you answer the high priest?' he demanded"* (John 18:22).

'Abdu'l-Bahá confirmed that Micah 5:4 referred to Jesus when he answered a question posed by American Bahá'ís, *"As to Micah, chapter 5, the 4th verse refers to Christ."²*

Many biblical scholars and Christians have dismissed the nativity of Jesus as given in the Gospels of Matthew and Luke as a story added later that was inspired by Mesopotamian astrology. However, Bahá'u'lláh commented on how a few of the Magi recognized the star of Jesus when it appeared in the night sky and followed it to the seat of Herod's kingdom, Jerusalem. There they asked where they could find the King of the Jews for they had come to worship him. Bahá'u'lláh explained the meaning of the signs in the visible heaven and the invisible heaven.

These Magi said: "Where is He that is born King of the Jews? for we have seen His star in the east and are come to worship Him!"* When they had searched, they found out that in Bethlehem, in the land of Judea, the Child had been born. This was the sign that was manifested in the visible heaven. As to the sign in the invisible heaven—the heaven of divine knowledge and understanding—it was Yahyá [John] son of Zachariah, who gave unto the people the tidings of the Manifestation of Jesus. Even as He hath revealed: "God announceth Yahyá to thee, who shall bear witness unto the

Word from God, and a great one and chaste."** By the term "Word" is meant Jesus, Whose coming Yahyá foretold. Moreover, in the heavenly Scriptures it is written: "John the Baptist was preaching in the wilderness of Judea, and saying, Repent ye: for the Kingdom of heaven is at hand."*** By John is meant Yahyá.[3]

* Matthew 2:2

** Qur'án 3:39

*** Matthew 3:1–2

THE NEW CYCLE

Amos, Hosea, Micah, and Isaiah all foresaw the new cycle that, as previously discussed, started in 1844 CE and includes the present day and millennia beyond. Speaking for the Lord, in just two verses Micah spoke of the gathering of the remnant and the coming of the Báb and Bahá'u'lláh.

> *I will surely gather all of you, Jacob;*
>> *I will surely bring together the remnant of Israel.*
> *I will bring them together like sheep in a pen,*
>> *like a flock in its pasture;*
>> *the place will throng with people.*
> **The One who breaks open the way** *will go up before them;*
>> *they will break through the gate and go out.*
> *Their* **King** *will pass through before them,*
>> *the* **LORD** *at their head.*
>
> (Micah 2:12–13, emphasis added)

There are many mentions of remnants and their redemption throughout the Hebrew Bible. The largest remnant emerged from Rome's defeat of Jerusalem in 70 CE and its destruction of the city and Temple. Most of the Jews were dispersed into what is called the Diaspora. Although a few Jews remained in the Holy Land throughout the centuries, the return of the Jews from the Diaspora had been only a trickle until it increased after the 1840 Edict of Gulhane was issued by the Ottoman government. This edict permitted ownership of property for all Ottoman citizens, including Jews.

In addition, the Ottoman Empire realized that its religious intolerance was a barrier to improved relations with Britain and other European powers. The Ottomans had been pursuing a process of internal development called *Tanzimat* which included provisions for ending its slave trade. However, religious freedom was not included. Muslims who converted to Christianity were executed for apostasy. The British pressured the Ottomans to stop the persecution of Christians. Therefore, on March 21, 1844, Ottoman authorities submitted a note to the British and French embassies promising to cease the executions of apostates from Islam. Christian missionaries soon named this note the Edict of Toleration. It's questionable as to what extent this policy was enforced since it was a minor part of the Tanzimat effort. Although the Jews were not mentioned in this new policy, though, it had the effect of extending a certain religious tolerance to them.[4]

Hushidar Motlagh provided his understanding of these two verses drawn from his biblical studies. Bolding is used to correlate words and phrases from various translations of Micah below with observations by Motlagh:

> A prophecy from Micah points to the gathering of the Jews and then to three figures. The first figure is called "a breaker," or "one who breaks open the way," who appears and goes through the gate before the others; the second figure is the king; and the third is the Lord.
>
> "I will surely gather all of you, O Jacob I will surely bring together the remnant of Israel. I will bring them together like sheep in a pen, like a flock in its pasture; the place will throng with people. The One who breaks open the way will go up before them; they will break through the gate and go out. Their King [Bahá'u'lláh] will pass through before them, the **LORD** [the Báb] at their head" (Micah 2:12–13, NIV).

The most significant book about the history of the advent of the Báb is called *The Dawn-Breakers*. The book relates events in the lives of the early believers in the Báb, but starts with the missions of two wise men, the first two "dawn-breakers," who predicted the coming of the Báb and prepared their followers for His advent. One of them was Siyyid Kázim, who met the Báb and died just before He declared His Mission. Siyyid Kázim knew who the Báb was before He had made any statement about His station. Does the title "one who breaks open the way" in Micah's prophecy refer to Him?

Here are two other translations of verse 13 of Micah's prophecy. In the first translation, the word "breaker" appears as it does in the title of the book (*The Dawn-Breakers*), which contains the story of Siyyid Kázim who "broke" the dawn of the new age for his followers:

> The breaker [Siyyid Kázim] is gone up before them [the new believers]: they [Siyyid Kázim's followers] have broken forth [from the confines of their own religion] and passed on to the gate [the Báb], and are gone out thereat [toward Bahá'u'lláh]; and their king [Bahá'u'lláh] is passed on before them [Bahá'u'lláh was a follower of the Báb], and Jehovah [the Báb] at the head of them (Micah 2:13, ARV).

> He who walks at their head will lead the way in front of them; he will walk at their head, they will pass through the gate and go out by it; their king will go on in front of them, Yahweh at their head (Micah 2:13, Jerusalem Bible).[5]

Motlagh points out that the station of Lordship refers to the Báb as well as to Bahá'u'lláh and quotes the Báb to this effect. *"All the keys of heaven God hath chosen to place on My right hand, and all the keys of hell on My left ... I am the Primal Point from which have been generated all created things. I am the countenance of God whose splendor can never be obscured, the light of God whose radiance can never fade."*[6]

Who was the king? Bahá'u'lláh referred to Himself as the King of Kings in His Most Holy Book, *The Kitáb-i-Aqdas*, in which He addressed the kings of the earth:

*Ye are but vassals, O kings of the earth! He Who is the **King of Kings** hath appeared, arrayed in His most wondrous glory, and is summoning you unto Himself, the Help in Peril, the Self-Subsisting. Take heed lest pride deter you from recognizing the Source of Revelation, lest the things of this world shut you out as by a veil from Him Who is the Creator of heaven. Arise, and serve Him Who is the Desire of all nations, Who hath created you through a word from Him, and ordained you to be, for all time, the emblems of His sovereignty.*[7] (emphasis added)

FROM SEA TO SEA, FROM MOUNTAIN TO MOUNTAIN

The prophets suffered from the burden of knowledge that they carried. Micah lamented, *"What misery is mine! I am like one who gathers summer fruit at the gleaning of the vineyard; there is no cluster of grapes to eat, none of the early figs that I crave"* (Micah 7:1). He anguished over the sins of the Israelites and gave his famous warning of the watchman. *"The best of them is like a brier, the most upright worse than a thorn hedge. The day God visits you has come, the day your watchmen sound the alarm. Now is the time of your confusion"* (7:4). The alert for the watchmen was later echoed by Jesus. *"Watch therefore, for ye know neither the day nor the hour your Lord doth come"* (Matt. 24:42, KJV).

It was at this point of despair that Micah reiterated his steadfastness: *"But as for me, I watch in hope for the Lord, I wait for God my Savior; my God will hear me"* (7:7).

Now comes a shift where Micah states that even though he has fallen, he will rise, and the Lord will be his light. The Lord will bring him out of darkness into the light where he can see the righteousness of the Lord. Micah may have been referring to the people rather than himself. He then gave a concise prophecy in four verses that seem to describe Bahá'u'lláh's travels in exile and how He would spiritually nourish mankind.

*In that day also he shall come even to thee **from Assyria**, and from the **fortified cities**, and **from the fortress even to the river**, and **from sea to sea**, and from **mountain to mountain**.*

*Notwithstanding the land shall be **desolate** because of them that dwell therein, for the fruit of their doings.*

***Feed thy people with thy rod**, the flock of thine heritage, which dwell solitarily in the wood, in the midst of Carmel: let them feed in Bashan and Gilead, as in the days of old.*

*According to the days of thy coming out of the land of Egypt will I shew unto him **marvellous things**.*
(7:12–15, KJV, emphasis added)

The distinguished scholar Adib Taherzadeh described how these four verses succinctly foretold the coming of Bahá'u'lláh and gave his insight into them:

Some three thousand years before, Micah, the prophet of Israel, had foretold the appearance of the Lord in these words:

In that day also he shall come even to thee from Assyria, and from the fortified cities, and from the fortress even to the river, and from sea to sea, and from mountain to mountain. (Micah 7:12)

How strikingly accurate was the fulfillment of this prophecy! Bahá'u'lláh came from Assyria; Constantinople and Akka are both fortified cities—the latter a fortress; He voyaged upon the Black Sea and the Mediterranean and journeyed from the mountains of Kurdistán to Mount Carmel.[8]

Micah said that on that day the Lord will come from *Assyria*. Bahá'u'lláh was banished from Teheran to Baghdad, the first of the four cities of His forty years of exile. Baghdad is located on the Euphrates River in the land of ancient Assyria. This first phase of exile lasted ten years, from early winter 1853 to the spring of 1863. Early in his banishment to Baghdad, Bahá'u'lláh retreated for two years to Sár-Galú, a mountain in Kurdistan. He first lived in poverty and obscurity in a cave, but He was soon recognized for His prodigious insight into Islamic theology and became esteemed by the local people. Toward the end of His life, Bahá'u'lláh visited Mount Carmel, where He designated the future location for the Shrine of the Báb and revealed the Tablet of Carmel, which laid the foundation for the Administrative Order of the Bahá'í Faith. He traveled from Sár-Galú in Kurdistan to Mount Carmel, *from mountain to mountain.*

The terms of banishment in each city were progressively more constricted and difficult and the locations were more remote. The second banishment of Bahá'u'lláh was from Baghdad to Constantinople (now Istanbul), Turkey, in 1863 and lasted four months. Istanbul is located on the Bosporus Straights between the Aegean and Black Seas. A series of defensive stone walls built by Constantine the Great had been revamped and enlarged over the centuries to become one of the most complex and elaborate fortifications ever built. The route by which Bahá'u'lláh was taken from Baghdad to Constantinople was first by land and then on the Black Sea from the port of Samsun, Turkey, to the port of Constantinople. Adrianople (now Edirne) in European Turkey was the third city of exile from late 1863 to 1868. Reaching the fourth and final place of exile, the fortified prison city of Akka, necessitated a voyage by steamboat on the Mediterranean Sea. Bahá'u'lláh went *from sea to sea,* from the Black Sea to the Mediterranean Sea, to reach the *fortified cities* of Constantinople and Akka.[9]

The land of Palestine was indeed *desolate* after centuries of corrupt governance by the Ottoman Empire and, incidentally, by the indiscriminate pasturage of goats. Akka was a penal city housing hardened criminals. Its prison fortress was massive and forbidding. Bahá'u'lláh's enemies hoped that He would not survive long there. Indeed, the air was so foul that it was said that a bird who flew over Akka would die. However, it did not go unnoticed that the currents in Akka Bay started to change direction after Bahá'u'lláh arrived, which greatly improved the air quality. Either the timing was coincidental for changes of the currents, or the spiritual power of Bahá'u'lláh was involved.

The phrase *from the fortress even to the river* could refer to Akka and the Na'mayn River flowing through "our Green Island" as discussed in Chapter 7.

Bahá'u'lláh followed the injunction *"Feed thy people with thy rod."* Moses used a wooden rod to strike the rock for water to quench the people's thirst. Since one meaning of water is spiritual sustenance, Moses's rod would be symbolic of His teaching the Israelites. An iron rod was expected to be used by the Jewish Messiah in a militaristic manner, but the rod of Jesus was His mouth. The rod of Bahá'u'lláh was His pen. *"We school you with the rod of wisdom and laws, like unto the father who educateth his son, and this for naught but the protection of your own selves and the elevation of your stations."*[10]

The power of the pen of Bahá'u'lláh now emanates from the Bahá'í World Centre on Mount Carmel, where His Writings are preserved in the archives and where the Seat of the Universal House of Justice is located. *The days of thy coming out of the land of Egypt* are a parallel between the forty years Moses taught His people in the wilderness and the forty years of the ministry of Bahá'u'lláh, which lasted from 1853 to 1892.

And lastly, God would show unto him *marvellous things*. Undoubtedly not everything Bahá'u'lláh was shown could be shared with a humanity that was not ready. However, over one hundred volumes of His writings have been preserved, volumes that cover innumerable aspects of our world. Shoghi Effendi described the body of Bahá'u'lláh's work as follows:

> With this book [*Epistle to the Son of the Wolf*], revealed about one year prior to His ascension, the prodigious achievement as author of a hundred volumes, repositories of the priceless pearls of His Revelation, may be said to have practically terminated—volumes replete with unnumbered exhortations, revolutionizing principles, world-shaping laws and ordinances,

dire warnings and portentous prophecies, with soul-uplifting prayers and meditations, illuminating commentaries and inter-pretations, impassioned discourses and homilies, all interspersed with either addresses or references to kings, to emperors and to ministers, of both the East and the West, to ecclesiastics of diverse denominations, and to leaders in the intellectual, polit-ical, literary, mystical, commercial and humanitarian spheres of human activity.[11]

William Sears, a preeminent scholar, wrote *The Half-Inch Prophecy*, a book about Micah 7:12–15. The title was inspired by these four verses measuring one-half an inch in his Bible. Sears finished his investigation of Micah 7:12–15 by summarizing as follows:

Bahá'u'lláh's wondrous travels had culminated in a glorious triumph, and the half-inch prophecy had been fulfilled to the last requirement.
1. He came from "Assyria".
2. He came from the "fortified cities".
3. He came from the "fortress to the river".
4. He came from "sea to sea".
5. He came from "mountain to mountain".[12]

THE HOUSE OF THE LORD

Micah was told that in the last days the mountain of the house of the Lord would be established and the days of global peace would come.

But in the last days it shall come to pass, that the mountain of the house of the Lord shall be established in the top of the mountains, and it shall be exalted above the hills; and people shall flow unto it.

And many nations shall come, and say, Come, and let us go up to the mountain of the Lord, and to the house of the God of Jacob; and he will teach us of his ways, and we will walk in his paths: for the law shall go forth of Zion, and the word of the Lord from Jerusalem.

And he shall judge among many people, and rebuke strong nations afar off; and they shall beat their swords into plowshares, and their spears into pruning hooks: nation shall not lift up a sword against nation, neither shall they learn war any more.

But they shall sit every man under his vine and under his fig tree; and none shall make them afraid: for the mouth of the Lord of hosts hath spoken it. (Micah 4:1–4, KJV)

Here we see similarities to Isaiah 2:1–4 as presented in Chapter 7. It is possible that both prophets received their verses separately, and it is also possible that editors copied them from one book to the other. We will never know.

While He was on Mount Carmel, Bahá'u'lláh revealed the Tablet of Carmel, which states, *"Ere long will God sail His Ark upon thee* [Mount Carmel] *and will manifest the people of Bahá who have been mentioned in the Book of Names."*[13] The Universal House of Justice, which is under the unerring guidance and protection of Bahá'u'lláh, the Lord of Hosts, was established in 1963 and its Seat was built on Mount Carmel. Sears commented on Micah 4:1 with the following insight:

The Ark of Noah, which Scripture foretold would take one hundred and twenty days to build, was also an impressive symbolic Ark which would shelter and protect all mankind against the storms and stresses of life and keep them safe forever. The one hundred and twenty days would be one hundred and twenty years according to Scriptural scholars: "a day as a year" being traditional with them.

What is fascinating about this story of the Ark is that it "sailed" on the side of God's holy Mountain in April 1963. The year 1963 of the Christian Calendar is identical to the year 120 of the Bahá'í Era.[14]

The book of Micah ends with God's gentle soliloquy of mercy. *"Who is a God like you, who pardons sin and forgives the transgression of the remnant of his inheritance? You do not stay angry forever but delight to show mercy"* (7:18). The voices of the prophets then went silent for several decades.

Much of the book of Deuteronomy was composed during these silent decades. Critical biblical scholarship indicates that much of Deuteronomy, especially what would be called the book of the law (Deut. 12–26, the Deuteronomic code) as discussed in the next chapter. The biblical scholar Ronald E. Clements noted that the main part of Deuteronomy was composed during the first half of the seventh century, during the reigns of Manasseh (697–642) and Josiah, and other elements of Deuteronomy were added after the death of Josiah (640–608).[15]

Deuteronomic scribes worked during these silent years as part of a reformist movement that seems to have been independent of court and temple. Judah would continue to wend her weary way through the seventh century, torn between the idolatrous culture of the Middle East and her yearning for the one God. The prophets Zephaniah, Nahum, Jeremiah, and Habakkuk would appear in the final preexilic years.

Chapter 10

Zephaniah – Apocalypse and Redemption Will Come

The transcendent Word of God is sanctified beyond time.
The past, the present, and the future are
all equal in relation to God.

'Abdu'l-Bahá[1]

THE LAST WAVE OF preexilic prophets appeared after a lull of several decades following Isaiah and Micah's time. Jeremiah's book would be long (fifty-six chapters) and filled with what might be called action-adventure. The three books of Zephaniah, Nahum, and Habakkuk would be short, each with only three chapters that brim over with rhetorical dialogues and searing condemnations paired with metaphorical accounts of hope for days to come.

Zephaniah, Nahum, and Habakkuk lived in preexilic Judah during the late seventh century BCE. The dates of their missions, as best known, indicate that they were contemporaries during at least a few overlapping years. They are among the lesser-known of the minor canonical prophets, but they made such a profound impression that their work became part of the living legacy of the Hebrew Bible.

Zephaniah believed that Judah's destiny was set and her deserved fate could not be avoided. Instead of imploring for reform to gain deliverance, he focused on the inevitable.

139

He was active during the reign of Josiah. As a descendant of Hezekiah, he would have belonged to the royal nobility and perhaps had access to the court. His familiarity with Jerusalem suggests that he lived there. The first verse of the book of Zephaniah, *"The word of the Lord that came to Zephaniah son of Cushi, the son of Gedaliah, the son of Amariah, the son of Hezekiah, during the reign of Josiah son of Amon king of Judah"* (Zeph. 1:1), put Zephaniah in the second half of the seventh century. His overall message was like that of Isaiah. The first words of the Lord that came upon Zephaniah were phrased in a grim, hyperbolic, and apocalyptic mode. (The word "apocalyptic" describes a foreboding imminent disaster or final doom.)

> *"I will sweep away everything*
>> *from the face of the earth,"*
>>> *declares the* LORD.
> *"I will sweep away both man and beast;*
>> *I will sweep away the birds in the sky*
>> *and the fish in the sea—*
>> *and the idols that cause the wicked to stumble."*

> *"When I destroy all mankind*
>> *on the face of the earth,"*
>>> *declares the* LORD,
> *"I will stretch out my hand against Judah*
>> *and against all who live in Jerusalem.*
> *I will destroy every remnant of Baal worship in this place,*
>> *the very names of the idolatrous priests—*
> *those who bow down on the roofs*
>> *to worship the starry host,*
> *those who bow down and swear by the* LORD
>> *and who also swear by Molek,*
>>> *those who turn back from following the* LORD
>>> *and neither seek the* LORD *nor inquire of him."*

(Zeph. 1:2–6)

These eschatological images are reminiscent of the Noah saga that tells of an ancient, all-encompassing catastrophe. (The word "eschatological describes the final events in the history of the world or of humankind.) Apocalyptic and eschatological imagery gets attention, and what could be more newsworthy than the destruction of Judah? Unexpectedly, the next verse seems to time-shift with a change in tone to a mystifying theme.

> *Be silent before the Sovereign LORD,*
>   *for the **day of the LORD** is near.*
> *The LORD has prepared a **sacrifice**;*
>   *he has consecrated those he has invited.*
> (1:7, emphasis added)

Several possibilities come to mind for verse 7. The ***day of the Lord*** is a standard reference to each new appearance by a Prophet of God, and ***sacrifice***, as used above, could allude to Jesus. Bahá'u'lláh wrote of Christ's sacrifice to a Christian bishop living in Constantinople: *"Know thou that when the Son of Man [Jesus] yielded up His breath to God, the whole creation wept with a great weeping. By sacrificing Himself, however, a fresh capacity was infused into all created things. Its evidences, as witnessed in all the peoples of the earth, are now manifest before thee."*[2]

The sacrifice might also apply to the decision of Mírzá Mihdí, a son of Bahá'u'lláh and the younger brother of 'Abdu'l-Bahá, to forgo the healing offered by his father after a terrible accident. Mírzá Mihdí chose to sacrifice his life for the furtherment of Bahá'u'lláh's Cause instead of accepting the offered healing and continuing his life on earth (see Vol. 1, Chapter 6).

Zephaniah announced the ***day of the Lord*** within an apocalyptic context of breathtakingly stark imagery:

> *The great **day of the LORD** is near—*
>   *near and coming quickly.*
> *The cry on the day of the LORD is bitter;*
>   *the Mighty Warrior shouts his battle cry.*

That day will be a day of wrath—
  a day of distress and anguish,
              a day of trouble and ruin,
    a day of darkness and gloom,
                a day of clouds and blackness—
    a day of trumpet and battle cry
*against the **fortified cities***
    and against the corner towers.

"I will bring such distress on all people
    that they will grope about like those who are blind,
    because they have sinned against the LORD.
Their blood will be poured out like dust
    and their entrails like dung.
Neither their silver nor their gold
    will be able to save them
    on the day of the LORD's *wrath."*

In the fire of his jealousy
    the whole earth will be consumed,
*for he will make a **sudden end***
    of all who live on the earth.
(1:14–18, emphasis added)

'Abdu'l-Bahá confirmed that Zephaniah was referring to the *day of the Lord* as that of Bahá'u'lláh when he wrote, *"In Zephaniah, Chapter 1, verses 14, 15, 16, 17 and 18 ... all these refer to the century of the Blessed Beauty."*[3] These apocalyptic verses can be frightening, even while keeping in mind that they may be more symbolic than literal. The stresses that are appearing at the transition from the Adamic Cycle to the Cycle of Fulfillment cannot be solved with gold and silver. The *sudden end of all who live on the earth* is not literal but is a warning that reliance on traditional belief systems will not be adequate as social institutions collapse and traditional standards of behavior and

142

morality fall. The chaos of transition is bringing an end to the world as we know it. The *fortified cities*, or the arms of modern militaries, will be no defense.

The Prophetic Cycle of six thousand years was closed with the advent of the Báb. The transition from the Prophetic Cycle to the Cycle of Fulfillment has been and will continue to be intensely painful because of the intransigence of man, even though all is being offered to him. Shoghi Effendi described the catastrophic times for this *day of the Lord:*

> *A tempest, unprecedented in its violence, unpredictable in its course, catastrophic in its immediate effects, unimaginably glorious in its ultimate consequences, is at present sweeping the face of the earth. Its driving power is remorselessly gaining in range and momentum. Its cleansing force, however much undetected, is increasing with every passing day. Humanity, gripped in the clutches of its devastating power, is smitten by the evidences of its resistless fury. It can neither perceive its origin, nor probe its significance, nor discern its outcome. Bewildered, agonized and helpless, it watches this great and mighty wind of God invading the remotest and fairest regions of the earth, rocking its foundations, deranging its equilibrium, sundering its nations, disrupting the homes of its peoples, wasting its cities, driving into exile its kings, pulling down its bulwarks, uprooting its institutions, dimming its light, and harrowing up the souls of its inhabitants.*[4]

On the other hand, mankind has been promised a future that is unimaginably glorious, as Bahá'u'lláh wrote to an individual: *"This is the Day in which God's most excellent favors have been poured out upon men, the Day in which His most mighty grace hath been infused into all created things. ... Soon will the present-day order be rolled up and a new one spread out in its stead."*[5]

Judeans were not caught up in a new day of the Lord or in any transition of cycles. They were confronted with imperial military forces, a common scourge in the Middle East. Zephaniah saw his people as living in grievous violation of the laws and teachings of their Prophet,

Moses. What would it take to bring Judah to her knees? Conquest and exile.

Idolatry would no longer be a major issue in postexilic times. After taking several hundred years for monotheism to firmly take hold, belief in the one God would be far more solid during the Restoration and when confronted with the Greek and Roman pantheons of deities, than it was in preexilic times. There is little mention in the postexilic books about idolatry and none in the Gospels. With monotheism firmly implanted in the Jewish psyche, Jesus could teach the people about their personal relationship with God, the promise of His kingdom, and the life everlasting.

Zephaniah addressed the problems of his time and poured out his fury. He was uncompromising in his condemnation of Jerusalem as he foretold why it would feel the wrath of God:

> *Woe to the city of oppressors,*
> *rebellious and defiled!*
> *She obeys no one,*
> *she accepts no correction.*
> *She does not trust in the LORD,*
> *she does not draw near to her God.*
> *Her officials within her*
> *are roaring lions;*
> *her rulers are evening wolves,*
> *who leave nothing for the morning.*
> *Her prophets are unprincipled;*
> *they are treacherous people.*
> *Her priests profane the sanctuary*
> *and do violence to the law,*
> *The LORD within her is righteous;*
> *he does no wrong.*
> *Morning by morning he dispenses his justice,*
> *and every new day he does not fail,*
> *yet the unrighteous know no shame.*
> (3:1–5)

Zephaniah heard the Lord's lament. *"Of Jerusalem I thought, 'Surely you will hear me and accept correction.' Then her place of refuge would not be destroyed, nor all my punishments come upon her. But they were still eager to act corruptly in all they did"* (3:7). Yet assurance was given that redemption would eventually come:

> *Therefore wait for me,"*
> > *declares the LORD,*
> > > *"for the day I will stand up to testify.*
> *I have decided to* **assemble the nations,**
> > *to gather the kingdoms*
>
> *and to pour out my wrath on them—*
> > *all my fierce anger.*
> *The* **whole world** *will be consumed*
> > *by the fire of my jealous anger.*
>
> *"Then I will* **purify the lips** *of the peoples,*
> > *that all of them may call on the name of the LORD*
> > *and serve him shoulder to shoulder.*
> (3:8–9, KJV, emphasis added)

The foregoing suggests our time because only now is it possible to *assemble the nations* of the world, and for the *whole world* to be caught up in a common horror. Never in human history have global catastrophes been encountered, one after another, as they are now—climate change; pandemics and plagues; breakdowns of cybersecurity; and breakdowns of cybersecurity; drought and famine; and war and destruction not seen since World War II. The world is slowly recognizing the need to develop a global capacity for enlightened, unified responses to perils.

To *purify the lips* means that the people will be brought back to God through prayer and meditation. Possibly to *purify the lips* could also refer to Bahá'u'lláh's instruction that a world auxiliary language be adopted. At some point in the future, not only will everyone learn his own native language as a young child, but also an agreed-upon universal auxiliary language and script will be taught in all schools. A global auxiliary language will ease communication that will be necessary to ensure peace and understanding among people.

> *In former Epistles We have enjoined upon the Trustees of the House of Justice either to choose one language from among those now existing or to adopt a new one, and in like manner to select a common script, both of which should be taught in all the schools of the world. Thus will the earth be regarded as one country and one home.*[6]

In addition, it is worth noting that the names of the Báb and Bahá'u'lláh are pronounced the same in all languages.

Zephaniah also foretold the ingathering of the remnant into Israel with honor and praise.

> *"I will remove from you*
>   *all who mourn over the loss of your appointed festivals,*
>   *which is a burden and reproach for you.*
> *At that time I will deal*
>   *with all who oppressed you.*
> *I will rescue the lame;*
>   *I will gather the exiles.*
> *I will give them praise and honor*
>   *in every land where they have suffered shame.*
> *At that time I will gather you;*
>   *at that time I will bring you home.*
> *I will give you honor and praise*
>   *among all the peoples of the earth*
> *when I restore your fortunes*
>   *before your very eyes,"*
>   *says the LORD.*

(3:18–20)

The first Zionist Congress was held in 1897 in Basel, Switzerland. In that same year, 'Abdu'l-Bahá commented directly on the return of Jews to Palestine:

You have asked Me a question with regard to the gathering of the children of Israel in Jerusalem in accordance with the prophecy. Jerusalem, the Holy of Holies, is a revered Temple, a sublime name, for it is the City of God ... The gathering of Israel at Jerusalem means, therefore, and prophesies, that Israel as a whole is gathering beneath the banner of God and will enter the Kingdom of the Ancient of Days. For the celestial Jerusalem, which has as its center, the Holy of Holies, is a City of the Kingdom, a Divine City. The East and West are but a small corner of that City. Moreover, materially as well (as spiritually), the Israelites will gather in the Holy Land. This is irrefutable prophecy, for the ignominy which Israel has suffered for well-nigh twenty-five hundred years will now be changed into eternal glory, and in the eyes of all, the Jewish people will become glorified to such an extent as to draw the jealousy of its enemies and the envy of its friends.[7]

The honor and fortunes of the Jews, whose ancestors had been scattered in the Diaspora and relentlessly persecuted, would thus be restored among the peoples of the earth with honor and praise.

Chapter 11

Nahum – Justice for Nineveh, Mercy for Judah

He will stretch out his hand against the north
and destroy Assyria, leaving Nineveh utterly desolate
and dry as the desert.

ZEPHANIAH 2:13

NO BIOGRAPHICAL INFORMATION IS given about Nahum except that his hometown was Elkosh, whose location has been much debated. Nahum is believed to have been active in the late seventh century either shortly before or after the Assyrian capital, Nineveh, fell to the Babylonians in 612 BCE. It's difficult to say whether Nahum's description of that defeat was history or prophecy. The book of Nahum is written in dramatic poetic form that emphasizes Nahum's obsession with the fall of Assyria. God is shown to be a powerful actor in human history. Graphic imagery depicts the depth of His wrath. Nahum also portrays the historic fall of Nineveh as part of the eternal fight between God and evil.

The book of Nahum has a terse start: *"A prophecy concerning Nineveh. The book of the vision of Nahum the Elkoshite"* (Nahum 1:1). This is the only instance in which a prophetic work in the Hebrew Bible refers to itself as a book. The theology of Nahum that runs through all three chapters is that a righteous God will destroy His enemies.

The Lord is a jealous and avenging God;
the Lord takes vengeance and is filled
with wrath.
The Lord takes vengeance on his foes
and vents his wrath against his enemies.
The Lord is slow to anger but great in power;
the Lord will not leave the guilty unpunished.
His way is in the whirlwind and the storm,
and clouds are the dust of his feet (1:2–3).

Who can withstand his indignation?
Who can endure his fierce anger?
His wrath is poured out like fire;
the rocks are shattered before him (1:6).

But for once the focus of God's wrath was not on Judah! It was on Assyria, whose empire would be ended, never to rise again. The Assyrian empire, stretching hundreds of miles from the Iranian plateau east of the Tigris River to Egypt, had reached its zenith during the first half of the seventh century. By the 630s, the empire was weakening internally from civil war and was losing control of its territories.

The Assyrian empire had been hated as no other because of its use of terror and cruelty as a mode of governance. Its conquered subjects had long despaired of deliverance when the unexpected was announced as follows:

The Lord is good,
a refuge in times of trouble.
He cares for those who trust in him,
but with an overwhelming flood
he will make an end of Nineveh;
he will pursue his foes into the realm
of darkness.

> *Whatever they plot against the L*ORD
>> *he will bring to an end;*
>> *trouble will not come **a second time.***
>
> (1:7–9, emphasis added)

A fall of Judah to the Assyrians would be *a second time* since the fall of Israel to the Assyrians was the first time for the Israelites. Nahum not only states that this second time would not happen but that Judah would experience the mercy of God!

> *This is what the L*ORD *says:*
>
> *"Although they have allies and are numerous,*
>> *they will be destroyed and pass away.*
>
> *Although I have afflicted you, Judah,*
>> ***I will afflict you no more.***
> *Now I will break their yoke from your neck*
>> *and tear your shackles away."*
>
> *The L*ORD *has given a command concerning you, Nineveh:*
>> *"You will have no descendants to bear your name.*
> *I will destroy the images and idols*
>> *that are in the temple of your gods.*
> *I will prepare your grave,*
>> *for you are vile."*
>
> (1:12–14, emphasis added)

Since the kingdom of Judah would be conquered by the Babylonians a little over a hundred years later, to say to the Judeans *I will afflict you no more* was patently inaccurate. This phrase was probably referring to a far-future time when the Jewish people would no longer be afflicted but would flourish in the State of Israel. However, the Babylonian defeat was not as devastating as an Assyrian one would have been. The Judahites of the Exile were allowed to remain together around Babylon, not dispersed to far corners of the empire.

Nahum then changes the focus from the destruction of Nineveh to a time when peace will be proclaimed.

> *Look, there on **the mountains**,*
> > *the feet of one who brings **good news**,*
> > *who proclaims peace!*
> (1:15, emphasis added)

The prophet of Second Isaiah wrote several decades after Nahum:

> *How beautiful on **the mountains***
> > *are the feet of those who bring **good news**,*
> *who proclaim **peace**,*
> > *who bring good tidings,*
> > *who proclaim salvation,*
> *who say to Zion,*
> > *"Your God reigns!"*
> (Isaiah 52:7, emphasis added)

The *good news* suggests the Gospels of Jesus and His blessing of the *peacemakers*. *"Blessed are the peacemakers, for they will be called children of God"* (Matt. 5:9). Jesus withdrew for forty days to a high *mountain* after His baptism. He is associated with Mount Tabor, believed to be the mountain of the Transfiguration, and He was often reported retreating to *mountains* to pray.

Possibly Nahum was also referring to the Báb, who was the herald of Bahá'u'lláh, the Prince of Peace. At a time when the Báb was under house arrest in Shiraz, some of his friends and followers waited for an opportunity to free him. It was not to be. The Báb refused their help by stating, *"'The **mountains** of Ádhirbáyján [the province in which Mákú and Chihríq are located] too have their claims,' was His confident reply as He lovingly advised them to abandon their project and return to their homes."*[1] The Báb's feet

THE COMING OF THE GLORY VOLUME II

blessed the mountains of Mákú and Chihriq, where He was imprisoned. His remains were also laid to final rest on a mountain, Mount Carmel.

After giving words of mercy to Judah, Nahum continues to prophesy the fate of the city, leaving no doubt at all of God's terrible anger against Nineveh. Nahum gave a graphic description of the armed invasion of Nineveh to come that includes the opening of the river gates to flood the city.

> *The chariots storm through the streets,*
>> *rushing back and forth through the squares.*
> *They look like flaming torches;*
>> *they dart about like lightning.*
>
> *Nineveh summons her picked troops,*
>> *yet they stumble on their way.*
> *They dash to the city wall;*
>> *the protective shield is put in place.*
> *The river gates are thrown open*
>> *and the palace collapses.*
> (Nahum 2:4–6)

Nineveh was a massive fortress city whose seven miles of twenty-foot walls had fifteen monumental gateways. If any city was impregnable, it was Nineveh. Yet it was defeated by a coalition of former subject peoples—the Babylonians, Medes, Persians, Armenians, Chaldeans, Scythians, and Cimmerians. Everyone hated the Assyrians! Nineveh, the largest city in the Middle East at that time, and possibly in the world, fell with little resistance allegedly after the city was flooded. Nahum left no doubt about Nineveh's fate:

> *"I am against you,"*
>> *declares the LORD Almighty.*
> *"I will burn up your chariots in smoke,*
>> *and the sword will devour your young lions.*

I will leave you no prey on the earth.
The voices of your messengers
will no longer be heard."
(2:13)

Although Nahum mentioned the river gates, or sluices, being opened to flood the city, there is little, if any, historical verification of this. It seems more likely that the flood was symbolic of God's rage against the Assyrians. Scenes of violent natural phenomena were often used in the Hebrew Bible as symbols of divine activity. Thunder roared and the winds swept Mount Sinai when Moses went to meet with God, and fire burst forth on Elijah's altar. Nineveh was the capital of a declining empire and had been under siege for three months when, in approximately 612 BCE, it fell for the usual reasons that cause sieged cities to fall.

C. L. Crouch, a professor at Fuller Theological Seminary, noted that there was no reason to understand the fall of Nineveh in literal terms. She noted that "the language of flood and of the rivers derives from a common ancient Near Eastern and biblical vocabulary of military defeat, colored by the conception of royal battle as reflecting the deity's ongoing conquest of chaotic waters through the use of natural phenomena."[2] The biblical scholar John D. W. Watts put it simply: "In Nahum, a historic event is presented as symbolic of the struggle between God and ultimate evil."[3]

Nahum's vision of Nineveh's demise would have comforted the people of Judah in his time. Little did they know that twenty-five hundred years of difficult, even tragic history, must be traversed before redemption in Israel.

Chapter 12

Habakkuk – A Dialogue with God

I know that my redeemer lives,
and that in the end he will stand on the earth.

JOB 24:1

THE BOOK OF HABAKKUK is profound and unique. The prophets we examined before Habakkuk served as conduits for divine messages to the people with minimal dialogue with the Source and questioning of Him. Habakkuk changed the *modus operandi* by using forthright dialogue with God that sought straight answers to his questions. Habakkuk poured out his overwhelming sorrow and rage at injustice and his impatience with God's plan. The Deity responded with hope for the future, complete with glimpses into both near- and far-future times when Habakkuk's issues would be addressed.

Some scholars believe that Habakkuk was active from the mid-seventh century to the late seventh. Other scholars believe that he wrote a little later, possibly between 609 and 598 BCE during the years of Babylonian invasions of Judah. Habakkuk's book contains no biographical data or call narrative, only a statement that he received a prophecy—*"The prophecy that Habakkuk the prophet received"* (Hab. 1:1). It is assumed that he lived in Jerusalem and belonged to the tribe of Levi, whose members served as musicians for the Temple, because the final chapter of his book is a song. If this assumption is accurate, Habakkuk might have been a prophet attached to the Temple and his oracles originally uttered or sung in Temple services.

Habakkuk cried out to God with the poignantly eternal "why" that is unsurpassed in its despair. Why must good succumb to evil? Why does the divine plan tolerate the evil committed in Judah? Why have evil, corruption, and inequity been tolerated for so long? When, oh when, will righteousness, justice, and peace ever come to Judah?

> *How long, LORD, must I call for help,*
> > *but you do not listen?*
> *Or cry out to you, "Violence!"*
> > *but you do not save?*
> *Why do you make me look at injustice?*
> > *Why do you tolerate wrongdoing?*
> *Destruction and violence are before me;*
> > *there is strife, and conflict abounds.*
> *Therefore the law is paralyzed,*
> > *and justice never prevails.*
> *The wicked hem in the righteous,*
> > *so that justice is perverted.*
> (1:2–4)

God responded to Habakkuk but did not give quite the comfort he wanted. Habakkuk was told to look at the nations and watch, *"For I am going to do something in your days that you would not believe, even if you were told"* (1:5). Yes, the Babylonians were being raised up but as a tool for justice. The Babylonians were described as *"that ruthless and impetuous people,"* a *"feared and dreaded people"* who *"fly like an eagle swooping to devour,"* and hordes who would *"advance like a desert wind and gather prisoners like sand,"* who would *"laugh at all fortified cities"* and *"sweep past like the wind and go on— guilty people, whose own strength is their god"* (1:6–11).

Habakkuk was told that the Babylonians would be the tool of God's justice for the people of Judah, who had rejected Him. Habakkuk accepted this divine punishment of Judah, but he couldn't understand

God's acceptance of the Babylonians' murderous cruelty and His use of them as an agent. Surely the Judeans were not as evil as the Babylonians!

> *Your eyes are too pure to look on evil;*
> *you cannot tolerate wrongdoing.*
> *Why then do you tolerate the treacherous?*
> *Why are you silent while the wicked*
> *swallow up those more righteous than themselves?*
>
> (1:13)

Habakkuk opened himself to God with an openness described as standing at his watch, stationed on the ramparts while waiting for an answer. *"I will look to see what he will say to me, and what answer I am to give to this complaint"* (2:1).

Then the LORD replied:

> *"Write down the revelation*
> *and make it plain on tablets*
> *so that **a herald may run with it**.*
> *For the revelation awaits an appointed time;*
> *it speaks of **the end***
> *and will not prove false.*
> *Though it **linger**, wait for it;*
> *it will certainly come*
> *and will not delay.*
>
> (2:2–3, emphasis added)

This is the first known record of a prophet being directed to write down a divine revelation. The phrase *a herald may run with it* suggests the Báb, Who was the *herald* for Bahá'u'lláh. If that is the case, *the end* means the end of the age, the year 1844 CE. The time for the coming of the Báb would *linger* for about twenty-five hundred years until 1844.

The scene then returned to Habakkuk's time as God assured him that He was acutely aware of the sins of the Babylonians. *"See, the enemy is puffed up; his desires are not upright—but the righteous person will live by his faithfulness"* and *"as greedy as the grave and like death is never satisfied"* (2:4–5). In time, the Babylonians would receive their due from their creditors because they *"have plundered many nations ... shed human blood ... destroyed lands and citizens and everyone in them"* (2:8). And woe to him *"who builds his house by unjust gain, setting his nest on high to escape the clutches of ruin!"* and to the Assyrians who *"laugh at all fortified cities; by building earthen ramps they capture them"* and *"sweep past like the wind and go on—guilty people, whose own strength is their god"* (2:9–11). Reference to *their god* was a hint of weak support for the Babylonian empire, which would collapse in a few decades. The next woe timeshifts far into the future.

> *Woe to him that buildeth a town with blood, and stablisheth a city by iniquity! Behold, is it not of the LORD of hosts that the people shall labour in the very fire, and the people shall weary themselves for very vanity?* ***For the earth shall be filled with the knowledge of the glory of the LORD, as the waters cover the sea.***
> (2:12–14, KJV, emphasis added)

Habakkuk's prophecy in verse 2:14 that *the earth shall be filled with the knowledge of the glory of the LORD as the waters cover the sea* is similar to Isaiah's following passage.

> *They shall not hurt nor destroy in all my holy mountain:* ***for the earth shall be full of the knowledge of the LORD, as the waters cover the sea.***
> (Isaiah 11:9, KJV, emphasis added)

The glory of the Lord is Bahá'u'lláh, Whose teachings will cover the earth. The waters of His spiritual knowledge are destined to reach all the peoples of the world. Bahá'u'lláh referred to His Dispensation as an ocean of Revelation. *"Praise and glory beseem the Lord of Names and the Creator of the heavens, He, the waves of Whose ocean of Revelation surge before the eyes of the peoples of the world."*[1]

The third chapter of Habakkuk is presented as a prayer and might have been sung by a temple choir.

A prayer of Habakkuk the prophet. On shigionoth*

> *LORD, I have heard of your fame;*
> > *I stand in awe of your deeds, LORD.*
> *Repeat them in our day,*
> > *in our time make them known;*
> > *in wrath remember mercy.*

> *God came from* **Teman**,
> > *the Holy One from* **Mount Paran**
> *His glory covered the heavens*
> > *and his praise filled the earth.*
> (Hab. 3:1–3, emphasis added)
> *Footnote: Probably a literary or musical term

Habakkuk may have been alluding to Moses's blessing of the tribes as reported in the book of Deuteronomy as follows:

This is the blessing that Moses the man of God pronounced on the Israelites before his death. He said:

> *"The LORD came from* **Sinai**
> > *and dawned over them from* **Seir**;
> > *he shone forth from* **Mount Paran.**
> (Deut. 33:1–2, emphasis added)

The Israelites had crossed the *Sinai* to reach their Promised Land. *Seir* was a town located at the northern edge of Judah, near Nazareth.[2] *Teman* was in Edom on the border of the Arabian Peninsula. The wilderness of *Paran*, known today as the Hejaz (the western province of Arabia that contains Mecca and Medina), refers to the desert that runs along the western edge of the Arabian desert on the east coast of the Red Sea. Hagar and Ishmael settled in the Paran, which was close to Mecca. It would seem that *Sinai* refers to Moses, *Seir* to Jesus, and *Paran* to Muḥammad.

Habakkuk described the divine power that was to come from Mount Paran, the symbol for Muḥammad and Islam:

> *His splendor was like the sunrise;*
> > *rays flashed from his hand,*
> > *where his power was hidden.*
> *Plague went before him;*
> > *pestilence followed his steps.*
> *He stood, and shook the earth;*
> > *he looked, and made the nations tremble.*
> *The ancient mountains crumbled*
> > *and the age-old hills collapsed—*
> > *but he marches on forever.*
> (Hab. 3:4–6)

Each Prophet of God appears on the horizon like the sunrise and slowly reveals His Dispensation as the sun rises and gains strength. Plagues and pestilence could refer to resistance to new teachings and to persecutions of a Prophet and His followers. The hills and mountains have many meanings, including mounds of traditional beliefs that tremble and crumble in the face of a new Dispensation from God.

Habakkuk finished with one of the most heartfelt, unequivocal statements of faith and praise in the face of adversity to be found in the Hebrew Bible, especially since it follows a gruesome account of what is described as the threshing of the nations. *"You split the earth with rivers; the mountains saw you and writhed … In wrath you strode through the earth and in anger you threshed the nations … You crushed the leader of the land of wickedness, you stripped him from head to foot … You trampled the sea with your horses, churning the great waters"* (3:9–10, 12–13, 15)

Habakkuk responded to the threshing of the nations with fear and trembling. *"I heard and my heart pounded, my lips quivered at the sound; decay crept into my bones, and my legs trembled"* (3:16). Yet he would wait patiently for God's plan to unfold.

> *Yet I will wait patiently for the day of calamity*
>   *to come on the nation invading us.*
> *Though the fig tree does not bud*
>   *and there are no grapes on the vines,*
> *though the olive crop fails*
>   *and the fields produce no food,*
> *though there are no sheep in the pen*
>   *and no cattle in the stalls,*
> *yet I will rejoice in the LORD,*
>   *I will be joyful in God my Savior.*
> *The Sovereign LORD is my strength;*
>   *he makes my feet like the feet of a deer,*
>   *he enables me to tread on the heights.*
> (3:17–19)

Habakkuk set a standard for steadfast faith in God when disaster loomed, society crumbled, and all seemed to be lost.

Chapter 13

Struggles for Judah

Hear this, you foolish and senseless people,
who have eyes but do not see, who have ears but do not hear:
Should you not fear me?" declares the LORD.
"Should you not tremble in my presence? ...
But these people have stubborn and rebellious hearts;
they have turned aside and gone away.

JEREMIAH 5:21–23

SAMARIA FELL AND THE kingdom of Israel was no more. Amos and Hosea were sadly vindicated. The book of 2 Kings lists the sins that led to the defeat of Israel—worshipping Asherah, the starry hosts, and Baal; practicing divination; sacrificing children to the fires of Molek; and forsaking the commands of the Lord. *"So the LORD was very angry with Israel and removed them from his presence. Only the tribe of Judah was left, and even Judah did not keep the commands of the LORD their God. They followed the practices Israel had introduced"* (2 Kings 17:18–19).

Hezekiah, the reformist king who did not heed Isaiah's advice to eschew alliances, was succeeded by his son Manasseh, an apple that fell far from the tree. He reigned for fifty-five years starting at age twelve, spending the first ten years as coregent with his father. Manasseh's concessions to, and even embrace of, polytheism and idolatry might have reflected a backlash against Hezekiah's reforms that obviously had not protected the Judean countryside and peasantry from Assyrian depredations. The book of 2 Chronicles catalogs his evils as follows:

He rebuilt the high places his father Hezekiah had demolished; he also erected altars to the Baals and made Asherah poles. He bowed down to all the starry hosts and worshiped them. He built altars in the temple of the LORD, of which the LORD had said, "My Name will remain in Jerusalem forever." In both courts of the temple of the LORD, he built altars to all the starry hosts. He sacrificed his children in the fire in the Valley of Ben Hinnom, practiced divination and witchcraft, sought omens, and consulted mediums and spiritists. He did much evil in the eyes of the LORD, arousing his anger.
(2 Chron. 33:3–6)

The sins laid at Manasseh's door might have been concessions to the Assyrians, who would not have tolerated domestic disturbances because of religious reforms. Possibly there was a ruler-vassal agreement that included recognition not only of the Assyrian king but also of the primary Assyrian god, Assur. Assyrian beliefs would have been spread throughout Judah by the Assyrian soldiers and officials who now came into the country. Judah's subservience to Assyria probably included Assyria's protection of the arts of magic and divination that had been expressly forbidden by Moses. *"But Manasseh led Judah and the people of Jerusalem astray, so that they did more evil than the nations the LORD had destroyed before the Israelites"* (33:9).

Concessions to Assyria helped to make the long reign of Manasseh peaceful. Prosperity returned while Judah was integrated into the Assyrian regional economy. The Hezekian reforms were not mentioned again in the Hebrew Bible, probably because they had had little or no effect on the rural people who practiced their own folk religion that combined the worship of traditional Canaanite gods and goddesses with the God of Abraham and Moses. Indeed, the reforms were soon forgotten in Jerusalem and the major cities. The religious and moral fabric of Judean society fell to its lowest level.

THE *"SEVEN TIMES OVER"* ACTIVATED

There is no mention of Manasseh pushing back against Assyrian vassalage. However, the book of 2 Chronicles states that he was taken prisoner by the Assyrians in about 676 BCE and taken to Babylon. It seems that two dynamics were at work—Assyrian concern for the loyalty of its vassal Manasseh, and the wrath of the Lord at the iniquities of Judah.

> *The LORD spoke to Manasseh and his people, but they paid no attention. So the LORD brought against them the army commanders of the king of Assyria, who took Manasseh prisoner, put a hook in his nose, bound him with bronze shackles and took him to Babylon. In his distress he sought the favor of the LORD his God and humbled himself greatly before the God of his ancestors. And when he prayed to him, the LORD was moved by his entreaty and listened to his plea; so he brought him back to Jerusalem and to his kingdom. Then Manasseh knew that the LORD is God.*
> (2 Chron. 33:10–13)

Scholars disagree as to whether Manasseh turned to the Lord in true repentance, but repentance could have been a wise career move, along with convincing the Assyrians that he would be a loyal vassal. Manasseh was returned to Judah and allowed to resume his reign. He is said to have tried to reverse the damage he'd done by removing idolatrous images from the Temple and idolatrous altars that he had built, and by urging Judah to serve the Lord, the God of Israel.

> *He got rid of the foreign gods and removed the image from the temple of the LORD, as well as all the altars he had built on the temple hill and in Jerusalem; and he threw them out of the city. Then he restored the altar of the LORD and sacrificed fellowship offerings and thank offerings on it, and told Judah to serve the LORD, the God of Israel. The people, however, continued to sacrifice at the high places, but only to the LORD their God.* (33:15–17)

Historians like to give dates to events, but these dates can be misleading. The conquest of a country is generally preceded by forays beyond the aggressor's boundaries and the conquest of a city by attacks in the surrounding area. The year 722 is given for the fall of the northern kingdom, the year its capital Samaria fell after a three-year siege. For decades afterward, the Assyrian army made incursions into Judah's countryside.

As previously discussed in Chapter 6, Isaiah had counseled Judah's King Ahaz when he was facing a threat from King Pekah of Israel and two other kings. One of Isaiah's remarks was that *"Within sixty-five years Ephraim will be too shattered to be a people"* (Isaiah 7:8). Sixty-five years later would have been 676 BCE. The three kings were threatening Ahaz during the first year of his reign, 732. Against Isaiah's counsel, Ahaz solved the problem by voluntarily putting Judah under vassalage to Assyria in return for protection.

What happened sixty-five years later in 676? It seems that the fourth, and last, of the major Assyrian incursions into Judah occurred that year,[1] resulting in the capture of Manasseh by the Assyrian emperor Esar-haddon. Some biblical scholars speculate whether the year 676 activated Moses's prophecy of *seven times over,* or 2,520 years. In biblical counting, a day is a year, and a time is also a year, and a year is 360 days. Therefore, seven times 360 equals 2,520 days/years, and 2,520 years added to 676 BCE ends at 1844 CE.

The "seven times over" comes from the Holiness Code found in Leviticus, Chapters 17–26 (see Vol. 1, Chapter 6). Thirty-six admonitions were given for worship and moral conduct (26:3–13). A long list of blessings was given for compliance with the Code, followed by a long list of curses for disobedience (26:14–39). The Lord's threats of dire punishments for disobedience were set forth.

"'But if you will not listen to me and carry out all these commands, and if you reject my decrees and abhor my laws and fail to carry out all my commands and so violate my covenant, then I will do this to you: I will bring on you sudden terror, wasting diseases and fever that will destroy your sight and sap your strength. You will plant seed in vain, because your enemies will eat it. I will set my face against you so that you will be defeated by your

enemies; those who hate you will rule over you, and you will flee even when
no one is pursuing you. If after all this you will not listen to me, I will
*punish you for your sins **seven times over.***"
(26:14–18, emphasis added)

Manasseh was generally considered to have been the evilest of
Judah's kings, and the year of his abduction was the low point in his
reign. A monarch's name was sometimes used, by extension, to mean
the people. If the *seven times over* started in 676, the 2,520 years ended
in 1844, the year of the declaration of the Báb. It was also the year the
Ottomans agreed not to execute Muslims for converting to Christianity,
which gave a measure of acceptance to religious minorities in Palestine.
The ancient homeland of the Jews thus became more hospitable to their
return. The long, sad history of reinforced vassaldom, the Diaspora, and
persistent persecution wherever the Jews went would eventually end for
those who returned to the Holy Land.

THE JOSIANIC REFORMATION

Manasseh was succeeded by his son Amon (642–640 BCE), who was
killed by his officials for reasons not given. Amon's eight-year-old son
Josiah (640–608) was heir to the throne. Josiah is believed to have had
a religious awakening as a teenager or young man, and he ordered that
the Temple be renovated. During the renovations, an ancient scroll of
the "book of the law," which is assumed to have been parts of Deuteronomy, was reportedly found by the high priest Hilkiah, who read it to
Josiah. The young king was so distressed by its instructions for religious
observance of the laws of Moses that he rent his robes. He ordered that
the Lord be inquired about what had been written in the discovered
scroll. The independent prophetess Huldah was duly consulted in Jerusalem, and the response she received was not comforting, as follows:

"This is what the LORD, the God of Israel, says: 'Tell the man who sent
you to me, "This is what the LORD says: I am going to bring disaster on this
place and its people, according to everything written in the book the king of

Judah has read. Because they have forsaken me and burned incense to other gods and aroused my anger by all the idols their hands have made, my anger will burn against this place and will not be quenched.'" Tell the king of Judah, who sent you to inquire of the LORD, 'This is what the LORD, the God of Israel, says concerning the words you heard: Because your heart was responsive and you humbled yourself before the LORD when you heard what I have spoken against this place and its people—that they would become a curse and be laid waste—and because you tore your robes and wept in my presence, I also have heard you, declares the LORD. Therefore I will gather you to your ancestors, and you will be buried in peace. Your eyes will not see all the disaster I am going to bring on this place'"
(2 Kings 22:15–20)

Was an ancient copy of Deuteronomy found in the Temple? Possibly. But there are many factors to keep in mind while pondering this episode. Biblical research indicates that the earlier books of the Hebrew Bible[2] were handled by many scribes who put pen to scroll to assemble the ancient written records and the oral traditions, of the teachings of Moses and Israelite history. Most of these books were not put into final form until exilic times when there was an agenda to favor certain aspects of Hebrew history, denigrate others, and come to terms with the demise of Judah.

One body of biblical thought contends that major portions of Deuteronomy were written during Manasseh's reign and this effort was continued early in Josiah's. The biblical scholar Ronald E. Clements noted that many scribes, including state officials, worked on this project. These writers were religiously motivated reformers drawn from a circle close to the centers of state administration but apparently were not associated with the king, the royal household, or the priesthood.[3] Clements continued with the recognition of the vital role of prophecy.

It is important to recognize the warm interest in prophecy and the belief that certain prophets continued to fulfill a role in Israel comparable to that of Moses. Such interest, which becomes more marked in the history that elaborates the lawbook, suggests that some prophetic element may also have contributed to the Deuteronomic movement for reform in Israel. Yet the understanding of prophecy is highly distinctive, and too removed from its most fundamental forms, for the authors of the book to have been prophets themselves. Prophecy is viewed essentially as a means of promoting the knowledge and claims of the Deuteronomic law.[4]

The reported discovery of an ancient scroll in the Temple during Josiah's reign raises many questions as to its source and age and even a possibility that it was "planted" by reformist individuals and brought to the attention of a religious king who was seeking spiritual meaning in his life. Whatever the situation, Josiah was stirred to the depths of his being. Perhaps it was the threats of frightening punishments for nonobservance of the law given in Deuteronomy 28:15–68 that spurred Josiah to action (see Vol. 1, Chapter 9). He launched a vigorous campaign of religious reform to purge non-Mosaic forms of worship, although the destiny of Judah, according to Huldah's message, was set.

The biblical narrative indicates that Josiah moved decisively. First, he gathered the priests, prophets, and people at the Temple and read to them the discovered manuscript, called the Book of the Covenant. *"The king stood by the pillar and renewed the covenant in the presence of the* LORD*—to follow the* LORD *and keep his commands, statutes and decrees with all his heart and all his soul, thus confirming the words of the covenant written in this book. Then all the people pledged themselves to the covenant"* (2 Kings 23:3).

It is written that Josiah ordered that all objects for the worship of Baal, Asherah, and the starry hosts be removed from the Temple and burned. He tore down the Temple quarters provided for the male prostitutes and the women who did weaving for Asherah. Josiah removed the horses and chariots dedicated to the sun from the entrance to the Temple. The idolatrous altars that had been erected by Ahaz were removed from the roof of the Temple. *"He desecrated Topheth, which was in the Valley of Ben Hinnom, so no one could use it to sacrifice their son or daughter in the fire to Molek"* (2 Kings 23:10).

The reforms spread throughout Judah with pagan altars pulled down and high places desecrated so that they could no longer be used for worship, especially for child sacrifices to appease the god Molek. The altars were polluted with human bones to make them unclean (23:7–14).

Internal divisions had been weakening the Assyrian empire since about 630 BCE, thus starting a gradual lessening of the Assyrian domination of Judah before the Assyrian empire succumbed to the Babylonians in 612. This enabled Josiah to carry his reformation campaign across the border into the former land of Israel. It is recorded that he destroyed the cult altar at Bethel that had been erected long before by Jeroboam, which fulfilled the prophecy of a man of God telling Jeroboam that a son named Josiah would be born to the House of David who would burn human bones on that altar (see Chapter 3 for discussion of 1 Kings 13:2–3). In Samaria, he destroyed all the shrines on the high places and then slaughtered their priests on the altars and burned their bones there (2 Kings 23:15, 19–20).

Josiah also tried to revive the teachings that he had learned from the discovered scroll about justice, social welfare, and protection of the weak and powerless. The Josianic reformation appears not to have been a half-hearted effort but one that went further than Hezekiah's had. Josiah even went after the mediums and spiritists, the household gods and their images. Josiah was compared to David in his utter loyalty to God. *"Neither before nor after Josiah was there a king like him who turned to the Lord as he did—with all his heart and with all his soul and with all his strength, in accordance with all the Law of Moses"* (23:25).

The prophet Jeremiah emerged on the scene in 626, the thirteenth year of Josiah's reign, and his ministry continued beyond the fall of Jerusalem and Judah in 586. Jeremiah's voice never deviated—trust in the Lord, cease your corrupt practices, do not make foreign alliances, and be warned of the Lord's punishment to come. His words never strayed from warning that the Josianic reforms had not changed Judah's fate.

Rather than ponder Jeremiah's warnings, Josiah saw the decline of the Assyrian empire and its partial withdrawal of troops as an opportunity to expand northward and reunite the two kingdoms under his

Davidic rule. Now was the time when the purported glorious past of the Israelites was to be renewed. The conquest of Israel would parallel that of the legendary conquest of Canaan, rendering Josiah a conquering hero like Joshua, Samuel, and David. Or so the thinking went.

Tragedy struck when Josiah made a disastrous mistake. Necho II of Egypt had been rushing his armies up the coast and across central Israel to reach Mesopotamia to help his Assyrian allies, who were in retreat from the Babylonians. Josiah took his army north to confront Necho II at Megiddo and thwart his assistance to Judah's enemy, Assyria. The pharaoh tried to dissuade Josiah from this ill-fated battle by sending messengers to him who stated that the pharaoh's quarrel was with the Babylonians, not with Judah. Josiah was not dissuaded. He took his army to the plain of Megiddo, where he was gravely wounded in battle and brought back to Jerusalem, where he died and was much lamented.

We can only surmise how deeply Josiah's death must have saddened and confused the religious community and the common people alike. The people must have felt bereft, especially those who had embraced the Josianic reforms. They were faced with wondering whether the Josianic reformation had "failed" because Josiah was dead and Judah was sliding into dissension and anarchy.

Josiah's reform movement had sparked a new religious identity. With the spread of literacy, written texts could be used more effectively to teach the people than during preceding centuries. This renewed religious zeal would enable some of the Judeans to keep their identity as monotheistic Hebrews during the Babylonian exile that would start in twenty-two years.

On the other hand, the independent prophets of the late seventh century seemed to agree that Judah was still a den of iniquity. Either the reforms had been only superficial, or the people had backslid fast.

JUDAH A VASSAL OF EGYPT AND BABYLONIA

Egypt replaced Assyria as vassal lord over Judah for a few years. It removed Josiah's son Jehoahaz (608 BCE) from the throne after three months and sent him to Egypt. Jehoiakim (608–597), another son of Josiah, was put on the throne. His reign was a balancing act between Egypt, to whom Jehoiakim owed his throne and paid tribute, and the Babylonians, who defeated the Assyrians in 612 and were on the move. The king, court, and advisers were intensely divided on the issue of alliances and how to protect the kingdom. The Babylonians settled the issue by decisively defeating the Egyptians in 605 at Carchemish on the Euphrates River and then invading Judah and demanding tribute. Jehoiakim's successor was his son, Jehoiachin (597), ruled only briefly when Nebuchadnezzar took him as a captive to Babylon along with his mother, wives, officials, and many prominent Judeans. Zedekiah (597–586), an uncle of Jehoiachin, was enthroned by the Babylonians and would preside over Judah's final act.

> *"Zedekiah was twenty-one years old when he became king, and he reigned in Jerusalem eleven years. He did evil in the eyes of the LORD his God and did not humble himself before Jeremiah the prophet, who spoke the word of the LORD. He also rebelled against King Nebuchadnezzar, who had made him take an oath in God's name. He became stiff-necked and hardened his heart and would not turn to the LORD, the God of Israel."*
> (2 Chron. 36:11–13)

These last years were a time of spiritual anguish and turmoil in Judah. How could God have allowed Josiah's death and the imposition of Egyptian power and then Babylonian? If the Josianic reformation had been in accord with God's will, why had God not allowed Judah to prosper? Had not a reunited monarchy under the Davidic kings been a praiseworthy goal whose time had come? Why were the Babylonians allowed to conquer a people that considered themselves to be righteous? The eternal questions why, why, why—the apparent victory of evil over good—were asked with anguish. Jeremiah addressed these questions in accordance with what the Lord told him.

Chapter 14
Jeremiah – If You Do Not Listen

Like a wind from the east, I will scatter them before their enemies;
I will show them my back and not my
face in the day of their disaster.

JEREMIAH 18:17

THE PROPHETIC SCENE WAS quiet for several decades of the seventh century BCE as though the curtain had come down on act one of a drama. But the words of the first four prophets (Amos, Hosea, Isaiah, and Micah) were preserved and disseminated by small groups of followers that might have developed into schools dedicated to this purpose. Indeed, the seventh century was a productive literary time in an increasingly literate society. Work progressed on recording and compiling the ancient records of Hebrew history including the books of Joshua, Judges, 1 and 2 Kings, and 1 and 2 Chronicles. This work was interrupted by the Babylonian conquest but was resumed during the Exile in the sixth century.

The book of Jeremiah is the longest of the prophetic books with fifty-two chapters, compared with thirty-nine chapters devoted to First Isaiah and forty-eight in the book of Ezekiel. As with Isaiah, Jeremiah can only be approached here in survey form that covers only highlights. In common with other prophetic books, it is not known how much survived of Jeremiah's original speeches and writings and how much was altered by successive editors. Fortunately, he had a faithful friend and scribe, Baruch ben Neriah. This assistance suggests that the book of Jeremiah is largely faithful to his words and ministry. The first three verses of the book of Jeremiah give his lineage and the exact years of his ministry:

> *"The words of Jeremiah son of Hilkiah, one of the priests at Anathoth in the territory of Benjamin. The word of the LORD came to him in the thirteenth year of the reign of Josiah son of Amon king of Judah, and through the reign of Jehoiakim son of Josiah king of Judah, down to the fifth month of the eleventh year of Zedekiah son of Josiah king of Judah, when the people of Jerusalem went into exile." (Jer. 1:1–3)*

Jeremiah was active for about forty years from 626 to the late 580s. He was a witness to the throes of religious reform with Josiah, vassaldom to Egypt and the Babylonian empire, and finally, conquest by the Babylonians followed by the Exile. The decline and fall of Judah were the backdrops for Jeremiah's ministry just as the demise of Israel had been for Isaiah. Parallels emerged between how Isaiah and Jeremiah each tried in vain to reason with their kings and countrymen before the final conquests by the Assyrians in the north and the Babylonians in the south. Jeremiah's writings are often correlated with specific years of a king's rule, a factor that provides dates and windows into Judah's history at particular times.

The book of Jeremiah states that he was born into a priestly family in Anathoth, which was located three miles north of Jerusalem. Jeremiah had family and property there, but he lived in Jerusalem as a member of an elite class. He has traditionally been called the "weeping prophet" for lamenting, *"If you do not listen, I will weep in secret because of your pride; my eyes will weep bitterly, overflowing with tears, because the LORD's flock will be taken captive"* (13:17).

The call narrative for Jeremiah is startling: *"Before I formed you in the womb I knew you, before you were born* I set you apart; I appointed you as a prophet to the nations" (1:5). This suggests many possibilities to ponder. Was he divinely endowed with superhuman insight, emotional endurance, and spiritual stamina? As a prophet to the nations, Jeremiah would speak far beyond the people and societies of his time, as far ahead as twenty-five centuries and more. When Jeremiah received his call, he protested that he was too young to know how to speak, but the Lord countered his protests.

> "Do not say, 'I am too young.' You must go to everyone I send you to and say whatever I command you. Do not be afraid of them, for I am with you and will rescue you," declares the LORD.

> Then the LORD reached out his hand and touched my mouth and said to me, "I have put my words in your mouth. See, today I appoint you over nations and kingdoms to uproot and tear down, to destroy and overthrow, to build and to plant." (1:7–10)

The word of the Lord came to Jeremiah asking what he saw, and Jeremiah answered that he saw the branch of an almond tree. "*The LORD said to me, 'You have seen correctly, for I am watching to see that my word is fulfilled'*" (1:12). (A footnote to this verse states that the Hebrew for *watching* sounds like the Hebrew for *almond tree.*) Again, the word of the Lord came to Jeremiah asking what he saw, and he answered that he saw a boiling pot tilting from the north.

> The LORD said to me, "From the north disaster will be poured out on all who live in the land. I am about to summon all the peoples of the northern kingdoms," declares the Lord.

> > "Their kings will come and set up their thrones
> > in the entrance of the gates of Jerusalem;
> > they will come against all her surrounding walls
> > and against all the towns of Judah.
> > I will pronounce my judgments on my people
> > because of their wickedness in forsaking me,

in burning incense to other gods
and in worshiping what their hands have made.

"Get yourself ready! Stand up and say to them whatever I command you.
Do not be terrified by them, or I will terrify you before them. Today I have
made you **a fortified city, an iron pillar and a bronze wall** *to*
stand against the whole land—against the kings of Judah, its officials, its
priests and the people of the land. They will fight against you but will not
overcome you, for I am with you and will rescue you," declares the LORD.
(1:14–19, emphasis added)

Thus, Jeremiah was given his mandate. The message he would deliver would be crystal clear and unequivocal. Judah's unrepentant idolatry and disobedience to Mosaic moral law had put her beyond the Lord's redemption; therefore, the Babylonians would come from the Fertile Crescent in the north to conquer Judah and its capital, Jerusalem. Jeremiah's protection was that the Lord would make him like *a fortified city, an iron pillar, and a bronze wall,* but this would only spare him from death. He would not be spared intense emotional and physical suffering and persecution. He would be ridiculed, beaten, put in the stocks, imprisoned, threatened with death, and thrown down a dry cistern to die. With few exceptions, the people responded to Jeremiah with ridicule, disbelief, and condemnation. Jeremiah's repeated, timeless lament was that *they would not listen.* This lament became his ministry's refrain, a despairing rebuke to the denialism that brought catastrophe upon Judah.

Jeremiah would be denied the comfort of marriage and children for the Lord told him: *"You must not marry and have sons or daughters in this place." For this is what the* LORD *says about the children born in this land and about the women who are their mothers and the men who are their fathers: "They will die of deadly diseases. They will not be mourned or buried but will be like dung lying on the ground. They will perish by sword and famine, and their dead bodies will become food for the birds and the wild animals"* (16:2–4).

Jeremiah was also denied the usual social outlets. He was not to attend funerals to mourn or show sympathy, and not to attend feasts and parties. *"For this is what the L*ORD *Almighty, the God of Israel, says: Before your eyes and in your days I will bring an end to the sounds of joy and gladness and to the voices of bride and bridegroom in this place"* (16:9).

I regard Jeremiah as the most intense and intriguing of the Hebrew prophets. His book combines brave exploits and stunning fulfillment of his mission with the severe sorrow of a prophet who was deprived of the comfort of family and most social outlets, and who felt sorrowfully and deeply to the marrow of his bones.

THE SINS OF JUDAH AND THE DESPAIR OF JEREMIAH

The first third of the book of Jeremiah is devoted to the sins of Judah and the depths of despair this brought to the Lord and to Jeremiah. The worst sin was idolatry. The Lord lamented about what fault the people had found in Him for *"They followed worthless idols and became worthless themselves"* (Jer. 2:5). The people of Israel were disgraced—their kings, officials, priests, and false prophets—as a thief is disgraced when caught.

> *"They say to wood, 'You are my father,'*
> *and to stone, 'You gave me birth.'*
> *They have turned their backs to me*
> *and not their faces;*
> *yet when they are in trouble, they say,*
> *'Come and save us!'*
> *Where then are the gods you made for yourselves?*
> *Let them come if they can save you*
> *when you are in trouble!*
> *For you, Judah, have as many gods*
> *as you have towns.*
> (2:27–28)

Jeremiah condemned the sins of Judah with zeal, outrage, and extraordinary steadfastness in the face of rebukes, ridicule, confrontations, threats of violence, and inflicted violence. He laid out the charges against Judah with passion and acerbity. *"Be appalled at this, you heavens, and shudder with great horror," declares the* LORD. *"My people have committed two sins: They have forsaken me, the spring of living water, and have dug their own cisterns, broken cisterns that cannot hold water"* (2:12–13).

The next sin was seeking foreign alliances rather than trusting God and being faithful to Him. *"'Now why go to Egypt to drink water from the Nile? And why go to Assyria to drink water from the Euphrates? Your wickedness will punish you; your backsliding will rebuke you. Consider then and realize how evil and bitter it is for you when you forsake the* LORD *your God and have no awe of me,' declares the Lord, the* LORD *Almighty"* (2:18–19).

Other evils included child sacrifice. *"They have built the high places of Topheth in the Valley of Ben Hinnom to burn their sons and daughters in the fire— something I did not command, nor did it enter my mind"* (7:31). The days would come, declared the Lord, when the Valley of Ben Hinnom would be called *"the Valley of Slaughter, for they will bury the dead in Topheth until there is no more room"* (7:32). Topheth was the cemetery where the sacrificed children were buried.

The false prophets who mostly served the court insisted that the House of David would be protected forever. Therefore, sins would be forgiven. Not so. The end was coming. *"A horrible and shocking thing has happened in the land: The prophets prophesy lies, the priests rule by their own authority, and my people love it this way. But what will you do in the end?"* (5:30–31).

Jeremiah was denied the solace of praying for the people. *"Then the* LORD *said to me, 'Do not pray for the well-being of this people. Although they fast, I will not listen to their cry; though they offer burnt offerings and grain offerings, I will not accept them. Instead, I will destroy them with the sword, famine and plague'"* (14:11–12). Jeremiah protested, *"Alas, Sovereign* LORD*! The prophets keep telling them, 'You will not see the sword or suffer famine. Indeed, I will give you lasting peace in this place'"* (14:13), and the Lord responded:

"The prophets are prophesying lies in my name. I have not sent them or appointed them or spoken to them. They are prophesying to you false visions, divinations, idolatries and the delusions of their own minds. There- fore this is what the LORD *says about the prophets who are prophesying in*

my name: I did not send them, yet they are saying, 'No sword or famine will touch this land.' Those same prophets will perish by sword and famine. And the people they are prophesying to will be thrown out into the streets of Jerusalem because of the famine and sword. There will be no one to bury them, their wives, their sons and their daughters. I will pour out on them the calamity they deserve."
(14:14–16)

Jeremiah lived in a social maelstrom, and sometimes a spiritual one. He implored the Lord: *"You are always righteous, Lord, when I bring a case before you. Yet I would speak with you about your justice: Why does the way of the wicked prosper? Why do all the faithless live at ease?"* (12:1).

And he lamented to himself, *"Cursed be the day I was born! May the day my mother bore me not be blessed!"* and *"Why did I ever come out of the womb to see trouble and sorrow and to end my days in shame?"* (20:14, 18).

Still, Jeremiah remained faithful in his mission to the end.

A MARRIAGE METAPHOR

The marriage metaphor was used to remind Judah of how *faithless Israel* had been severed from the Lord and how *her unfaithful sister Judah* had returned to the Lord *only in pretense.*

*During the reign of King Josiah, the LORD said to me, "Have you seen what **faithless Israel** has done? She has gone up on every high hill and under every spreading tree and has committed adultery there. I thought that after she had done all this she would return to me but she did not, and **her unfaithful sister Judah** saw it. I gave faithless Israel her certificate of divorce and sent her away because of all her adulteries. Yet I saw that her unfaithful sister Judah had no fear; she also went out and committed adultery. Because Israel's immorality mattered so little to her, she defiled the land and committed adultery with stone and wood. In spite of all this, her unfaithful sister Judah did not return to me with all her heart, **but only in pretense,"** declares the LORD.*
(Jer. 3:6–10, emphasis added)

Perhaps the phrase *but only in pretense* best describes the ultimate result of the Josianic reformation in Judah. Continuing with the marriage analogy, Jeremiah gave the words of conciliation from the Lord.

> *"Return, faithless people,"* declares the LORD, *"for I am your husband. I will choose you—one from a town and two from a clan—and bring you to* **Zion.** *Then I will give you* **shepherds** *after my own heart, who will lead you* **with knowledge and understanding.** *In those days, when your numbers have increased greatly in the land,"* declares the LORD, *"people will no longer say, 'The ark of the covenant of the LORD.' It will never enter their minds or be remembered; it will not be missed, nor will another one be made. At that time they will call Jerusalem the* **Throne of the LORD,** *and* **all nations will gather in Jerusalem** *to honor the name of the LORD. No longer will they follow the stubbornness of their evil hearts. In those days the people of Judah will join the people of Israel, and together they will come from* **a northern land to the land I gave your ancestors** *as an inheritance.*
> (3:14–18, emphasis added)

Jeremiah knew that the kingdom of Judah was doomed and the Babylonian conquest could not be avoided. Therefore, the return of a few to *Zion*, whose symbolic significance evolved to mean the Holy Land, may have referred to the Restoration under the Persian king Cyrus II in the fifth century BCE. It may also have pointed to events in the distant future when the return to the Holy Land led to the establishment of the modern state of Israel. However, the phrases *the throne of the Lord* and *all nations will gather in Jerusalem* also suggest a new Dispensation because Jerusalem is symbolic of the new word of God, a new religion.

Religious leaders are the *shepherds* who take care of the flock, the people. New shepherds, new Prophets of God, would come to continue humanity's spiritual education *with knowledge and understanding*. Bahá'u'lláh mentioned the establishment of the *Throne of your Lord* in the following excerpt from His preeminent theological work, *The Kitáb-i-Íqán*, surnamed the Book of Certitude.

*Say: The Word of God can never be confounded with the words of His creatures. It is, in truth, the King of words, even as He is Himself the sovereign Lord of all, and His Cause transcendeth all that was and all that shall be. Enter, O people, the City of Certitude wherein the **throne of your Lord**, the All-Merciful, hath been established. Thus biddeth you the Pen of the All-Glorious, as a token of His unfailing grace.*[1] (emphasis added)

Coming from *a northern land to the land I gave your ancestors* suggests the Zionist movement that developed in Russia and eastern Europe. The phrase *all nations will gather in Jerusalem* could suggest a time when Bahá'u'lláh and the Bahá'í Faith are recognized by people in all nations.

PROPHETIC IMMUNITY TESTED

During the first year of the reign of Jehoiakim (608 BCE), Jeremiah was told by the Lord to deliver His message in the Temple courtyard to the people, as follows:

*Early in the reign of Jehoiakim son of Josiah king of Judah, this word came from the LORD: "This is what the LORD says: 'Stand in the courtyard of the LORD's house and speak to all the people of the towns of Judah who come to worship in the house of the LORD. Tell them everything I command you; do not omit a word. Perhaps they will listen and each will turn from their evil ways. Then I will relent and not inflict on them the disaster I was planning because of the evil they have done.' This is what the LORD says: 'If you do not listen to me and follow my law, which I have set before you, and if you do not listen to the words of my servants the prophets, whom I have sent to you again and again (though **you have not listened**), then I will make this house like Shiloh and this city a curse among all the nations of the earth.'"*
(Jer. 26:2–6, emphasis added)

Jeremiah duly presented the Lord's words in the Temple courtyard. Outraged priests, court prophets, and bystanders seized Jeremiah and

181

insisted that he be put to death. They took their case to the court offi-cials, who assembled at the New Gate to hear the evidence. *"This man should be sentenced to death because he has prophesied against this city. You have heard it with your own ears!"* (26:11). Jeremiah responded that the Lord had sent him to state everything that was heard, especially, *"Now reform your ways and your actions and obey the LORD your God. Then the LORD will relent and not bring the disaster he has pronounced against you"* (26:13).

This event tested prophetic immunity. The court officials ruled for Jeremiah after being reminded by some of the elders of the prophet Micah's case.

> *Some of the elders of the land stepped forward and said to the entire assembly of people, "Micah of Moresheth prophesied in the days of Hezekiah king of Judah. He told all the people of Judah, 'This is what the LORD Almighty says:*
>
> > *"Zion will be plowed like a field,*
> > *Jerusalem will become a heap of rubble,*
> > *the temple hill a mound overgrown with thickets."**
> > *Micah 3:12
>
> *"Did Hezekiah king of Judah or anyone else in Judah put him to death? Did not Hezekiah fear the LORD and seek his favor? And did not the LORD relent, so that he did not bring the disaster he pronounced against them? We are about to bring a terrible disaster on ourselves!"* (26:17–19)

Jeremiah was set free but prophetic immunity was not uniformly enforced. At that time there was another independent prophet named Uriah who was called by God to deliver similar warnings to Judah. Uriah fled to Egypt to escape Jehoiakim's wrath, but the king's men chased him there and brought him back. *"They brought Uriah out of Egypt and took him to King Jehoiakim, who had him struck down with a sword and his body thrown into the burial place of the common people"* (26:23).

THE TEMPLE SERMON

Jeremiah was again instructed by the Lord to deliver His message to the public, this time at the Temple gate. This probably meant one of the three gates that separated the inner portion of the Temple from the outer. On certain days, such as fast days, the outer court would have been the most crowded place in Jerusalem. Imagine the courage it must have taken for Jeremiah to deliver the Lord's message in the outer court, a message that is called the Temple Sermon. The Temple Sermon contained the essence of what Jeremiah had preached and would continue to preach for many years:

> *"Hear the word of the LORD, all you people of Judah who come through these gates to worship the LORD. This is what the LORD Almighty, the God of Israel, says: Reform your ways and your actions, and I will let you live in this place. Do not trust in deceptive words and say, 'This is the temple of the LORD, the temple of the LORD, the temple of the LORD!' If you really change your ways and your actions and deal with each other justly, if you do not oppress the foreigner, the fatherless or the widow and do not shed innocent blood in this place, and if you do not follow other gods to your own harm, then I will let you live in this place, in the land I gave your ancestors for ever and ever. But look, you are trusting in deceptive words that are worthless.*
>
> *"Will you steal and murder, commit adultery and perjury, burn incense to Baal and follow other gods you have not known, and then come and stand before me in this house, which bears my Name, and say, 'We are safe'—safe to do all these detestable things? Has this house, which bears my Name, become a den of robbers to you? But I have been watching! declares the LORD.*
>
> *"Go now to the place in Shiloh where I first made a dwelling for my Name, and see what I did to it because of the wickedness of my people Israel. While you were doing all these things, declares the LORD, I spoke to you again and again, but **you did not listen**; I called you, but you did not answer. Therefore, what I did to Shiloh I will now do to the house that bears my Name, the temple you trust in, the place I gave to you and your*

ancestors. **I will thrust you from my presence, just as I did
all your fellow Israelites, the people of Ephraim."**
(7:3–15, emphasis added)

Deliverance from the Babylonians was not an option. Instead, if the
people of Judah changed their ways and actions and dealt with each
other justly, they would be allowed to continue living in the land the Lord
gave their ancestors forever and ever; if they did not, they would not.

As with Isaiah, Jeremiah was also told not to pray for this people or
try to intercede for them. *"So do not pray for this people nor offer any plea or
petition for them; do not plead with me, for I will not listen to you"* (7:16). Can you
not see, the Lord asked Jeremiah, what is going on in the towns of Judah
and streets of Jerusalem? Jeremiah was reminded that families worked
together to their own detriment preparing cakes to offer to the Queen of
Heaven and making drink offerings to other gods. *"Therefore this is what the
Sovereign LORD says: My anger and my wrath will be poured out on this place—on
man and beast, on the trees of the field and on the crops of your land—and it will
burn and not be quenched"* (7:20).

THE RIGHTEOUS BRANCH

Despite Jeremiah's unrelenting condemnation of the kings and religious leaders of his time, he sometimes moved from judgment to the
theme of prophetic deliverance in a far-future time. For example, all
thirty verses of Chapter 22 are devoted to a denunciation of the sins of
the Judean kings Shallum (Jehoahaz), Jehoiakim, and Jehoiachin, which
must have been written in either 597 or a little later. Then Chapter 23
starts abruptly with a "woe" followed by prophecies for the far future.

*"Woe to the **shepherds** who are destroying and scattering the **sheep**
of my pasture!" declares the LORD. Therefore this is what the LORD, the
God of Israel, says to the shepherds who tend my people: "Because you
have scattered my **flock** and driven them away and have not bestowed
care on them, I will bestow punishment on you for the evil you have done,"
declares the LORD. "I myself will gather the **remnant** of my flock out*

184

of all the countries where I have driven them and will bring them back to their pasture, where they will be fruitful and increase in number. I will place shepherds over them who will tend them, and they will no longer be afraid or terrified, nor will any be missing," declares the LORD.

"The days are coming," declares the LORD,
  *"when I will raise up for David a righteous **Branch**,*
a King who will reign wisely
  and do what is just and right in the land.
In his days Judah will be saved
  and Israel will live in safety.
This is the name by which he will be called:
  The LORD Our Righteous Savior.

*"So then, the days are coming," declares the LORD, "when people will no longer say, 'As surely as the LORD lives, who brought the Israelites up out of Egypt,' but they will say, 'As surely as the LORD lives, who brought the descendants of Israel up out of the land of the north and out of all **the countries where he had banished them**.' Then they will live in their own land."*
(Jer. 23:1–8, emphasis added)

The *shepherds* represent the priesthood of the Mosaic Dispensation that misled and oppressed the people. The *flock* and the *sheep* would be the people, as Jesus so often used these terms. *"Do not be afraid, little flock, for your Father has been pleased to give you the kingdom"* (Luke 12:32), and *"Feed my sheep"* (John 21:17). The word *remnant* is sometimes used to mean the Hebrews lost to the various exiles and the Diaspora who would eventually be restored to Israel (see Chapter 9 for Micah's verses on the gathering of the remnant).

As discussed at length in Chapter 8 with commentary from 'Abdu'l-Bahá, the *Branch* is Bahá'u'lláh, who was descended from Abraham, David, and Yazdirgird III, the last emperor of the Persian Sasanian dynasty (224–651 CE), on His father's side, and from Abraham on His mother's side.[2] The *countries where he had banished them* could refer to the various Babylonian deportations culminating in the Exile, and also to the Diaspora, the dispersion of the Jews from the Holy Land in all directions after the Roman conquest of 70 CE after a five-month siege. The ingathering from the Diaspora started with the Zionist movement in the nineteenth century. The modern state of Israel is considered by Jews to be *their own land* that was promised to them by Abraham. *The King* is one of the titles of Bahá'u'lláh, the King of Glory (see Appendix F). 'Abdu'l-Bahá left no doubt that Bahá'u'lláh was the *Branch* foreseen by Jeremiah.

> *That incomparable Branch will gather together all Israel, that is, in His Dispensation Israel will be gathered in the Holy Land, and the Jewish people who are now scattered in the East and the West, the North and the South, will be assembled together.*[3]

Bahá'u'lláh verified Jeremiah's glimpse of the days to come. *"Hearken with thine inner ear unto the Voice of Jeremiah, Who saith: 'Oh, **for great is that Day**, and it hath no equal. Wert thou to observe with the eye of fairness, thou wouldst perceive the greatness of the Day.'"*[4]

Promises persist throughout the book of Jeremiah that the people of Israel and Judah will be restored to their own land and will prosper there. There would be redemption and restoration. This restoration would not mean an end to the people's struggles, but they were not to fear. They would have peace and security. They would be restored to health, their fortunes would be restored, and honor brought to them.

> *"So you will be my people,*
>   *and I will be your God."*
> *See, the storm of the LORD*
>   *will burst out in wrath,*
> *a driving wind swirling down*
>   *on the heads of the wicked.*
> *The fierce anger of the LORD will not turn back*
>   *until he fully accomplishes*
>   *the purposes of his heart.*

In days to come
   you will understand this."
(30:22–24)

Jeremiah had been working up to the glorious news of a new covenant with the people of Israel and Judah. *"For there shall be a day, that the*
*watchmen upon the mount Ephraim shall cry, Arise ye, and let us go **up to Zion***
unto the Lord *our God,"* (31:6, emphasis added), and *"Behold, the days come,*
saith the Lord, *that I will make **a new covenant** with the house of Israel, and*
with the house of Judah" (31:31, emphasis added).

As discussed previously, Zion sometimes refers to Mount Carmel.
There would be a different covenant, not the one made with their ancestors. *"This is the covenant I will make with the people of Israel after that time,"*
declares the Lord. *"I will put my law in their minds and write it on their hearts. I will*
be their God, and they will be my people" (31:33).

THE SCORN OF JEHOIAKIM

In the fourth year of Jehoiakim's reign (604 BCE), Jeremiah received
a daunting writing assignment from the Lord, Who knew the perfidy of
this king and how the ensuing drama would play out, but Who wanted
to give the Judahites yet another chance.

> *In the fourth year of Jehoiakim son of Josiah king of Judah, this word came*
> *to Jeremiah from the* Lord: *"Take a scroll and write on it all the words*
> *I have spoken to you concerning Israel, Judah and all the other nations from*
> *the time I began speaking to you in the reign of Josiah till now. Perhaps when*
> *the people of Judah hear about every disaster I plan to inflict on them, they*
> *will each turn from their wicked ways; then I will forgive their wickedness*
> *and their sin."* (Jer. 36:1–3)

Jeremiah dutifully dictated the words to Baruch, his friend and
scribe. By then, Jeremiah was not allowed on the Temple grounds so
it was Baruch who went to the New Gate of the Temple on a fast day,
when a great number of people would be there. He read aloud the words

of the Lord on the ninth month of the fifth year of Jehoiakim's reign (604/603). The narration of this event does not give the contents of the scroll, but we can surmise that Baruch delivered a message like the Temple Sermon.

Temple officials informed court officials of this effrontery, who requested that Baruch read the scroll to them. Baruch did so and the court officials were filled with fear and warned him, *"You and Jeremiah, go and hide. Don't let anyone know where you are"* (36:19). Jeremiah must have had friends at the court. The scroll was left in the room of the secretary, from where it was retrieved by a court official and read to the king.

Jehoiakim was sitting by a fire in his winter apartment with members of his court. After three or four columns of the scroll were read, Jehoiakim cut them and threw them into the fire. The entire scroll was thus burned against the advice of at least three of his officials. Jehoiakim then ordered the arrest of Jeremiah and Baruch, *"But the LORD had hidden them"* (36:26).

God instructed Jeremiah to take another scroll and rewrite on it all that had been written on the first one. Writing a scroll was a long, laborious process. It had taken about a year for Baruch to inscribe Jeremiah's dictation on the first scroll. This time there was an addition to the scroll, an addition that could be perilous to Jeremiah.

*"Also tell Jehoiakim king of Judah, 'This is what the LORD says: You burned that scroll and said, "Why did you write on it that the king of Babylon would certainly come and destroy this land and wipe from it both man and beast?"' Therefore this is what the LORD says about Jehoiakim king of Judah: 'He will have no one to sit on the throne of David; his body will be thrown out and exposed to the heat by day and the frost by night. I will punish him and his children and his attendants for their wickedness; I will bring on them and those living in Jerusalem and the people of Judah every disaster I pronounced against them, **because they have not listened.**'"*
(36:29–31, emphasis added)

Five or six years later in 597, the Babylonians put Jerusalem under siege for three months. Jehoiakim died during the siege and his body was thrown over the wall, his fate probably an inside job on the part of his courtiers or army officers. The vassaldom of Judah was reinforced.

AN ORACLE FOR BABYLON

Toward the end of the book of Jeremiah are six chapters of oracles against various foreign nations: Egypt, Philistia, Moab, Ammon, Edom, Damascus, Kedar and Hazor, Elam, and Babylon. Maledictions were pronounced on all of them for various reasons and probably delivered at various times, not together as presented in Chapters 46 through 51. Judah had not been the only nation that aggravated the Lord!

The sins of Babylon especially provoked the Lord. The forty-six verses of Chapter 50 are mostly a diatribe against Babylon that starts with *"Announce and proclaim among the nations, lift up a banner and proclaim it; keep nothing back, but say, 'Babylon will be captured; Bel will be put to shame, Marduk filled with terror' because 'A nation from the north will attack her and lay waste her land'"* (Jer. 50:2–3).

The diatribe against Babylon continues with predicting the disasters to come upon it for its sins and prophesying its coming defeat. *"The LORD will carry out his purpose, his decree against the people of Babylon. You who live by many waters and are rich in treasures, your end has come, the time for you to be destroyed"* (Jer. 51:12–13). The tirade against Babylon continues in apocalyptic language that goes far beyond Babylon the city. Jeremiah seems to have made Babylon a symbol for sinful cities everywhere.

Jeremiah gave a scroll with these warnings to a staff officer named Seraiah, who was traveling to Babylon on official business, and instructed him to read the scroll aloud in Babylon. Then Seraiah was to finalize the reading by saying, *"LORD, you have said you will destroy this place, so that neither people nor animals will live in it; it will be desolate forever." When you finish reading this scroll, tie a stone to it and throw it into the Euphrates. Then say, "So will Babylon sink to rise no more because of the disaster I will bring on her. And her people will fall."* (51:62–64)

Babylon fell to the Medes, the Persians, and their allies in 539. The city steadily declined for many centuries until the desert sands reclaimed it in the seventh century CE.

AN ORACLE FOR ELAM

The oracle for Elam is as short as the oracle for Babylon is long, but it gives a remarkable prophecy.

This is the word of the LORD that came to Jeremiah the prophet concerning Elam, early in the reign of Zedekiah king of Judah:

> *This is what the LORD Almighty says:*
> *"See, I will break the bow of **Elam**,*
> *the mainstay of their might.*
> *I will bring against Elam the four winds*
> *from the four quarters of heaven;*
> *I will scatter them to the four winds,*
> *and **there will not be a nation***
> *   **where Elam's exiles do not go.***
> *I will shatter **Elam** before their foes,*
> *before those who want to kill them;*
> *I will bring disaster on them,*
> *even my fierce anger,"*
> *declares the LORD.*
> *"I will pursue them with the sword*
> *until I have made an end of them.*
> *I will set **my throne** in **Elam***
> *and destroy her **king and officials**,"*
> *declares the LORD.*
> *"Yet I will restore the fortunes of **Elam***
> *in days to come,"*
> *declares the LORD.*

(49:34–39, emphasis added)

Elam was the name of an ancient province in the southwest corner of Persia. The Báb was born in 1819 CE in Shiraz, a city in Elam.

The word *throne* is often used in sacred texts to denote the power and glory of God. The *king and officials* may refer to the shah of Persia, Nási-ri'd-dín-Sháh, and his officials who persecuted and imprisoned the Báb and then had Him executed.

The following text from the writings of the Báb equates the Tree of divine truth (the Tree of Life, see Vol. 1, Chapter 4) as *the throne* from which issue succeeding Revelations from the Prophets of God.

> *The Revelation of the Divine Reality hath everlastingly been identical with its concealment and its concealment identical with its revelation. That which is intended by "Revelation of God" is the Tree of divine Truth that beto-keneth none but Him, and it is this divine Tree that hath raised and will raise up Messengers, and hath revealed and will ever reveal Scriptures. From eternity unto eternity this Tree of divine Truth hath served and will ever serve as **the throne** of the revelation and concealment of God among His crea-tures, and in every age is made manifest through whomsoever He pleaseth.* [5]

The ancient Persian province of Elam would see the Tree of divine truth raise up a Messenger of God and see *the throne* of the Bábí Dispensation. The exiles from Elam refer to the Bábís who fled the persecution in Persia and Bahá'ís who now live in every nation and territory of the world with only one or two exceptions.

Chapter 15

Jeremiah – The End
of the Davidic Kingdom

Obey me, and I will be your God and you will be my people.
Walk in obedience to all I command you,
that it may go well with you.
But they did not listen or pay attention;
instead, they followed the stubborn
inclinations of their evil hearts.
They went backward and not forward.

JEREMIAH 7:23–24

WAITING FOR THE END must have been a long, agonizing process for Jeremiah, especially since it came in three stages—the three sieges of Jerusalem in 605, 597, and 586 BCE. Josiah, the hope of Judah, was dead, and his son and heir, Jehoahaz, offended his Egyptian ally, Pharaoh Necho, who imposed a massive fine on Judah and took Jehoahaz to Egypt, where he died. Another son of Josiah, Jehoiakim, became king for eleven years and was succeeded by Jehoiachin, who lasted three months before being deported to Babylon.

The Babylonians had defeated the Egyptians, Judah's ally, in 605 at Carchemish to the north of Damascus. The intermittent resistance of Judah to vassaldom, and her switching of allegiances between Egypt and Babylonia, tried the patience of Nebuchadnezzar II (605–562). He tried to subdue Judah in 605 by deporting to Babylon some of Jerusalem's nobility and elite citizens, including a priest named Daniel. The next deportation in 597 included more royalty, military officers, craftsmen, smiths, and a young man named Ezekiel. At that time, Nebuchadnezzar II made Zedekiah, another son of Josiah, king of Judah. The siege of Jerusalem in 586 resulted in its complete destruction and massive deportations that would be called the Babylonian Exile.

PROPHET TO THE EARLY EXILES

Jeremiah extended his mission to the deportees who had been taken to Babylon in 605 and with Jehoiachin in 597.

> *This is what the LORD Almighty, the God of Israel, says to all those I carried into exile from Jerusalem to Babylon: "Build houses and settle down; plant gardens and eat what they produce. Marry and have sons and daughters; find wives for your sons and give your daughters in marriage, so that they too may have sons and daughters. Increase in number there; do not decrease. Also, seek the peace and prosperity of the city to which I have carried you into exile. Pray to the LORD for it, because if it prospers, you too will prosper."*
> (Jer. 29:4–7)

In other words, Jeremiah told the Hebrews in exile to settle down and thrive. However, prophets were agitating them with false predictions that they would soon return, even within two years. Jeremiah set them straight.

> *Yes, this is what the LORD Almighty, the God of Israel, says: "Do not let the prophets and diviners among you deceive you. Do not listen to the dreams you encourage them to have. They are prophesying lies to you in my name. I have not sent them," declares the LORD.*
> (29:8–9)

The plan of the Lord was for the Hebrews to prosper in Babylon. He had plans to give them hope and a future.

*Then you will call on me and come and pray to me, and I will listen to you. You will seek me and find me when you seek me with all your heart. I will be found by you," declares the LORD, "and will bring you back from captivity. I will gather you from **all the nations and places where I have banished you**," declares the LORD, "and will bring you back to the place from which I carried you into exile."*
(29:12–14, emphasis added)

The Restoration with Ezra would include only Hebrews from Babylonia and surrounding areas. The Zionist movement and the influx of Jews to Palestine, and later to Israel, would include Jews from *all the nations and places where I have banished you,* the Diaspora. In the next verse, Jeremiah returned to his time and again warned of false prophets in Judah.

*You may say, "The LORD has raised up prophets for us in Babylon," but this is what the LORD says about the king who sits on David's throne and all the people who remain in this city, your fellow citizens who did not go with you into exile—yes, this is what the LORD Almighty says: "I will send the sword, famine and plague against them and I will make them like figs that are so bad they cannot be eaten. I will pursue them with the sword, famine and plague and will make them abhorrent to all the kingdoms of the earth, a curse and an object of horror, of scorn and reproach, among all the nations where I drive them. For **they have not listened** to my words," declares the LORD, "words that I sent to them again and again by my servants the prophets. And you exiles **have not listened either**," declares the LORD.*
(29:15–19, emphasis added)

Jeremiah was on the job, steadfast in his mission, which included counseling the last Davidic king throughout the travails of Judah.

SUBMIT TO THE BABYLONIANS AND LIVE

Jeremiah was told by the Lord to make a yoke of straps and crossbars and to put it on his neck. He was then to send the following message to the neighboring kings of Edom, Moab, Ammon, Tyre, and Sidon through their envoys.

> *"Give them a message for their masters and say, 'This is what the Lord Almighty, the God of Israel, says: "Tell this to your masters: With my great power and outstretched arm I made the earth and its people and the animals that are on it, and I give it to anyone I please. Now I will give all your countries into the hands of my servant Nebuchadnezzar king of Babylon; I will make even the wild animals subject to him. All nations will serve him and his son and his grandson until the time for his land comes; then many nations and great kings will subjugate him."'*
> (Jer. 27:4–7)

> *"'If, however, any nation or kingdom will not serve Nebuchadnezzar king of Babylon or bow its neck under his yoke, I will punish that nation with the sword, famine and plague, declares the Lord, until I destroy it by his hand. So do not listen to your prophets, your diviners, your interpreters of dreams, your mediums or your sorcerers who tell you, 'You will not serve the king of Babylon.' They prophesy lies to you that will only serve to remove you far from your lands; I will banish you and you will perish. But if any nation will bow its neck under the yoke of the king of Babylon and serve him, I will let that nation remain in its own land to till it and to live there, declares the Lord.'"*
> (27:8–11)

Jeremiah not only proclaimed this message to Zedekiah, the priests, and the people, but he also walked his talk. He moved about the streets of Jerusalem wearing the wooden yoke that symbolized that the people must submit to the yoke of Babylon. Endless were his skirmishes with the false prophets of the establishment. One of them, Hananiah, broke Jeremiah's wooden yoke and claimed: *"This is what the Lord says: 'In the same way I will break the yoke of Nebuchadnezzar king of Babylon off the neck of all the nations within two years'"* (28:11). As Jeremiah walked away the word of the Lord came to him:

"Go and tell Hananiah, 'This is what the LORD says: You have broken a wooden yoke, but in its place you will get a yoke of iron. This is what the LORD Almighty, the God of Israel, says: I will put an iron yoke on the necks of all these nations to make them serve Nebuchadnezzar king of Babylon, and they will serve him. I will even give him control over the wild animals.'"
(28:12–14)

Although enraged by Jeremiah, Zedekiah repeatedly turned to him for counsel as the Babylonian army approached and then laid siege to Jerusalem, a siege that would last about two years. Two factors must have been colliding in Zedekiah's head—he could end the rebellion and resubmit Judah to vassalage under Nebuchadnezzar, or he could give in to the more reckless and patriotic members of the court who wanted an uprising, even though that had not worked well for Jehoiachin. Although Zedekiah had been made king by Nebuchadnezzar, he rebelled against the Babylonians by making an alliance with the Egyptians. When the Egyptian army marched into Judah to battle the Babylonian army, Nebuchadnezzar withdrew from the siege. Zedekiah asked Jeremiah, not directly but through two intermediaries, for prayers. *"Please pray to the LORD our God for us"* (37:3). Thus, the word of the Lord came to Jeremiah:

"This is what the LORD, the God of Israel, says: Tell the king of Judah, who sent you to inquire of me, 'Pharaoh's army, which has marched out to support you, will go back to its own land, to Egypt. Then the Babylonians will return and attack this city; they will capture it and burn it down.'
"This is what the LORD says: Do not deceive yourselves, thinking, 'The Babylonians will surely leave us.' They will not! Even if you were to defeat the entire Babylonian army that is attacking you and only wounded men were left in their tents, they would come out and burn this city down."
(37:6–10)

The Babylonians defeated the Egyptians and turned back to Jerusalem to renew the siege.

A DESPERATE MEASURE

As Nebuchadnezzar and the Babylonian army were returning, the word came to Jeremiah as follows:

> *"This is what the LORD, the God of Israel, says: Go to Zedekiah king of Judah and tell him, 'This is what the LORD says: I am about to give this city into the hands of the king of Babylon, and he will burn it down. You will not escape from his grasp but will surely be captured and given into his hands. You will see the king of Babylon with your own eyes, and he will speak with you face to face. And you will go to Babylon."*
> (Jer. 34:2–3)

All but three fortified cities—Jerusalem, Lachish, and Azekah—had fallen. The end of the two-year siege of Jerusalem was imminent. Zedekiah tried a desperate measure to reverse God's plan by making a covenant with the people in Jerusalem to obey one—just one—law of Moses. Zedekiah chose the seventh-year freeing of Hebrew slaves, which had long not been observed. Everyone was to free his Hebrew slaves.

> *So all the officials and people who entered into this covenant agreed that they would free their male and female slaves and no longer hold them in bondage. They agreed, and set them free. But afterward they changed their minds and took back the slaves they had freed and enslaved them again.*
> (34:10–11)

There would be punishment for this faithlessness—a certain *freedom* for the slaveowners.

> *"Therefore this is what the LORD says: You have not obeyed me; you have not proclaimed **freedom** to your own people. So I now proclaim '**freedom**' for you, declares the LORD — '**freedom**' to fall by the sword, plague and famine. I will make you abhorrent to all the kingdoms of the earth."*
> (34:17, emphasis added)

THEY WOULD NOT LISTEN

Over the centuries, messages from the classical prophets had been routinely ignored. It was no different with Jeremiah. The kings, the priests, and the people *would not listen*. Dissonant noise interfered with receipt of divine guidance. Had the people ever really listened to the prophets?

> *"To whom can I speak and give warning?* **Who will listen to me?** *Their ears are closed so they cannot hear. The word of the* Lord *is offensive to them; they find no pleasure in it. But I am full of the wrath of the* Lord, *and I cannot hold it in."*
> (Jer. 6:10–11, emphasis added)

> *"While you were doing all these things, declares the* Lord, *I spoke to you again and again, but* **you did not listen***; I called you, but you did not answer."*
> (7:13, emphasis added)

> *"From the time I brought your ancestors up from Egypt until today, I warned them again and again, saying, 'Obey me.' But* **they did not listen** *or pay attention; instead, they followed the stubbornness of their evil hearts."*
> (11:7–8), emphasis added)

> *"I warned you when you felt secure, but you said,* **'I will not listen!'** *This has been your way from your youth; you have not obeyed me."*
> (22:21, emphasis added)

> *"And though the* Lord *has sent all his servants the prophets to you again and again,* **you have not listened** *or paid any attention."*
> (25:4, emphasis added)

> "Listen! I am going to bring on Judah and on everyone living in Jerusalem every disaster I pronounced against them. I spoke to them, but **they did not listen**; I called to them, but they did not answer."
> (35:17, emphasis added)

The Israelites did not listen in their time. How well are people listening in the twenty-first century?

A RIGHTEOUS BRANCH TO SPRING
FORTH FROM DAVID

The end was close; the Babylonian army was camped outside Jerusalem preparing for the siege. Zedekiah had had Jeremiah imprisoned in the palace court of the guard because his warnings were bad for morale. However, Jeremiah would not be subdued. He found an opportunity to prophesy for the future while being held prisoner. Here's the episode.

Jeremiah's cousin Hanamel arrived at the gate to tell him to buy his field in Anathoth. This was Jeremiah's right or duty under the law of redemption. As explained in Leviticus 25:23–25, land could not be sold permanently because it belonged to God and *"you are only strangers and residents with Me."* Therefore, every piece of property had a means of redemption after a sale. For example, if land was sold by a destitute man, his closest redeemer, a relative, could buy the land and return it. If there was no redeemer, the seller still had the option of earning the funds to buy the property back. If that was not possible, at the year of jubilee the land ownership would revert to the impoverished seller.

Jeremiah bought the land for seventeen silver shekels. He signed and sealed the deed and gave the sealed deed of purchase and a copy to Baruch in the presence of Hanamel, the signatory witnesses, and the people who were sitting in the courtyard. Then he gave Baruch instructions before these witnesses for the preservation of these documents. *"This is what the LORD of armies, the God of Israel says: 'Take these deeds, this sealed deed of purchase and this open deed, and put them in an earthenware jar, so that they may last a long time.' For this is what the LORD of armies, the God of Israel says: 'Houses and fields and vineyards will again be purchased in this land'"* (Jer. 32:14–15, emphasis added).

Jeremiah was confused. The Babylonian siege mounds had been built up to the city, which would fall *by sword, famine, and plague.* Why,

200

he prayed to God, had he been directed to not only purchase the land but go to great lengths to protect the purchase papers when all the land would soon be taken over by the Babylonians?

The Lord responded first with the rhetorical question: was anything too hard for Him? Jerusalem was indeed being given into the hands of the Chaldeans and the king of Babylon *by sword, famine, and plague.* However, great hope was given for the future.

> *Behold, I am going to gather them out of **all the lands to which I have driven them** in My anger, in My wrath, and in great indignation; and I will bring them back to this place and have them live in safety. They shall be My people, and I will be their God; and I will give them **one heart and one way**, so that they will fear Me always, for their own good and for the good of their children after them. I will make **an everlasting covenant** with them that I will not turn away from them, to do them good; and I will put the fear of Me in their hearts, so that they will not turn away from Me.*
> (32:37–40)

There is more than one approach to understanding the above. It may have foreseen the Restoration to Jerusalem under King Cyrus II of Persia and Ezra. The *one heart and one way* and *an everlasting covenant* suggest Bahá'u'lláh, Whose Dispensation teaches the oneness of humanity and the oneness of religion with a covenant that is destined to last five hundred centuries.

This divine message continued that He would plant the people in this land with all His heart and all His soul. Just as He had brought great disaster on the people, so He was going to bring on them all the good that He promised them. The land would be desolate, but people *"will buy fields for money, sign and seal deeds, and call in witnesses in the land of Benjamin, in the areas surrounding Jerusalem, in the cities of Judah, in the cities of the hill country, in the cities of the lowland, and in the cities of the Negev; for I will restore their fortunes,' declares the LORD"* (32:44). This sounds like a projection of nineteenth- and twentieth-century Jewish immigration to Palestine and the modern state of Israel.

"'The days are coming,' declares the LORD, 'when I will fulfill the good promise I made to the people of Israel and Judah.

> *"'In those days and at that time*
> *I will make a righteous **Branch** sprout from David's line;*
> *he will do what is just and right in the land.*
> *In those days Judah will be saved*
> *and Jerusalem will live in safety.*
> *This is the name by which it will be called:*
> *The LORD Our Righteous Savior.'"*

(33:14–16, emphasis added)

This is the second time that the Lord promised to Jeremiah that *a righteous Branch* for David would be raised up (see above, also Chapter 8 for a full commentary on the theme of the *Branch* from Isaiah 11:1–12, the *Branch* being Bahá'u'lláh).

THE LAST DAYS OF JUDAH

The Babylonians were laying siege to Jerusalem. Jeremiah was beaten by soldiers and imprisoned in a dungeon, after which Zedekiah had him brought to the palace for a private conversation. He wanted new, more positive, prophecies that did not require him to change his course of action. *"Is there any word from the LORD? And Jeremiah said, 'There is!' Then he said, 'You will be delivered into the hands of the king of Babylon'"* (37:17).

Jeremiah asked in what way he had sinned against the king or the people, prompting Zedekiah to imprison him. *"And where are your prophets who prophesied to you, saying, 'The king of Babylon will not come against you or against this land?'"* (37:19). Fearful that he would die in the prison dungeon, Jeremiah begged that he not be returned there. Hence, Zedekiah once again put him in the courtyard of the guardhouse where he would receive one loaf of bread a day as long as the siege lasted.

Jeremiah still would not stop preaching and prophesying. So, the officials asked Zedekiah to have him killed because he was discouraging the soldiers and the people who were left in the city. The king told them to do as they liked, so they lowered Jeremiah into a deep, dry cistern to die. Fortunately, one Ebed-melech, a court official, asked permission of Zedekiah to rescue Jeremiah. A remorseful Zedekiah assigned three men to help with the rescue.

Zedekiah soon had Jeremiah brought to him one last time and said, *"I am going to ask you something; do not hide anything from me"* (38:14). Jeremiah reminded him that the last time Zedekiah had sent for him he had said the same thing. *"If I tell you, will you not certainly put me to death? Besides, if I give you advice, you **will not listen** to me"* (38:15, emphasis added). Zedekiah swore that he would not have him killed or handed over to those who would, so Jeremiah forged ahead.

> *"This is what the LORD God Almighty, the God of Israel, says: 'If you surrender to the officers of the king of Babylon, your life will be spared and this city will not be burned down; you and your family will live. But if you will not surrender to the officers of the king of Babylon, this city will be given into the hands of the Babylonians and they will burn it down; you yourself will not escape from them.'"*
> (38:17–18)

The exchanges between Jeremiah and Zedekiah had become repetitive with Jeremiah reciting the same message and Zedekiah not listening. The walls of Jerusalem were breached. Zedekiah fled the city on horseback with companions, but with spies everywhere they were soon captured and taken to Nebuchadnezzar. These two kings undoubtedly had an interesting conversation before Zedekiah was forced to watch as his sons were killed by the sword. He was then blinded and taken to Babylon to live out his life. Jerusalem was burned and razed to the ground. The Temple was destroyed. Captives were lined up and chained for the walk into the Exile, a walk that would have taken about four months.

Walter Brueggemann, a theologian who was ordained in the United Church of Christ, summarized concisely the mindset of the Judean kings that led to their bad decisions and degradation: "Kings in Jerusalem noticed Babylon but missed Yahweh's sovereignty. In the end, they missed everything."[1]

EGYPT—REVERSING THE METAPHOR

The fall of Jerusalem in 586 BCE ended the preexilic era. Broadly speaking, the upper classes went into exile, and the lower classes remained in Judah. After a few decades, the Persian king Cyrus II would give permission for all Hebrews who wished to do so to return to Jerusalem and rebuild their Temple. But the Exile would always be remembered as a deep trauma with no equal until the utter defeat by the Romans in 70 CE and its consequent Diaspora, and then the European Holocaust of the twentieth century.

This third deportation was not as massive as it was later remembered. Those taken into the Exile were nobles, priests, skilled laborers, merchants, and some of the people who had already surrendered to the Babylonians. These deportees constituted only a small percentage of the population, but the wealth and power structure of Judah was destroyed as potential leaders of revolt were killed or exiled. This is how defeated people are rendered harmless so that their labor on the land can profit the conqueror.

Jeremiah recorded the numbers of the deportees in 605, 597, and after the fall of Jerusalem as follows:

> So Judah went into captivity, away from her land. This is the number of the people Nebuchadnezzar carried into exile:
>
> in the seventh year, 3,023 Jews;
> in Nebuchadnezzar's eighteenth year,
>   832 people from Jerusalem;
> in his twenty-third year,
>   745 Jews taken into exile by Nebuzaradan
>   the commander of the imperial guard.
>   There were 4,600 people in all.
> (52:27-30)

Since only men were counted, the number of wives and children added to 4,600 men of the three deportations would have brought the total count to about 14,000 to 18,000 people. The poor, who represented no threat, were given an opportunity to start life over with vineyards and fields that were given to them. The irony is that some of these lands may once have belonged to the ancestors of these poor who had been defrauded by the rich, whose descendants were now walking in chains to Babylon. Retributive justice in that respect was brought by the Babylonians.

Nebuzaradan, the commander of the Babylonian guard, found Jeremiah bound in chains with captives being taken into exile. Imperial intelligence sources had reported Jeremiah's tireless advocacy of submission to the Babylonians. Therefore, Nebuzaradan freed Jeremiah and offered him a choice—he could go to Babylon and be protected there, or he could go anywhere in Judah he wished.

Jeremiah chose to stay in Judah, and Nebuzaradan asked him to report to Gedaliah, the newly appointed Judean governor. Gedaliah came from a powerful and respected Jerusalem family that had taken a moderate political attitude concerning Babylon. The mandate Gedaliah had been given by Nebuchadnezzar was to restore Judah, now called the province of Yehud, to an economically productive level. Gedaliah seems to have been a wise man who took a pragmatic course to achieve this end. He warmly welcomed back many Judeans who had fled to neighboring countries and urged loyalty to Nebuchadnezzar in return for prosperity, peace, and security.

Jeremiah demonstrated submission to Nebuchadnezzar by assisting Gedaliah, a course of action that was consistent with his teachings. Gedaliah probably appreciated Jeremiah and listened to him. But on one vital issue, Gedaliah did not listen. Johanan, a military officer loyal to Gedaliah, reported an assassination plot against Gedaliah led by a returned military officer, Ishmael. Gedaliah didn't believe it until he was assassinated at dinner by Ishmael's men. Ishmael and his men successfully sought refuge with the Ammonites, forcibly taking Jeremiah with them.

Jeremiah was again a prisoner, this time a prisoner of militant rebels. Fearing imperial wrath, the perpetrators planned to flee to Egypt. They had the *hutzpah* to seek Jeremiah's prayers to God for this plan with a beguiling promise: *"May the LORD be a true and faithful witness against us if we do not act in accordance with everything the LORD your God sends you to tell us"* (42:5). Ten days later, the answer came to Jeremiah.

> *"This is what the LORD, the God of Israel, to whom you sent me to present your petition, says: 'If you stay in this land, I will build you up and not tear you down; I will plant you and not uproot you, for I have relented concerning the disaster I have inflicted on you. Do not be afraid of the king of Babylon, whom you now fear. Do not be afraid of him, declares the LORD, for I am with you and will save you and deliver you from his hands. I will show you compassion so that he will have compassion on you and restore you to your land.'*
>
> *"However, if you say, 'We will not stay in this land,' and so disobey the LORD your God, and if you say, 'No, we will go and live in Egypt, where we will not see war or hear the trumpet or be hungry for bread,' then hear the word of the Lord, you remnant of Judah. This is what the LORD Almighty, the God of Israel, says: 'If you are determined to go to Egypt and you do go to settle there, then the sword you fear will overtake you there, and the famine you dread will follow you into Egypt, and there you will die. Indeed, all who are determined to go to Egypt to settle there will die by the sword, famine and plague; not one of them will survive or escape the disaster I will bring on them.'"*
> (42:9–17)

The rebels *did not listen*. Jeremiah and Baruch were forcibly taken to Egypt. Yet even from Egypt, and in his indefatigable manner, Jeremiah continued to warn this remnant of the disaster they were courting. Thus, he delivered God's judgment:

> *"I will take away the remnant of Judah who were determined to go to Egypt to settle there. They will all perish in Egypt; they will fall by the sword or die from famine. From the least to the greatest, they will die by*

sword or famine. They will become a curse and an object of horror, a curse and an object of reproach. I will punish those who live in Egypt with the sword, famine and plague, as I punished Jerusalem. None of the remnant of Judah who have gone to live in Egypt will escape or survive to return to the land of Judah, to which they long to return and live; none will return except a few fugitives."
(44:12–14)

A reverse flight to Egypt symbolized denial of the Mosaic Covenant and spiritual regression. Those Jews who resettled in Egypt continued their idolatrous worship. After all, they convinced themselves, hadn't disaster come upon Judah because they had stopped burning incense to the Queen of Heaven and pouring out drink offerings to her? (44:15–18)

Among Jeremiah's last words of record were, *"Those who escape the sword and return to the land of Judah from Egypt will be very few. Then the whole remnant of Judah who came to live in Egypt will know whose word will stand—mine or theirs"* (44:28).

Jeremiah's stentorian voice has been a clarion call down the ages for morality and justice, for obedience to God. *To listen!* Jeremiah *was a prophet to the nations.* He presented timeless prophecies of what happens when the Word of God is denied, when people refuse *to listen* to the eternal verities that have been repeatedly brought to humanity. Disobedience to God and His laws, as taught by all the Manifestations of God, is bringing destruction today to individuals, families, and societies. Slowly, but inexorably.

'Abdu'l-Bahá wrote an engaging description of the rise and fall of Israelite civilization in accordance with the Israelites' initial adherence to, then disobedience of, the Word of God (see Appendix I).

Epilogue

THE KINGDOM OF ISRAEL fell and its people, the ten tribes of Israel, were deported to far lands for assimilation into the Assyrian empire, never to be heard from again. Over a century later, the kingdom of Judah fell, and the Davidic kingdom on earth came to its prophesied end. Jerusalem and Solomon's Temple were razed.

The Hebrew people had been chosen to be the recipients of the Mosaic Revelation, the most spiritually advanced yet given to humanity. The Mosaic codes of conduct were the most advanced yet given, and they fostered the development of a more just society. As habitually happens in religious history, though, corruption set in.

The preexilic prophets repeatedly and relentlessly foretold the results of disobeying the Mosaic Covenant. They assured the people that serving God and remaining faithful to the Mosaic Covenant would bring His blessings, whereas failure to do so would bring His punishment. God spoke through the prophets of the Mosaic Dispensation, but His words could not move individuals who chose not to listen.

Jeremiah was a transitional prophet between preexilic and postexilic times who spoke from Judah. Ezekiel was a transitional prophet who spoke from Babylon and would bring strong messages of hope for the future. The prophet Daniel would conduct his ministry from an area outside Babylon and give five time-specific prophecies for Christianity, Islam, and the Bahá'í Faith. Second Isaiah and Obadiah would speak from the Exile, Second Isaiah with joyous praise of God and wondrous times to come, and Obadiah with rage and anguish about the perfidy of Edom toward Jewish refugees during the Babylonian conquest.

The Restoration served as a religious filter. When the Jews were free to return to rebuild Jerusalem and the Temple, only the most steadfast responded. Those who had assimilated into Babylonian culture, and had mostly adopted the local pantheon of deities, were not motivated to join the arduous trek back to Jerusalem. Despite the Restoration, the winter of the Mosaic Dispensation would renew its grip in the former land of Judah. However, castigation for sins would not be the focus of the postexilic prophets because punishment had already been rendered. A stronger future emphasis would emerge, as well as encouragement and assurance of the love of God.

One sign of the winding down of the era of the classical Hebrew prophets is the relative brevity of the books of Haggai, Zechariah, Malachi, and Joel, although their words would ring for millennia. Haggai would write of a spiritual temple filled with glory and the mystical connotations of a signet ring. His contemporary, Zechariah, would remind the people of their sinful past and their disregard of the prophets, but would then move on to the day of redemption, the day when two anointed beings would fulfill the seven major religions.

Malachi would also go through the paces of citing the sins of the people and the sorrow of God. He advocated for the righting of social wrongs and for the status and security of women. From there he focused on the day of the Lord and the coming of twin Prophets. Joel would issue a clarion call that reverberates today, to blow the trumpet in Zion and sound the alarm on God's holy hill because the day of the Lord was coming.

Volume 3 of *The Coming of the Glory* covers the last phase of the saga of the Hebrew prophets and how the plan of God was revealed through the Hebrew Scriptures.

Appendix A
The Báb – Herald of the Bahá'í Faith

AN ATMOSPHERE OF RELIGIOUS expectancy reached fever pitch simultaneously in the Protestant Christian and the Shi'a Islamic worlds during the 1830s and early 1840s CE. In the West, many Christians expected the Second Coming, the return of Jesus Christ, a belief based on Daniel 8:14: *"It will take 2,300 evenings and mornings; then the sanctuary will be reconsecrated."* With the biblical counting system of a day representing a year, and the count starting in 457 BCE, the year Persian King Artaxerxes issued his decree to rebuild Jerusalem, the 2,300 days ended in 1844. When Jesus did not return in the manner expected, His apparent nonappearance became known as the Great Disappointment.

Meanwhile, in Persia (today's Iran) and Iraq, Shi'a Muslims expected the imminent return of the twelfth Imam, who was called the Qa'im ("He who will arise") or the Promised One. Descended from Muḥammad, he was the twelfth in the line of imams who were the Prophet's spiritual and political successors. Shi'a tradition states that the Qa'im disappeared at age five under mysterious and disputed circumstances in the year 874 and remained alive throughout the centuries in occultation (a state of being hidden). He would return in a thousand years to usher in the Day of Judgment and establish the kingdom of God on earth. According to the Islamic lunar calendar, the thousand years would culminate in the year 1844.

Mullá Ḥusayn (1813–1849), a Persian Shi'a Muslim and dedicated student of this prophecy, had been ardently looking for the Promised One. He felt pulled to Shiraz, Persia, where on May 22, 1844, a young

211

merchant named Siyyid 'Alí Muḥammad Shírází (1819–1850) divulged
to Mullá Ḥusayn that He was that Messenger of God, the Qa'im—the
Báb, the Gate of God, the Gate of Bahá'u'lláh. The title of the Báb has
many symbolic, layered meanings. The basic understanding is that the
Báb's purpose was to serve as the gate between Islam's expectancy of the
return of the Promised One, the Qa'im, and the coming of Bahá'u'lláh.
The Báb described the purpose of His Revelation as follows:

> *The purpose underlying this Revelation, as well as those that preceded it, has,*
> *in like manner, been to announce the advent of the Faith of Him Whom God*
> *will make manifest. And this Faith—the Faith of Him Whom God will make*
> *manifest—in its turn, together with all the Revelations gone before it, have as*
> *their object the Manifestation destined to succeed it. And the latter, no less than*
> *all the Revelations preceding it, prepare the way for the Revelation which is yet to*
> *follow. The process of the rise and setting of the Sun of Truth will thus indef-*
> *initely continue—a process that hath had no beginning and will have no end.*[1]

Shoghi Effendi, who translated and edited Nabil-i-Aazám's chronicle of the early years of the Bábí and Bahá'í Faiths, *The Dawn-Breakers:*
Nabil's Narrative of the Early Days of the Bahá'í Revelation, wrote:
From the beginning, the Báb must have divined the reception which
would be accorded by His countrymen to His teachings, and the fate
which awaited Him at the hands of the mullás [Islamic clergy]. But He
did not allow personal misgivings to affect the frank enunciation of His
claims nor the open presentation of His Cause. The innovations which
He proclaimed, though purely religious, were drastic; the announcement of His own identity startling and tremendous. He made Himself
known as the Qa'im, the High Prophet or Messiah so long promised,
so eagerly expected by the Muhammadan world. He added to this the
declaration that he was also the Gate (that is, the Báb) through whom
a greater Manifestation than Himself was to enter the human realm.[2]
The Báb's mission was twofold—to make a complete break from
Islam through a new religion that came to be called the Bábí Faith, and
to proclaim the coming of *Him Whom God will make manifest*. Just as Jesus

was severely opposed by the Jewish priestly authorities, and Muḥammad by the idol-worshipping Meccans, so was the Báb by the Islamic clergy, many of whom feared change as a threat to their station and livelihood. The Báb was either under house arrest or imprisoned for most of His six-year ministry from 1844 to 1850, while His disciples and followers taught His Faith throughout Persia.

In July 1848, the Báb was taken from His mountain prison in Chihriq to the city of Tabriz for examination before the Crown Prince of Persia and foremost ecclesiastics. He seated Himself in the seat reserved for the Crown Prince and started reciting verses of Divine Revelation. The clerics cut the Báb off and begged Him to abandon His mission. They asked Whom He claimed to be and what was the message He brought. *"I am, I am"* thrice exclaimed the Báb, *"I am the Promised One! I am the One whose name you have for a thousand years invoked, at whose mention you have risen, whose advent you have longed to witness, and the hour of whose Revelation you have prayed God to hasten."*[3]

The assemblage of notables was enraged and humiliated. Fear struck. Its most hardened members prevailed in having the Báb tortured and then returned to His prison cell in Chihriq. But the news of the Báb's proclamation spread throughout Persia and invigorated supporters of His Cause. Despite tragic upheavals and persecutions, the spirit of this new religion continued to blaze.

The Grand Vizier for the shah, N'asari'd-Dín-Sháh, succeeded in having the Báb put to death. On July 9, 1850, a firing squad executed the Báb in Tabriz in front of thousands of witnesses.[4]

The Báb had come to one of the most morally degraded societies in the world. His announcement that humanity stood at the threshold of a new era of spiritual and moral reformation aroused excitement and hope among the population. But ruthless persecution of the Bábís, including the massacre of about twenty thousand believers during the Báb's ministry and in the years immediately after His execution, drove this new religion underground.

The Dispensation of the Báb lasted nine years, from May 1844 to late 1852, making it the shortest in religious history. Two years before

His execution, the Báb had bestowed upon one of His disciples, Mírzá Ḥusayn-'Alí Núrí (1817–1892), the name *Bahá*, which means Glory.[5] He, therefore, became known as Bahá'u'lláh, which translates from Arabic to "the Glory of God."

Never before in known religious history had one Manifestation of God heralded another Who was His contemporary. Adib Taherzadeh commented, "Because He was a Manifestation of God, the Báb had true knowledge of the station of Bahá'u'lláh, a knowledge which is beyond the reach of all humanity."[6] Interestingly, the Báb and Bahá'u'lláh never met in this world, although they lived about five hundred miles apart— the Báb in Shiraz in southwestern Persia when He wasn't in prison, and Bahá'u'lláh in Tehran in the north.

Shoghi Effendi quoted the Báb as follows regarding the *year nine*:

"In the year nine," He, referring to the date of the advent of the promised Revelation, has explicitly written, *"ye shall attain unto all good." "In the year nine, ye will attain unto the presence of God." "Ere nine will have elapsed from the inception of this Cause,"* He more particularly has stated, *"the realities of the created things will not be made manifest. All that thou hast as yet seen is but the stage from the moist germ until We clothed it with flesh. Be patient, until thou beholdest a new creation. Say: 'Blessed, therefore, be God, the most excellent of Makers!'"*[7]

As the Báb had foreseen, the *year nine* in the Islamic lunar calendar corresponded with 1852, in the autumn of which Bahá'u'lláh received the divine confirmation of His identity and mission in a vision during His imprisonment in the infamous pit in Tehran, the Síyáh-Chál.

Appendix B
The Exiles of Bahá'u'lláh

BAHÁ'U'LLÁH WAS EXILED TO Baghdad in the depths of an exceptionally severe winter after four months of imprisonment in a dreaded pit of blackness, the Síyáh-Chál. He had been shackled with a heavy yoke and chains for four months. He revealed in prayer His sufferings and those of His family and followers.

My God, My Master, My Desire! ... Thou hast created this atom of dust through the consummate power of Thy might, and nurtured Him with Thine hands which none can chain up ... Thou hast destined for Him trials and tribulations which no tongue can describe, nor any of Thy Tablets adequately recount. The throat Thou didst accustom to the touch of silk Thou hast, in the end, clasped with strong chains, and the body Thou didst ease with brocades and velvets Thou hast at last subjected to the abasement of a dungeon. ... How many the nights during which the weight of chains and fetters allowed Me no rest, and how numerous the days during which peace and tranquility were denied Me, by reason of that wherewith the hands and tongues of men have afflicted Me! Both bread and water which Thou hast, through Thy all-embracing mercy, allowed unto the beasts of the field, they have, for a time, forbidden unto this servant, and the things they refused to inflict upon such as have seceded from Thy Cause, the same have they suffered to be inflicted upon Me, until, finally, Thy decree was irrevocably fixed, and Thy behest summoned this servant to depart out of Persia, accompanied by a number of frail-bodied men and children of tender age, at this time when the cold is so

215

*intense that one cannot even speak, and ice and snow so abundant that it
is impossible to move.*[1]

Because Bahá'u'lláh's father had been a court vizier, Persian authorities did not have the option of executing Bahá'u'lláh. Therefore, the
Persian government persuaded the Ottoman authorities to accept Him
in exile in Baghdad. January 1853 marked the beginning of Bahá'u'lláh's
forty years of exile and imprisonment that ended with His death in May
1892. To the consternation of Persian authorities, though, Bahá'u'lláh
attracted attention in Baghdad as a spiritual leader. After ten years, the
Persian government persuaded the Ottoman authorities to exile Him
farther away to Constantinople (now Istanbul), Turkey, and then to Adrianople (now Edirne), in European Turkey. Just days before His departure
from Baghdad in 1863, Bahá'u'lláh publicly announced that He was the
one foretold by the Báb. The year of this proclamation was 1863, the
year nineteen that the Báb had indicated.[2]

> *"Be attentive,"* He, referring in a remarkable passage to the year
> nineteen, has admonished, *"from the inception of the Revelation till the
> number of Vahíd (19)." "The Lord of the Day of Reckoning,"* He, even
> more explicitly, has stated, *"will be manifested at the end of Vahíd (19)
> and the beginning of eighty (1280 A.H.)."*[3]

During His exile in Adrianople, and later from Akka, Bahá'u'lláh
wrote a series of tablets (letters) to the world's major religious and political
leaders.[4] One addressed the kings of the world collectively, while others
were individually addressed to Abdu'l-i-Aziz, the Sultan of Turkey; Alexander II, Czar of Russia; N'asari'd-Dín-Sháh, the Shah of Persia; Napoleon III; the Catholic pontiff, Pope Pius IX; and Queen Victoria.

Bahá'u'lláh proclaimed in these missives His station and covered
many subjects, two of which were exhortations to the rulers to greatly
reduce their expenditures on armaments and to care for their people
with justice and mercy. For example, He wrote in a tablet addressed to
the kings of the earth:

Fear the sighs of the poor and of the upright in heart who, at every break of day, bewail their plight, and be unto them a benignant sovereign. They, verily, are thy treasures on earth. It behoveth thee, therefore, to safeguard thy treasures from the assaults of them who wish to rob thee. Inquire into their affairs, and ascertain, every year, nay every month, their condition, and be not of them that are careless of their duty.[5]

Bahá'u'lláh wrote repeatedly of the dawn of a new age of universal peace that would come. However, if His teachings and warnings were ignored, the establishment of that peace would be preceded by cataclysmic upheavals in the world's political, religious, economic, and social order. History tells us what decisions the rulers made. Today we are living with the consequences.

The exile to the prison city of Akka began in 1868. The purpose of this ultimate imprisonment with its harsh sanctions was to cause Bahá'u'lláh's death and, until then, to isolate Him from His followers by denying all visitor contacts. However, in time, some of the Turkish authorities and Islamic clergy in Akka became His devoted admirers and eased the severe conditions of his confinement. After nine years, two spent within the prison itself and seven within the city walls, Bahá'u'lláh was allowed to live outside Akka in a country setting where He was visited by people from all walks of life.

One might ask why a Manifestation of God would voluntarily submit to persecution, torture, and imprisonment. The answer is found in a tablet that Bahá'u'lláh wrote from Akka to an early Bahá'í, in which He states that His sacrifices are for the redemption of mankind, thus conveying the themes of atonement and sacrifice that are familiar to Christians.

The Ancient Beauty hath consented to be bound with chains that mankind may be released from its bondage, and hath accepted to be made a prisoner within this most mighty Stronghold that the whole world may attain unto true liberty. He hath drained to its dregs the cup of sorrow, that all the peoples of the earth may attain unto abiding joy, and be filled with gladness. This is of the mercy of your Lord, the Compassionate, the Most Merciful.

We have accepted to be abased, O believers in the Unity of God, that ye may be exalted, and have suffered manifold afflictions, that ye might prosper and flourish.[6]

Taherzadeh noted that Bahá'u'lláh revealed some of His most momentous writings during these dire years in Akka. He also explained, "And, significantly, it was during these calamitous years, and as a direct result of the afflictions and sufferings which were heaped upon the Supreme Manifestation of God in this Most Great Prison, that enormous spiritual forces were released causing humanity to be freed of all fetters which had been placed upon it in the course of past ages and centuries."[7]

Bahá'u'lláh passed away in 1892. His remains were put to rest beneath a garden room in a small house located steps from the mansion of Bahji where He spent His final years. This Shrine of Bahá'u'lláh is, for Bahá'ís, the holiest place on earth.

Appendix C
The Two Cycles

PROGRESSIVE REVELATION UNFOLDED IN human history through a succession of Prophets of God, each with His own Revelation—also called His Book, whether written or oral. This progression formed what is called the Adamic Cycle, also called the Prophetic Cycle and the Prophetic Era, which started with Adam and culminated with the advent of the Báb.

The Bahá'í Cycle, also known as the Cycle of Fulfillment, started with the missions of the Báb and Bahá'u'lláh, whose teachings are designed to bring humankind to spiritual maturity. The coming of the Báb in 1844 was the link between the Adamic and the Bahá'í Cycles. Muḥammad was, indeed, the Seal of the Prophets because He was the last Prophet in the Adamic Cycle. While Prophets will continue to appear at various intervals according to the will of God, they will conduct their ministries within the parameters of the Bahá'í Cycle, in the same manner that Prophets from Adam to Muḥammad worked within the parameters of the Adamic Cycle.

Each Prophet foretold the coming of the next, and all of them foretold the coming of the supreme Manifestation of God, Bahá'u'lláh. As 'Abdu'l-Bahá explained:

> Each of the Manifestations of God has likewise a cycle wherein His religion and His law are in full force and effect. When His cycle is ended through the advent of a new Manifestation, a new cycle begins. Thus, cycles are inaugurated, concluded, and renewed, until a universal cycle is completed in the world of existence and momentous events transpire which efface every record

219

and trace of the past; then a new universal cycle begins in the world, for the realm of existence has no beginning.

Briefly, our claim is that a universal cycle in the world of existence comprises a vast span of time and countless ages and epochs. In such a cycle, the Manifestations of God shine forth in the visible realm until a universal and supreme Manifestation makes the world the focal centre of divine splendours and, through His revelation, brings it to the stage of maturity. The duration of the cycle He ushers in is very long indeed. Other Manifestations will arise in the course of that cycle under His shadow and will renew, according to the needs of the time, certain laws pertaining to material affairs and transactions, but They will remain under His shadow. We are in the cycle which began with Adam and whose universal Manifestation is Bahá'u'lláh.[1]

Bahá'u'lláh came for many reasons, the foremost of which was to unify humanity. The core tenet of Bahá'í belief is unity—God is one, His Prophets are one, and humankind is one. Only when these three "onenesses" are recognized will world peace be achieved.

A basic theme of this book is that God has always been, and will always be, an actor in history. The world is vibrating with His message if we listen.

This is the Day which the Pen of the Most High hath glorified in all the holy Scriptures. There is no verse in them that doth not declare the glory of His holy Name, and no Book that doth not testify unto the loftiness of this most exalted theme. Were We to make mention of all that hath been revealed in these heavenly Books and holy Scriptures concerning this Revelation, this Tablet would assume impossible dimensions.[2]

And lastly, let's keep in mind that the Báb wrote: *"God hath raised up Prophets and revealed Books as numerous as the creatures of the world, and will continue to do so to everlasting."*[3] While the Hebrew Bible may seem overwhelming with its vast reservoir of divine guidance and human experience, it's only a fraction of the divine wisdom and guidance that has been poured into human history.

Appendix D

Talk Given by 'Abdu'l-Bahá on April 13, 1912

PRAISE BE TO GOD! This is a radiant gathering. The faces are brilliant with the light of God. The hearts are attracted to the Kingdom of Bahá. I beg of God that day by day your faces may become brighter; day by day you may draw nearer to God; day by day you may take a greater portion from the outpourings of the Holy Spirit so that you may become encircled by the bounties of heaven.

The spiritual world is like unto the phenomenal world. They are the exact counterpart of each other. Whatever objects appear in this world of existence are the outer pictures of the world of heaven. When we look upon the phenomenal world, we perceive that it is divided into four seasons; one is the season of spring, another the season of summer, another autumn and then these three seasons are followed by winter. When the season of spring appears in the arena of existence, the whole world is rejuvenated and finds new life. The soul-refreshing breeze is wafted from every direction; the soul-quickening bounty is everywhere; the cloud of mercy showers down its rain, and the sun shines upon everything. Day by day we perceive that the signs of vegetation are all about us. Wonderful flowers, hyacinths and roses perfume the nostrils. The trees are full of leaves and blossoms, and the blossoms are followed by fruit. The spring and summer are followed by autumn and winter. The flowers wither and are no more; the leaves turn gray and life has gone. Then comes another springtime; the former springtime is renewed; again a new life stirs within everything.

The appearances of the Manifestations of God are the divine springtime. When Christ appeared in this world, it was like the vernal bounty; the outpouring descended; the effulgence of the Merciful encircled all things; the human world found new life. Even the physical world partook of it. The divine perfections were upraised; souls were trained in the school of heaven so that all grades of human existence received life and light. Then by degrees these fragrances of heaven were discontinued; the season of winter came upon the world; the beauties of spring vanished; the excellences and perfections passed away; the lights and quickening were no longer evident; the phenomenal world and its materialities conquered everything; the spiritualities of life were lost; the world of existence became life unto a lifeless body; there was no trace of the spring left.

Bahá'u'lláh has come into this world. He has renewed that springtime. The same fragrances are wafting; the same heat of the Sun is giving life; the same cloud is pouring its rain, and with our own eyes we see that the world of existence is advancing and progressing. The human world has found new life.

I hope that each and all of you may become like unto verdant and green trees so that through the breezes of the divine spring, the outpouring of heaven, the heat of the Sun of Truth, you may become eternally refreshed; that you may bear blossoms and become fruitful; that you may not be as fruitless trees. Fruitless trees do not bring forth fruits or flowers. I hope that all of you may become friends of the paradise of Abhá, appearing with the utmost freshness and spiritual beauty. I pray in your behalf and beg of God confirmation and assistance.[1]

Appendix E

"End of the World –
Possibly the World's Greatest
Translation Error" by Jay Tyson

I'D LIKE TO NOMINATE "End of the World" as the most significant translation error of all time.

This translation is found in several places in the King James version of the Bible in the Gospel of Matthew (13:39-40, 49, 24:3, and 28:20). If translated correctly, it would have been the "end of the eon" or age, according to Strong's Exhaustive Concordance, which gives the Greek equivalent of each word.

In the original Greek Bible, the term used was the Greek word *aion* from which we get the English word "eon," that is, a long period of time. When King James asked his scholars to create a reliable English version of the Bible back in 1611 AD, *they somehow decided that the end of an eon was also the end of the world.* But if the Greeks had intended to say "the end of the world," they would have used the term *kosmos.* Elsewhere in the New Testament, kosmos is used for describing the physical world.

The unforeseen results of this error are astounding to contemplate. It suggested that Christian followers did not need to look carefully for the signs of the end of the *age.* If *the world itself* was ending, no one could possibly miss it! There would be no need to make the effort to search, as the wise men of the East had searched for the King of the Jews (Matt. 2:1–2).

And thus, much of Protestant Christianity, in the English-speaking world at least, proceeded along with a false premise that Christ's return was associated with the ending of the physical world.

Paul's letter to the Hebrews (9:26) provides clear evidence of his understanding of the term: In the KJV, he notes that his own time ("now") was "the end of the world." Clearly, the physical world did not end during Paul's lifetime. In the Greek Bible, he is using the same term, *aion*, and he was correct because the *age of Judaism* was gradually ending during his lifetime and within the first century after Jesus's crucifixion. The Jewish temple was destroyed by the Romans in 70 AD during the First Jewish-Roman War and the Jewish people were barred from living in the Holy Land after the Bar Kokhba Revolt in 132-136 AD. Paul clearly understood that *the Hebrew age* had ended, but the *world* itself would not end.

And, in case you have any doubts, look at more recent English translations of the Bible. For ease of reference, you can find many different translations of the above verses at http://www.biblegateway.com. The scholars of the Christian world have adjusted their translations because they have recognized that the dramatic end-of-the-world was never predicted in the Bible. The only prediction was for "the end of the age."

But alas, the error was realized too late! Many Christian ministers and missionaries had used the concept so often that it became woven into their theology and written into their books and teachings. This was particularly true of the newer denominations that have appeared since the 1830s in America, which were built on "end times" theology. These ideas were spread extensively by Adventists and Jehovah's Witnesses and a host of smaller evangelical churches, which grew particularly in America in the later 1800s, and which led to the modern evangelical movement within Christianity. In the twentieth century, they carried these teachings around the world.

So, although the errant translation in 1611 might have seemed minor at the time, it has created a world-encircling misunderstanding since then. The signs of the end of the previous *age* have occurred regularly since the 1830s—the spread of Christ's gospel to all nations (Matt. 24:14), the ending of the period of Gentile control of Jerusalem

(Luke 21:24), as well as more outward evidence such as the invention of millions of modern devices that have transformed our world, and the creation of a host of modern problems that have ensued. But the mistranslated end-of-the-world has not occurred. For nearly 200 years, religious leaders have told us to wait because "it is coming soon."

Now, as several generations have come and gone, many people have realized that something was wrong with this understanding. Many are realizing that the time has come to go back and re-evaluate some fundamental assumptions, including the real meaning of "the end of the world." Many are looking to see if they or their forebearers might have missed something. Is there a reasonable way out of this conundrum?

And this is why *The Wise Men of the West* was written.[1]

Appendix F
The Titles of Bahá'u'lláh

SHOGHI EFFENDI RECORDED THE extensive list of titles by which Bahá'u'lláh was known:

He was formally designated Bahá'u'lláh, an appellation specifically recorded in the Persian Bayán, signifying at once the light, and the splendor of God and was styled the *"Lord of Lords,"* the *"Most Great Name,"* the *"Ancient Beauty,"* the *"Pen of the Most High,"* the *"Hidden Name,"* the *"Preserved Treasure,"* *"He Whom God will make manifest,"* the *"Most Great Light,"* the *"All-Highest Horizon,"* the *"Most Great Ocean,"* the *"Supreme Heaven,"* the *"Pre-Existent Root,"* the *"Self-Subsistent,"* the *"Day-Star of the Universe,"* the *"Great Announcement,"* the *"Speaker on Sinai,"* the *"Sifter of Men,"* the *"Wronged One of the World,"* the *"Desire of the Nations,"* the *"Lord of the Covenant,"* the *"Tree beyond which there is no passing."* He derived His descent, on the one hand, from Abraham (the Father of the Faithful) through his wife Katurah, and on the other from Zoroaster, as well as from Yazdigird, the last king of the Sásáníyán dynasty. He was moreover a descendant of Jesse, and belonged, through His father, Mírzá Abbás, better known as Mírzá Buzurg—a nobleman closely associated with the ministerial circles of the Court of Fath-'Alí Sháh—to one of the most ancient and renowned families of Mazindarán.[1]

Shoghi Effendi also listed the various ways Bahá'u'lláh was titled by the Hebrew prophets:

To Him Isaiah, the greatest of the Jewish prophets, had alluded as the *"Glory of the Lord,"* the *"Everlasting Father,"* the *"Prince of Peace,"* the *"Wonderful,"* the *"Counsellor,"* the *"Rod come forth out of the stem of Jesse"* and the *"Branch grown out of His roots,"* Who *"shall be established upon the throne of David,"* Who *"will come with strong hand,"* Who *"shall judge among the nations,"* Who *"shall smite the earth with the rod of His mouth, and with the breath of His lips slay the wicked,"* and Who *"shall assemble the outcasts of Israel, and gather together the dispersed of Judah from the four corners of the earth."* Of Him David had sung in his Psalms, acclaiming Him as the *"Lord of Hosts"* and the *"King of Glory."* To Him Haggai had referred as the *"Desire of all nations,"* and Zachariah as the *"Branch"* Who *"shall grow up out of His place,"* and *"shall build the Temple of the Lord."* Ezekiel had extolled Him as the *"Lord"* Who *"shall be king over all the earth,"* while to His day Joel and Zephaniah had both referred as the *"day of Jehovah,"* the latter describing it *as "a day of wrath, a day of trouble and distress, a day of wasteness and desolation, a day of darkness and gloominess, a day of clouds and thick darkness, a day of the trumpet and alarm against the fenced cities, and against the high towers."* His Day Ezekiel and Daniel had, moreover, both acclaimed as the *"day of the Lord,"* and Malachi described as *"the great and dreadful day of the Lord"* when *"the Sun of Righteousness"* will *"arise, with healing in His wings,"* whilst Daniel had pronounced His advent as signalizing the end of the *"abomination that maketh desolate."*[2]

Bahá'u'lláh referred to Himself in one section of *Gleanings of the Writings of Bahá'u'lláh* as the

- Day Spring of the Pen of the All-Merciful
- Tongue of the Ancient of Days
- Him Who is the Sovereign Truth
- Pen of Him Who causes the dawn to break
- Most Great Name
- Pen of the Ancient of Days
- Tongue of Grandeur
- Him Who is the object of the adoration of all worlds
- Him Whose face hath shed illumination upon all who are in the heavens and who are on the earth
- Pen of the Most Great Name[3]

Appendix G

Excerpts from Abdu'l-Bahá's Talk on June 16, 1912

IF CHRISTIANS OF ALL denominations and divisions should investigate reality, the foundations of Christ will unite them. No enmity or hatred will remain, for they will all be under the one guidance of reality itself. Likewise, in the wider field if all the existing religious systems will turn away from ancestral imitations and investigate reality, seeking the real meanings of the Holy Books, they will unite and agree upon the same foundation, reality itself. As long as they follow counterfeit doctrines or imitations instead of reality, animosity and discord will exist and increase. Let me illustrate this. Moses and the prophets of Israel announced the advent of the Messiah but expressed it in the language of symbols. When Christ appeared, the Jews rejected Him, although they were expecting His manifestation and in their temples and synagogues were crying and lamenting, saying, "O God, hasten the coming of the Messiah!" Why did they deny Him when He announced Himself? Because they had followed ancestral forms and interpretations and were blind to the reality of Christ. They had not perceived the inner significances of the Holy Bible. They voiced their objections, saying, "We are expecting Christ, but His coming is conditioned upon certain fulfillments and prophetic announcements. Among the signs of His appearance is one that He shall come from an unknown place, whereas now this claimant of Messiahship has come from Nazareth. We know his home, and we are acquainted with his mother.

"Second, one of the signs or Messianic conditions is that His scepter would be an iron rod, and this Christ has not even a wooden staff.

229

"Third, He was to be seated upon the throne of David, whereas this Messianic king is in the utmost state of poverty and has not even a mat.

"Fourth, He was to conquer the East and the West. This person has not even conquered a village. How can he be the Messiah?

"Fifth, He was to promulgate the laws of the Bible. This one has not only failed to promulgate the laws of the Bible, but he has broken the law of the sabbath.

"Sixth, the Messiah was to gather together all the Jews who were scattered in Palestine and restore them to honor and prestige, but this one has degraded the Jews instead of uplifting them.

"Seventh, during His sovereignty even the animals were to enjoy blessings and comfort, for according to the prophetic texts, He should establish peace to such a universal extent that the eagle and quail would live together, the lion and deer would feed in the same meadow, the wolf and lamb would lie down in the same pasture. In the human kingdom warfare was to cease entirely; spears would be turned into pruning hooks and swords into plowshares. Now we see in the day of this would-be Messiah such injustice prevails that even he himself is sacrificed. How could he be the promised Christ?"

And so they spoke infamous words regarding Him.

Now inasmuch as the Jews were submerged in the sea of ancestral imitations, they could not comprehend the meaning of these prophecies. All the words of the prophets were fulfilled, but because the Jews held tenaciously to hereditary interpretations, they did not understand the inner meanings of the Holy Bible; therefore, they denied Jesus Christ, the Messiah. The purpose of the prophetic words was not the outward or literal meaning, but the inner symbolical significance. For example, it was announced that the Messiah was to come from an unknown place. This did not refer to the birthplace of the physical body of Jesus. It has reference to the reality of the Christ—that is to say, the Christ reality was to appear from the invisible realm—for the divine reality of Christ is holy and sanctified above place.

His sword was to be a sword of iron. This signified His tongue which should separate the true from the false and by which great sword of attack He would conquer the kingdoms of hearts. He did not conquer by the physical power of an iron rod; He conquered the East and the West by the sword of His utterance.

He was seated upon the throne of David, but His sovereignty was neither a Napoleonic sovereignty nor the vanishing dominion of a Pharaoh. The Christ Kingdom was everlasting, eternal in the heaven of the divine Will.

By His promulgating the laws of the Bible, the reality of the law of Moses was meant. The Sinaitic law is the foundation of the reality of Christianity. Christ promulgated it and gave it higher, spiritual expression.

He conquered and subdued the East and West. His conquest was effected through the breaths of the Holy Spirit, which eliminated all boundaries and shone from all horizons.

In His day, according to prophecy, the wolf and the lamb were to drink from the same fountain. This was realized in Christ. The fountain referred to was the Gospel, from which the water of life gushes forth. The wolf and lamb are opposed and divergent races symbolized by these animals. Their meeting and association were impossible, but having become believers in Jesus Christ those who were formerly as wolves and lambs became united through the words of the Gospel.

The purport is that all the meanings of the prophecies were fulfilled, but because the Jews were captives of ancestral imitations and did not perceive the reality of the meanings of these words, they denied Christ; nay, they even went so far as to crucify Him. Consider how harmful is imitation. These were interpretations handed down from fathers and ancestors, and because the Jews held fast to them, they were deprived.

It is evident, then, that we must forsake all such imitations and beliefs so that we may not commit this error. We must investigate reality, lay aside selfish notions and banish hearsay from our minds. The Jews consider Christ the enemy of Moses, whereas, on the contrary, Christ promoted the Word of Moses. He spread the name of Moses throughout the Orient and Occident. He promulgated the teachings of Moses. Had it not been for Christ, you would not have heard the name of Moses;

and unless the manifestation of Messiahship had appeared in Christ, we would not have received the Old Testament.

The truth is that Christ fulfilled the Mosaic law and in every way upheld by Moses; but the Jews, blinded by imitations and prejudices, considered Him the enemy of Moses.[1]

Appendix H

'Abdu'l-Bahá, Shoghi Effendi, and the Bahá'í Covenant

BAHÁ'U'LLÁH APPOINTED HIS OLDEST son, Abbás Effendi (1844–1921), in His will as His successor, the Head of the Bahá'í Faith, and the sole authorized interpreter of the Sacred Texts. 'Abbás Effendi had taken the name 'Abdu'l-Bahá early in life. This name translates in Arabic to servant ('Abdu'l) of the glory (Bahá). He chose this name to indicate his lifelong dedication to his father, which began even before He accompanied his father and family into their forty-year exile at age nine. He expressed the meaning of his name this way:

> *My name is 'Abdu'l-Bahá, my identity is 'Abdu'l-Bahá, my qualification is 'Abdu'l-Bahá, my reality is 'Abdu'l-Bahá, my praise is 'Abdu'l-Bahá. Thraldom to the Blessed Perfection is my glorious and refulgent diadem; and servitude to all the human race is my perpetual religion. No name, no title, no mention, no commendation hath he nor will ever have except 'Abdu'l-Bahá. This is my longing. This is my supreme apex. This is my greatest yearning. This is my eternal life. This is my everlasting glory!*[1]

'Abdu'l-Bahá's imprisonment in Ottoman custody ultimately lasted for fifty-six years, sixteen years beyond His father's death. At age sixty-four, in 1908, He was among the Ottoman Empire's religious and political prisoners who were freed during the Young Turks Revolution. In the years after the passing of Bahá'u'lláh, 'Abdu'l-Bahá guided the development of the Faith as it expanded from the Middle East into Asia, Africa,

Europe, and North America. He became known as an ambassador of peace throughout the East and West, an exemplary human being, and the leading exponent of the Bahá'í Faith. He also devoted much of His ministry to serving the poor in Akka and its neighboring city across the bay, Haifa.

During the same period, 'Abdu'l-Bahá planned and started construction of the Shrine of the Báb for the interment of His remains in 1909. These remains had been quietly transported from Persia to Haifa decades after His execution. Bahá'u'lláh had shown 'Abdu'l-Bahá the location on Mount Carmel where the Báb was to be interred.

Despite His age and poor health, 'Abdu'l-Bahá undertook a grueling three-year (1911–1913) lecture tour through Europe, Canada, and the United States. He foresaw World War I and, upon His return to Palestine, worked tirelessly to promote the cultivation and storage of grain to feed the populace in Ottoman Palestine during the coming conflict. He stayed in Palestine throughout the war, continuing both his local work for the poor and his guidance of the international Bahá'í community. He withstood Allied bombardments of Turkish positions and threats from the Turkish commander to crucify him on Mount Carmel, the steep slope on which much of Haifa stands, before the British troops arrived. 'Abdu'l-Bahá was dubbed a Knight of the British Empire (KBE) in April 1920 in recognition for His humanitarian efforts during the war.

'Abdu'l-Bahá died eighteen months later in November 1921. Thousands of mourners accompanied his casket from his home in Haifa to the Shrine of the Báb on Mount Carmel, where He was laid to rest in a burial chamber next to that of the Báb. Six speakers from the Christian, Muslim, and Jewish communities offered eulogies.

As of this writing, the Shrine of 'Abdu'l-Bahá is being completed in a location equidistant between the Shrine of Báb on Mount Carmel and the Shrine of Bahá'u'lláh outside Akka. The remains of 'Abdu'l-Bahá will be transferred to His Shrine.

The Will and Testament of 'Abdu'l-Bahá named twin successors— the Universal House of Justice, which had not yet been elected, and his eldest grandson, Shoghi Effendi Abbás (1897–1957), who took the most humble title he could find, that of Guardian of the Faith. 'Abdu'l-Bahá also designated Shoghi Effendi the sole interpreter of the Sacred Texts of the Faith and bestowed upon him the responsibility for completing the construction of the Shrine of the Báb.

Shoghi Effendi was educated at the American School in Beirut, Lebanon, and at Oxford University, England. He had a brilliant mind and was self-disciplined beyond measure. He wrote in Arabic, Persian, and English—a language of which he displayed an exquisite, erudite, and compelling command. His writings, which include an incomparable history of the Faith from 1844 to 1944 (*God Passes By*), and innumerable volumes of his letters and commentaries offer profound insights into the spiritual dimensions of civilization and the dynamics of social change.

With infinite patience and encouragement, Shoghi Effendi guided the progress of the Faith and its global spread with painstaking attention, one small victory at a time. He labored without pause for the development of the buildings and gardens of the Bahá'í World Centre on the slopes of Mount Carmel in Haifa, which became part of the newly formed nation of Israel during his lifetime. He also translated many of the works of the Báb and Bahá'u'lláh into exquisite English. The adoration and appreciation that the Bahá'í world had for him were reflected in frequent references to him as the "beloved Guardian."

Shoghi Effendi's unexpected death in November 1957 left the Bahá'í world bereft. He had not been able to appoint a successor in accordance with the provisions of the Will and Testament of 'Abdu'l-Bahá since He and his wife, Amatu'l-Bahá Rúhíyyih Khánum (the former Mary Maxwell of Canada) had no children. Fortunately, Shoghi Effendi had continued the practice instituted by Bahá'u'lláh, and followed by 'Abdu'l-Bahá, of recognizing specific individuals for their tireless devotion to the protection and expansion of the Bahá'í Faith with the title Hands of the Cause of God. At the time of Shoghi Effendi's passing, there were twenty-seven surviving Hands of the Cause. All but one of them met together soon after Shoghi Effendi's funeral and elected nine of their number to temporarily conduct the affairs of the Faith from the Bahá'í World Centre in Haifa. This decision was subsequently endorsed unanimously by the National Spiritual Assemblies, the highest governing bodies of the Faith at that time.

In April 1963—the centenary of the public declaration of Bahá'u'lláh—the Universal House of Justice was elected by members of the fifty-six National Spiritual Assemblies that had been established in the world. The Hands of the Cause had declared themselves ineligible for election. As the highest institution of the Faith, the House of Justice is composed of nine members who are elected every five years by members of all National Assemblies. The nine-member National Assemblies themselves are elected by secret ballot by delegates who are elected by the Bahá'ís of their countries, also by secret ballot. The Universal House of Justice is responsible for applying the principles of the Faith within the global Bahá'í community, protecting the Faith from those who wish it harm, teaching the Faith in various global endeavors, and administering the affairs of the worldwide community.

The succession after Bahá'u'lláh of 'Abdu'l-Bahá, Shoghi Effendi, and the Universal House of Justice constitutes the Bahá'í Covenant. For the first time in the history of revealed religions, a covenant of succession—a provision for the protection and leadership of a new faith—was enacted to prevent schism into competing sects. The Faith has remained undivided and free of schism—a most necessary condition for it to work effectively and credibly for global unity.

For an excellent article on the life and work of Shoghi Effendi, see "The Life and Work of Shoghi Effendi," https://www.bahai.org/shoghi-effendi/life-work-shoghi-effendi.

Appendix I

'Abdu'l-Bahá, Excerpts from
The Secret of Divine Civilization

"THEY [THE HEBREWS IN Egypt] continued on in this anguish [slavery] until suddenly Moses, the All-Beauteous, beheld the Divine Light streaming out of the blessed Vale, the place that was holy ground, and heard the quickening voice of God as it spoke from the flame of that Tree 'neither of the East nor of the West,'* and He stood up in the full panoply of His universal prophethood. In the midst of the Israelites, He blazed out like a lamp of Divine guidance, and by the light of salvation He led that lost people out of the shadows of ignorance into knowledge and perfection. He gathered Israel's scattered tribes into the shelter of the unifying and universal Word of God, and over the heights of union He raised up the banner of harmony, so that within a brief interval those benighted souls became spiritually educated, and they who had been strangers to the truth, rallied to the cause of the oneness of God, and were delivered out of their wretchedness, their indigence, their incomprehension and captivity and achieved a supreme degree of happiness and honor. They emigrated from Egypt, set out for Israel's original homeland, and came to Canaan and Philistia. They first conquered the shores of the River Jordan, and Jericho, and settled in that area, and ultimately all the neighboring regions, such as Phoenicia, Edom and Ammon, came under their sway. In Joshua's time there were thirty-one governments in the hands of the Israelites, and in every noble human attribute—learning, stability, determination, courage, honor, generosity—this people came to surpass all the nations of the earth. When

237

in those days an Israelite would enter a gathering, he was immediately singled out for his many virtues, and even foreign peoples wishing to praise a man would say that he was like an Israelite.

"It is furthermore a matter of record in numerous historical works that the philosophers of Greece such as Pythagoras, acquired the major part of their philosophy, both divine and material, from the disciples of Solomon. And Socrates after having eagerly journeyed to meet with some of Israel's most illustrious scholars and divines, on his return to Greece established the concept of the oneness of God and the continuing life of the human soul after it has put off its elemental dust. Ultimately, the ignorant among the Greeks denounced this man who had fathomed the inmost mysteries of wisdom and rose up to take his life; and then the populace forced the hand of their ruler, and in council assembled they caused Socrates to drink from the poisoned cup.

After the Israelites had advanced along every level of civilization, and had achieved success in the highest possible degree, they began little by little to forget the root-principles of the Mosaic Law and Faith, to busy themselves with rites and ceremonials and to show forth unbecoming conduct. In the days of Rehoboam, the son of Solomon, terrible dissension broke out among them; one of their number, Jeroboam, plotted to get the throne, and it was he who introduced the worship of idols. The strife between Rehoboam and Jeroboam led to centuries of warfare between their descendants, with the result that the tribes of Israel were scattered and disrupted. In brief, it was because they forgot the meaning of the Law of God that they became involved in ignorant fanaticism and blameworthy practices such as insurgence and sedition. Their divines, having concluded that all those essential qualifications of humankind set forth in the Holy Book were by then a dead letter, began to think only of furthering their own selfish interests, and afflicted the people by allowing them to sink into the lowest depths of heedlessness and ignorance. And the fruit of their wrong doing was this, that the old-time glory which had endured so long now changed to degradation, and the rulers of Persia, of Greece, and of Rome, took them over. The banners of their sovereignty were reversed; the ignorance, foolishness, abasement and self-love of their religious leaders and their scholars were brought to light in the coming of Nebuchadnezzar, King of Babylon, who destroyed them. After a general massacre, and the sacking and razing of their houses and even the uprooting of their trees, he took captive whatever remnants his sword had spared and carried them off to Babylon.

"Our purpose is to show how true religion promotes the civilization and honor, the prosperity and prestige, the learning and advancement of a people once abject, enslaved and ignorant, and how, when it falls into the hands of religious leaders who are foolish and fanatical, it is diverted to the wrong ends, until this greatest of splendors turns into blackest night."[1]

* Qur'án 24:35.

Notes

INTRODUCTION

1 Stephen Lambden, "The Word Bahá: Quintessence of the Greatest Name," *Baháí Studies Review* 3:1, note no. 7, 1993.

2 Gary Selchert, "The Concept of Sacred Justice in Hebrew Eschatology," *Lights of Irfan*, Book 1, 111.

3 Bahá'u'lláh, "Words of Wisdom," *Tablets of Bahá'u'lláh Revealed after the Kitáb-i-Aqdas*, 157.

4 Helen Hornby, *Lights of Guidance*, no. 1688, 502. From a letter written on behalf of Shoghi Effendi to the National Spiritual Assembly of the United States and Canada, July 28, 1936: *Baháí News*, No. 103, 1, October 1936.

5 *The Bible: Extracts on the Old and New Testaments*. Cited in a letter dated January 31, 1955, written on behalf of Shoghi Effendi to an individual.

6 Ibid. Cited in a letter dated August 9, 1984, written on behalf of the Universal House of Justice to an individual.

7 Bahá'u'lláh, *The Kitáb-i-Íqán*, no. 53, 49.

8 Abdu'l-Bahá, *The Promulgation of Universal Peace*, 155.

9 Bahá'u'lláh, *Gleanings from the Writings of Bahá'u'lláh*, no. 139, 175. Written in a tablet to Shaykh Maḥmúd, Muftí of Akka. A *muftí* is a Muslim legal expert. Anthony Joy, *Exploring Gleanings*, 121.

10 Mírzá Abu'l-Faḍl Gulpáygání, *Miracles and Metaphors*, 9.

11 Ibid.

12 'Abdu'l-Bahá, *Some Answered Questions*, no. 39:7, 178.

13 Ibid., no. 47:1, 207.

14 Ibid., no. 38:4, 172–73.

15 Ibid., no. 35:2–4, 156–57.

16 Leslie McFall, "Has the chronology of the Hebrew kings been finally settled?" *Melios,* vol. 17, no. 1, The Gospel Coalition, https://www.thegospelcoalition.org/themelios/article/has-the-chronology-of-the-hebrew-kings-been-finally-settled/

17 *Promulgation of Universal Peace,* 201.

CHAPTER 1: THE WRITING PROPHETS

1 R. N. Whybray, "Prophets: Ancient Israel," *The Oxford Companion to the Bible,* Bruce M. Metzger and Michael D. Coogan, eds., 1st ed., 620.

2 The NAS Old Hebrew Lexicon, s.v. "balak", website Bible Study Tools.

3 William Schniedewind, *How the Bible Became a Book,* 8485. William Schniedewind is Professor of Hebrew Bible and Northwest Semitic Languages in the Department of Near Eastern Languages and Cultures at the University of California, Los Angeles.

4 Ibid., 85.

5 'Abdu'l-Bahá, *Some Answered Questions,* 43:4–6, 187–88.

6 Ibid., 5:2, 17.

7 Abraham Heschel, *The Prophets,* 5–6.

8 Ibid., 12.

9 Ibid., 29.

10 Michael Sours, *Understanding Biblical Prophecy,* vol. 3, 5–6.

11 Ibid., 6.

CHAPTER 2: JONAH – A MOST RELUCTANT PROPHET

1 Mitch Albom, https://www.goodreads.com/quotes/208923-adam-hid-in-the-garden-of-eden-moses-tried-to. Quoted from *Have a Little Faith: A True Story.* Mitchell Albom is an American author, journalist, and musician. Having achieved national recognition for sports writing in his early career, he is perhaps best known for the inspirational stories and themes that are woven through his books, plays, and films.

2   Gwendolyn Leick, *Mesopotamia: The Invention of the City*, 242.

3   Ibid, 243.

4   Ibid., 219.

5   R. Baruch, "Hebrew Numerology and the Bible," 4, website Love Israel, November 13, 2015. Rabbi Baruch holds a PhD in Jewish Studies with an emphasis in biblical languages. He earned rabbinical ordination as an Orthodox Rabbi in 1998. He and his family have lived in Israel since 2002, where he teaches at the Zera Avraham Institute, a congregation of Messianic Jews who believe that Jesus is Israel's promised Messiah, as well as the Israel College of the Bible, a Hebrew-speaking, private messianic Bible college located in Netanya, Israel.

6   Michael E. Hunt, "The Significance of Numbers in Scripture," May 2012, website Agape Catholic Bible Study.

7   James L. Crenshaw, "The Book of Jonah," *The Oxford Companion to the Bible*, Bruce M. Metzger and Michael, Coogan, eds., 381.

8   Geoffrey Dennis, Rabbi, "Judaism and Numbers: The Jewish numerology tradition, known as gematria, values some numbers more than others," website My Jewish Heritage. Dennis was ordained by the Hebrew Union College-Jewish Institute of Religion for Reform Judaism. He is also an adjunct professor of rabbinic literature in the Jewish Studies Program at the University of North Texas, teaching courses in the Bible, Kabbalah, and modern Israel.

9   Baruch, "Hebrew Numerology and the Bible," website Love Israel, 17.

10 Hunt, "The Significance of Numbers in Scripture," website Agape Catholic Bible Study, May 2012.

11 'Abdu'l-Bahá, *Selections from the Writings of 'Abdu'l-Bahá*, no. 138.2, 167.

CHAPTER 3: ISRAEL SEVERED FROM JUDAH

1   Israel Finkelstein and Neil Asher Silberman, *The Bible Unearthed*, 238.

2   Israel Finkelstein and Neil Asher Silberman, *David and Solomon*, 97.

3 Hillel Geva cited in Hershel Shanks, "Ancient Jerusalem: The Village, the Town, the City," *Biblical Archaeology Review*, May/June 2016. Geva is the Director of the Israel Exploration Society and holds a PhD from The Hebrew University in Jerusalem. He specializes in the archeology of ancient Jerusalem, and he edits and publishes *Jewish Quarter Excavations in the Old City of Jerusalem*, the reports from those excavations having produced five volumes to date.

4 'Abdu'l-Bahá, *Some Answered Questions*, no. 43:5–6, 188.

5 The talent was the heaviest and largest biblical unit of coins, weighing about 75 pounds or 35 kilograms. A shekel contained 575 grams of silver, or about 1.25 pounds, and 1,000 talents equaled 35,000 kilograms of silver. With 1,000 grams to a kilogram, 3,500,000 grams of silver would be needed for 6,089 silver shekels. It would take 122 people paying 50 shekels per year to pay the tribute.

6 *The Bible Unearthed*, 214. Samaria was the capital city of the kingdom of Israel.

7 K. Lawson Younger, Jr., "Israelites and Judahites in Assyria According to the Cuneiform Sources," slide 16, Lanier Theological School, Deerfield, IL. This 82-page slideshow, with charts and photographs, presents many aspects of the deportations into the Assyrian empire.

CHAPTER 4: AMOS – YET YOU DID NOT RETURN TO ME

1 Jennifer M. Dines, "Amos," *The Oxford Bible Commentary*, 582.

2 Bari Weiss, "Can an Archaeological Dig Change the Future of Jerusalem?" *The New York Times*, March 30, 2019. Papyrus scrolls were wrapped in cords and secured with a bit of clay called a bulla, or seal, which could be inscribed.

3 Sycamore trees were a type of fig tree. Its figs were slashed in order to hasten their ripening.

4 Adam Eliyahu Berkowitz, "Scientific Proof for King Uzziah's Earthquake," *Breaking Israel News*, January 8, 2019.

5 At that time, there were lions and bears in the Middle East, so they were apt metaphors for danger.

6 Bahá'u'lláh, *Epistle to the Son of the Wolf*, 145. The word *kerem* (carmel) translates from both Hebrew and Arabic as vineyard. The quotation *"Our God will come, and He will not be silent."* is from the Quran.

7 Shoghi Effendi, *God Passes By*, 194.

8 Bahá'u'lláh, *The Proclamation of Bahá'u'lláh*, "The Great Announcement to Mankind," 111.

9 The Assyrians often put hooks through their captives' lips to control them.

10 Adib Taherzadeh, *The Revelation of Bahá'u'lláh: Vol. 2, Adrianople 1863–68*, 2. Taherzadeh gives the attribution: Bahá'u'lláh, *Má'idiy-i-Ásamání*, (Writings of Bahá'u'lláh), Vol. VII, 192. Compiled from the Writings of Baha'u'llah by Abdu'l-Hamid-i-Ishraq Khavari. Taherzadeh explains that the 1280 A.H. in the Islamic calendar is 1863 AD, the year that Bahá'u'lláh publicly declared His identity and was exiled to Constantinople.

11 Nabíl-i-A'zam, *The Dawn-Breakers: Nabil's Narrative of the Early Days of the Bahá'í Revelation*, 515.

12 "Balfour Declaration Letter written," website *This Day In History*, November 2, 1917. "On November 2, 1917, Foreign Secretary Arthur James Balfour writes an important letter to Britain's most illustrious Jewish citizen, Baron Lionel Walter Rothschild, expressing the British government's support for a Jewish homeland in Palestine. The letter would eventually become known at the Balfour Declaration."

13 Resolution Adopted on the Report of the Ad Hoc Committee on the Palestinian Question Resolution, United Nations Documents, November 29, 1947.

14 Law of Return 5710–1950, Israel Ministry of Foreign Affairs. The word *oleh* means immigrant to Israel.

CHAPTER 5: HOSEA – REAPING THE WHIRLWIND

1 The massacre at Jezreel was King Jehu's murder of the family of Ahab. See Vol. 1, Chapter 3.

2 Bahá'u'lláh, *Epistle to the Son of the Wolf*, 179.

3 'Abdu'l-Bahá, *Selections from the Writings of 'Abdu'l-Bahá*, no. 139.9, 170.

4 'Abdu'l-Bahá, *Some Answered Questions*, no. 9:15, 37–38.

5 Hushidar Motlagh, *Lord of Lords*, 256–57. Motlagh is professor emeritus at Central Michigan University. He is the author of about fifty volumes relating to the knowledge of God, understanding the Bible, the Qur'án, and the fulfillment of prophecies in the advent of the Bahá'í Faith, available at https://globalperspective.org/.

6 William Sears, *Thief in the Night*, 144. William Sears (1911–1992) was a writer and a popular television and radio personality in various shows but he left television popularity for lifelong service to the Bahá'í Faith.

CHAPTER 6: JUDAH ON HER OWN

1 Israel Finkelstein and Neil Asher Silberman, *The Bible Unearthed*, 235, 238.

2 Hillel Geva, "Ancient Jerusalem: The Village, the Town, the City," *Biblical Archaeology Review*, May/June 2016.

3 *The Bible Unearthed*, 241–43. *"You, Judah, have as many gods as you have towns; and the altars you have set up to burn incense to that shameful god Baal are as many as the streets of Jerusalem"* (Jer. 11:13). The word "syncretistic" is the adjective for syncretism, which means the merging of religions, cultures, or schools of thought.

4 William G. Dever, *The Lives of Ordinary People in Ancient Israel*, 250. Dever is professor emeritus of Near Eastern archeology and anthropology at the University of Arizona, Tucson, with more than fifty years of experience in the field.

5 Ibid., 291.

6   *"He made the Sea of cast metal, circular in shape, measuring ten cubits from rim to rim and five cubits high"* (1 Kings 7:23). The Sea was one of the Temple's furnishings. It was cast in bronze and sat atop a huge bronze basin supported by twelve bulls, one for each of the twelve tribes of Israel, three facing north, three facing west, three facing south, and three facing east. The Sea was circular in shape and represented the waters of the Red Sea.

7   Translation from Old Hebrew dated to the late eighth or seventh century: " … [when the tunnel] was driven through. And this was the way in which it was cut through: While [the quarrymen were] still […] axes, each man toward his fellow, and while there were still three cubits to be cut through, [there was heard] the voice of a man calling to his fellow, for there was an overlap in the rock on the right [and on the left]. And when the tunnel was driven through, the quarrymen hewed [the rock], each man towards his fellow, axe against axe; and the water flowed from the spring toward the reservoir for 1,200 cubits, and the height of the rock above the heads of the quarrymen was a hundred cubits." Jona Lendering, "The Siloam Inscription," Livius.org, revised October 4, 2020.

CHAPTER 7: FIRST ISAIAH – THE DAY OF THE LORD OF HOSTS

1   Shoghi Effendi, *The World Order of Bahá'u'lláh*, 205.

2   Hushidar Motlagh, *Lord of Lords*, 459–60.

3   Bahá'u'lláh, *Gleanings from the Writings of Bahá'u'lláh*, no. 10.1, 12–13.

4   *Some Answered Questions*, no. 13.1, 3, 76–77.

5   *Gleanings*, no. 10.2, 13–14. Anthony Joy states that *Gleanings* no. 10 was written to the Bahá'ís of Khurasan to address Isaiah 2:10–11. *Exploring Gleanings*, 15.

6   "The Will of the divine Testator is this: It is incumbent upon the Aghsán, the Afnán and My Kindred to turn, one and all, their faces towards the Most Mighty Branch. Consider that which We have revealed in Our Most Holy Book: 'When the ocean of My presence hath ebbed and the Book of My Revelation is ended, turn your

faces toward Him Whom God hath purposed, Who hath branched from this Ancient Root.' The object of this sacred verse is none other except the Most Mighty Branch ['Abdu'l-Bahá]." *Tablets of Bahá'u'lláh Revealed after the Kitáb-i-Aqdas,* 221).

7   Ibid., 4.

8   Shoghi Effendi, *God Passes By,* 94–95. These names have different relevancies in the Mosaic and Christian sacred texts.

9   Bahá'u'lláh, "Súrih-i-Haykal" (Súrih of the Temple), *The Summons of the Lord of Hosts,* no. 102, 54–55.

10   Ibid., no. 121, 63.

11   Ibid., no. 128, 66.

12   "Ishráqát" (Splendours), *Tablets of Bahá'u'lláh Revealed after the Kitáb-i-Aqdas,* 122.

13   Adib Taherzadeh, *The Revelation of Bahá'u'lláh: Mazra'ih & Bahjí 1877–92,* vol. 4, 13.

CHAPTER 8: A CHILD, A ROD, AND A BRANCH

1   'Abdu'l-Bahá, *Some Answered Questions,* no. 71.2, 291.

2   'Abdu'l-Bahá, *The Promulgation of Universal Peace,* 199–200.

3   *Some Answered Questions,* no. 9.15, 37.

4   Bahá'u'lláh, Suríh of the Temple (to Pope Pius IX), *The Summons of the Lord of Hosts,* no. 122, 63.

5   'Abdu'l-Bahá, *Selections from the Writings of 'Abdu'l-Bahá,* no. 201.1, 257–58.

6   'Abdu'l-Bahá, quoted by Shoghi Effendi, *World Order of Bahá'u'lláh,* 133.

7   Bahá'u'lláh, Lawḥ-i-Aqdas (Tablet to the Christians), *Tablets of Bahá'u'lláh Revealed after the Kitáb-i-Aqdas,* 12.

8   William Sears, *Thief in the Night,* 150–51.

9   *Some Answered Questions,* no. 12.2–10, 71–75.

10   Bahá'u'lláh, *Tablets of Bahá'u'lláh Revealed after the Kitáb-i-Aqdas,* "Tarazát" (Ornaments), 30.

11   *Tablets of Bahá'u'lláh Revealed after the Kitáb-i-Aqdas,* "Lawḥ-i-Maqṣúd" (Tablet of Maqṣúd), 169.

12 *Tablets of Bahá'u'lláh Revealed after the Kitáb-i-Aqdas*, 247.

13 Dr. Youness Afroukteh, *Memories of Nine Years in Akka*, 260.

14 'Abdu'l-Bahá, cited by Rúḥíyyih Rabbaní, *The Priceless Pearl*, 12.

15 Ibid.

16 Ibid.

CHAPTER 9: MICAH – HE WATCHED IN HOPE FOR THE LORD

1 Refer to vol. 1, chapter 9, *The Coming of the Glory*, for discussions on the Covenant Code (Exodus 20:22–23:33), the Holiness Code (Lev. 17–26), and the Deuteronomic Code (Deut. 12–26).

2 'Abdul-Bahá, *Star of the West*, vol. 10, no. 12: June 4, 1919, 232.

3 Bahá'u'lláh, *The Kitáb-i-Íqán*, no. 70, 59–60. Yaḥyá is Arabic for John.

4 In 1839, a forward-thinking Ottoman sultan started the process of *Tanzimat*, a reorganization plan that lasted from 1839 to 1876. The Edict of Gulhane was issued in 1840 and gave the right of all Ottoman citizens to own property. This included the Jews in Palestine. The tradition of executing apostates from Islam to Christianity was abrogated in 1833. Suggested reading is the article "The 1844 Ottoman 'Edict of Toleration' by Michael W. Sours, *Journal of Bahá'í Studies*, August 3, 1998, 53–80. Available at https://bahai-library.com/sours_ottoman_edict_toleration

5 Hushidar Motlagh, *Lord of Lords*, 393–94. ARV refers to the American Revised Version, an English translation that was completed in 1901. The Jerusalem Bible is an English translation released in 1966.

6 *Selections from the Writings of the Báb*, nos. 3 and 4, 14. Cited by Motlagh, *Lord of Lords*, 259–60.

7 Bahá'u'lláh, *The Kitáb-i-Aqdas*, no. 82, 49.

8 Adib Taherzadeh, *The Revelation of Bahá'u'lláh: Adrianople 1863–68*, Vol. 2, 2.

9 The citadel in Akka was built during the Ottoman period over the ruins of a twelfth-century Crusader fortress. It was used at various

times as a government building, army barracks, and arms warehouse, and was last used as a prison under the British Mandate during the Arab revolts of the 1930s. Also imprisoned at the time were members of the Irgun, a Zionist paramilitary organization that fought for freedom from the British from 1931 to 1948. Recently, this part of the prison was renovated by the government of Israel and made into a museum commemorating the imprisonment and execution of Irgun soldiers. Respectfully included in the renovations were the cells where Bahá'u'lláh, His family, and followers were kept. The prison is visited by Bahá'í pilgrims and is a point of interest for many tourists.

10   *The Kitáb-i-Aqdas*, no. 45, 36.
11   Shoghi Effendi, *God Passes By*, 220.
12   William Sears, *The Half-Inch Prophecy*, 82–83.
13   *Tablets of Bahá'u'lláh Revealed after the Kitáb-i-Aqdas*, 5.
14   *The Half-Inch Prophecy*, 117. The Bahá'í Era began in 1844.
15   Ronald E. Clements, "The Book of Deuteronomy," *The Oxford Companion to the Bible*, Bruce M. Metzger and Michael D. Coogan, eds., 1st ed., 65.

CHAPTER 10: ZEPHANIAH – APOCALYPSE AND REDEMPTION

1   'Abdu'l-Bahá, *Some Answered Questions*, no. 28:3, 130.
2   Bahá'u'lláh, *Gleanings from the Writings of Bahá'u'lláh*, no. 36.1, 85.
3   'Abdu'l-Bahá, *Star of the West*, vol. 10, no. 12, June 4, 1919, 232.
4   Shoghi Effendi, *The Promised Day Is Come*, 3.
5   *Gleanings*, no. 4.1–2, 6–7.
6   *Tablets of Bahá'u'lláh Revealed after the Kitáb-i-Aqdas*, 127.
7   Helen Bassett Hornby, *Lights of Guidance: A Bahá'í Reference File*, No. 1677, 500. (According to information received by the National Spiritual Assembly of the United States several years ago, this tablet was revealed by the Master in 1897 to a Jewish community in the Orient: *Bahá'í News*, No. 250, December 1951, p. 5).

CHAPTER 11: NAHUM – JUSTICE FOR NINEVEH, MERCY FOR JUDAH

1   Nabil-i-Azam, *The Dawn-Breakers: Nabil's Narrative of the Early Days of the Bahá'í Revelation*, 23.

2   C. L. Crouch, "On Floods and the Fall of Nineveh: A Note on the Origins of a Spurious Tradition," *New Perspectives on Old Testament Prophecy and History: Essays in Honour of Hans M. Barstad*, 216.

3   John D. W. Watts, "The Book of Nahum," *The Oxford Companion to the Bible*, Bruce M. Metzger and Michael E. Coogan, eds., p. 545. Watts (1921–2013) was a Baptist theologian, Old Testament scholar, and professor at Fuller Theological Seminary, Pasadena, California, and the International Baptist Theological Institute in Prague, Czech Republic.

CHAPTER 12: HABAKKUK – A DIALOGUE WITH GOD

1   Bahá'u'lláh, *Tablets of Bahá'u'lláh Revealed after the Kitáb-i-Aqdas*, Tarazát (Ornaments), 33.

2   *Selections from the Writings of 'Abdu'l-Bahá*, no. 145.5, 180.

CHAPTER 13: STRUGGLES FOR JUDAH

1   The first Assyrian incursion was under Tiglath-pileser during the reign of Menahem (Azariah in Judah), who bought him off with a huge ransom (2 Kings 15:19–20). The second was under Tiglath-pileser during the reign of Pekah (Ahaz) in 741. The northern region was captured, and many people were deported (1 Chron. 5:26, 2 Kings 15:29). The third invasion was under Shalmaneser in 723 during the reigns of Hoshea in Israel and Hezekiah in Judah and ended in 722 or 721 (dates vary) with the fall of Samaria and the kingdom (2 Kings 17:3). The fourth was into Judah under Esarhaddon in 676 (2 Chron. 33:11, Ezra 4:2). *The Assyrian Invasions and Deportations of Israel* by J. Llewellyn Thomas, F.R.C.S., Table No. II, 35.

2   Primarily, but not limited, to Genesis, Exodus, Leviticus, Numbers, Deuteronomy, Joshua, Judges, Ruth, 1 and 2 Samuel, 1 and 2 Kings,

1 and 2 Chronicles, Esther, Job, Psalms Proverbs, Ecclesiastics, and the Song of Solomon.

3 Ronald E. Clements, "The Book of Deuteronomy," *The Oxford Companion to the Bible*, Bruce M. Metzger and Michael D. Coogan, eds., 1st ed., 167. Clements states that "Jeremiah's prophecies are presented as the final proof of the Deuteronomic interpretation as the reasons for the collapse of Israel as a nation; they serve also as the vehicle of hope and guidance for the nation's renewal and eventual restoration." Clements was a fellow of Fitzwilliam College and Lecturer in Old Testament Literature and Theology at the University of Cambridge, before becoming the Samuel Davidson Professor of Old Testament at King's College London.

4 Ibid, 167–68.

CHAPTER 14: JEREMIAH –
IF YOU DO NOT LISTEN

1 Bahá'u'lláh, *The Summons of the Lord of Hosts*, no. 53, 28.

2 'Abdu'l-Bahá, *Some Answered Questions*, no. 57:6, 247. Frances Worthington, *Abraham: One God, Three Wives, Five Religions*, chart, 182–83.

3 *Some Answered Questions*, no. 12:7, 75.

4 Bahá'u'lláh, *Epistle to the Son of the Wolf*, 144.

5 The Báb, *Selections from the Writings of the Báb*, no. 3:39, 145.

CHAPTER 15: JEREMIAH – THE END
OF THE DAVIDIC KINGDOM

1 Walter Brueggemann, *A Commentary on Jeremiah: Exile and Homecoming*, 29.

APPENDIX A: THE BÁB – HERALD
OF THE BAHÁ'Í FAITH

1 The Báb, *Selections from the Writings of the Báb*, no. 3:34, 136–37.

2 Shoghi Effendi, Introduction to *The Dawn-Breakers: Nabíl's Narrative of the Early Days of the Bahá'í Revelation* by Nabil-i-A'zam, xxix.

3 Nabil-i-A'zam, *The Dawn-Breakers*, 315–16.

4   The complete account of the events surrounding the trial and execution of the Báb is described in *The Dawn-Breakers*, 500–26.

5   "Considered alone, Bahá is a verbal-noun meaning radiant ‹glory›, ‹splendour›, 'light', 'brilliancy', 'beauty', 'excellence', 'goodliness', 'divine majesty' - there are other shades of meaning also." Lambden, "The Word Bahá: Quintessence of the Greatest Name," *Bahá'í Studies Review*, 3:1.

6   Adib Taherzadeh, *The Revelation of Bahá'u'lláh*, vol. 1, 297.

7   The Báb, cited by Shoghi Effendi, *God Passes By*, 29.

APPENDIX B: THE EXILES OF BAHÁ'U'LLÁH

1   Bahá'u'lláh, cited by Shoghi Effendi, *God Passes By*, 109.

2   Adib Taherzadeh wrote, "On the other hand, the Báb also referred to the year nineteen, a year coinciding with the Declaration of Bahá'u'lláh in Baghdád, which occurred at the end of nineteen lunar years from the inception of the Bahá'í Era." *The Revelation of Bahá'u'lláh*, Vol. 1, 299.

3   The Báb, cited in *God Passes By*, 29.

4   These tablets are published in *The Summons of the Lord of Hosts*.

5   Bahá'u'lláh, *The Summons of the Lord of Hosts*, Súriy-i-Mulúk (Súrih to the Kings), no. 68, 213.

6   Bahá'u'lláh, *Gleanings from the Writings of Bahá'u'lláh*, no. 45, 99–100. The Ancient Beauty is one of the titles of Bahá'u'lláh.

7   Taherzadeh, *The Revelation of Bahá'u'lláh*, vol. 3, 420.

APPENDIX C: THE TWO CYCLES

1   'Abdu'l-Bahá, *Some Answered Questions*, no. 41:3, 183.

2   Bahá'u'lláh, *Gleanings from the Writings of Bahá'u'lláh*, no. 10.2, 13.

3   The Báb, *Selections from the Writings of the Báb*, no. 4:10:2, 160–61.

APPENDIX D: TALK GIVEN BY 'ABDU'L-BAHÁ ON APRIL 13, 1912

1   'Abdu'l-Bahá, *The Promulgation of Universal Peace*, 10.

NOTES

APPENDIX E: "END OF THE WORLD – POSSIBLY THE WORLD'S GREATEST TRANSLATION ERROR" BY JAY TYSON

1   Tyson, Jay, Blog #4"End of the World"?? Possibly the world's greatest translation error, December 24, 2021, https://wisemenofthewest.com/posts-for-the-wise-men-of-the-west/ Jay Tyson is the author of the two-volume *The Wise Men of the West*, the search for the Promised One in the East.

APPENDIX F: TITLES OF BAHÁ'U'LLÁH

1   Shoghi Effendi, *God Passes By*, 94.
2   Ibid., 95.
3   *Gleanings from the Writings of Bahá'u'lláh*, no. 115:1, 2, 3, 6, 10, 11, 12, and 13, 241–45.

APPENDIX G: EXCERPTS FROM ABDU'L-BAHÁ'S TALK ON JUNE 16, 1912

1   'Abdu'l-Bahá, *The Promulgation of Universal Peace*, 198–200.

APPENDIX H: 'ABDU'L-BAHÁ, SHOGHI EFFENDI, AND THE BAHÁ'Í COVENANT

1   'Abdu'l-Bahá, *Tablets of 'Abdu'l-Bahá*, Vol. 2, 430.

APPENDIX H: ABDU'L-BAHÁ, EXCERPTS FROM *THE SECRET OF DIVINE CIVILIZATION*

1   'Abdu'l-Bahá, *The Secret of Divine Civilization*, 75–80.

Bibliography

WORKS OF THE BÁB

Selections from the Writings of the Báb. The Universal House of Justice. Compiled by the Research Department of the Universal House of Justice and translated by Habib Taherzadeh with the assistance of a Committee at the Bahá'í World Centre. Haifa, Israel. First pocket-size edition. Wilmette, IL: Bahá'í Publishing Trust, 2006.

WORKS OF BAHÁ'U'LLÁH

Epistle to the Son of the Wolf. Translated by Shoghi Effendi. 1st pocket-size ed. Wilmette, IL: Bahá'í Publishing Trust, 1988.

Gleanings from the Writings of Bahá'u'lláh. First pocket-size edition. Translated by Shoghi Effendi. Wilmette, IL: Bahá'í Publishing Trust, 1983.

The Kitáb-i-Aqdas: The Most Holy Book. Haifa: Bahá'í World Centre, 1992.

The Kitáb-i-Íqán: The Book of Certitude. Translated by Shoghi Effendi. New pocket-sized edition with paragraph numbers. Wilmette, IL: Bahá'í Publishing Trust, 2003.

The Proclamation of Bahá'u'lláh. Wilmette, IL: Bahá'í Publishing Trust, 1978.

The Summons of the Lord of Hosts: Tablets of Bahá'u'lláh. Haifa: Bahá'í World Centre, 2002.

Tablets of Bahá'u'lláh Revealed after the Kitáb-i-Aqdas. Compiled by the Research Department of the Universal House of Justice. Translated by Habib Taherzadeh et al. Wilmette, IL: Bahá'í Publishing Trust, 1988.

WORKS OF 'ABDU'L-BAHÁ

Paris Talks: Addresses Given by 'Abdu'l-Bahá in Paris in 1911. 11th ed. London: Bahá'í Publishing Trust, 1995.

The Promulgation of Universal Peace: Talks Delivered by 'Abdu'l-Bahá during His Visit to the United States and Canada in 1912. Compiled by Harold McNutt. Wilmette, IL: Bahá'í Publishing Trust, 2007.

The Secret of Divine Civilization. National Spiritual Assembly of the United States, 1990. First pocket-sized edition Translated from the Persian by Marziel Gail in consultation with Ali Kuli-Khan.

Selections from the Writings of 'Abdu'l-Bahá. Compiled by the Research Department of the Universal House of Justice and translated by a committee at the Bahá'í World Centre and by Marzieh Gail, and originally published by the Universal House of Justice in Haifa, Israel, in 1978. Wilmette: Bahá'í Publishing Trust, 1997.

Some Answered Questions. Compiled and translated from the Persian by Laura Clifford Barney. Newly revised by a committee at the Bahá'í World Centre. Haifa, Israel: Bahá'í World Centre, 2014.

WORKS OF SHOGHI EFFENDI

Citadel of Faith: Messages to America 1947–1957. Wilmette, IL: Bahá'í Publishing Trust, 1965.

God Passes By. Wilmette, IL: Bahá'í Publishing Trust, Revised ed., 1974.

The Promised Day Is Come. First pocket-size ed. Wilmette, IL: Bahá'í Publishing Trust, 1996.

The World Order of Bahá'u'lláh: Selected Letters. 2nd rev. ed. Wilmette, IL: Bahá'í Publishing Trust, 1974.

COMPILATIONS

Bahá'u'lláh, 'Abdu'l-Bahá, Shoghi Effendi, and the Universal House of Justice. *The Bible: Extracts on the Old and New Testaments.* Research Department of the Universal House of Justice. (publication date not given) https://bahai-library.com/uhj_old_new_testaments

Lights of Guidance: A Baháʼí Reference File. Compiled by Helen Bassett Hornby. 3rd revised ed. New Delhi, India: Baháʼí Publishing Trust, 1994.

HOLY SCRIPTURES
The Bible, King James Version
The Bible, New International Version

OTHER SOURCES
Albom, Mitch. *Have a Little Faith: A True Story.* New York: Hatchette Books, 2011.

"Balfour Declaration Letter written." *This Day in History,* November 2, 1917. Website History.com. https://www.history.com/this-day-in-history/the-balfour-declaration

Baruch, R. "Hebrew Numerology and the Bible," website Love Israel, November 13, 2015. https://www.loveisrael.org/articles/2015/11/13/hebrew-numerology-and-the-bible

Berkowitz, Adam Eliyahu. "Scientific Proof for King Uzziah's Earthquake," *Breaking Israel News,* January 8, 2019. https://www.breakingisraelnews.com/119954/scientists-agree-earthquake-days-amos/

Bible Study Tools. https://www.biblestudytools.com/encyclopedias/isbe/balak.html

Brueggemann, Walter. *A Commentary on Jeremiah: Exile and Homecoming.* Grand Rapids, MI: Wm. B. Eerdsman Publishing Co., 1998.

_____. *Hopeful Imagination: Prophetic Voices in Exile.* Philadelphia, PA: Fortress Press, 1986.

Clements, Ronald E. "The Book of Deuteronomy," *The Oxford Companion to the Bible.* Bruce M. Metzger and Michael David Coogan, eds, 1st ed. Oxford Companions series. New York: Oxford University Press, 1993.

Crenshaw, James L. "The Book of Jonah," *The Oxford Companion to the Bible,* Bruce M. Metzger and Michael, Coogan, eds., 381.

257

BIBLIOGRAPHY

Crouch, C. L. "On Floods and the Fall of Nineveh: A Note on the Origins of a Spurious Tradition." *New Perspectives on Old Testament Prophecy and History: Essays in Honour of Hans M. Barstad.* 10.1163/9789004293274_017. Series: Vetus Testamentum, Supplements, Volume: 168. Eds. Rannfrid I. Thelle, Terje Stordalen and Mervyn E.J. Richardson. Brill: Leiden, 2015.

Dennis, Rabbi Geoffrey. "Judaism and Numbers: The Jewish numerology tradition, known as gematria, values some numbers more than others." https://www.myjewishlearning.com/article/judaism-numbers/

Dever, William G. *The Lives of Ordinary People in Ancient Israel: Where Archaeology and the Bible Interact.* Grand Rapids, MI: William B. Eerdsman Publishing Company, 2012.

Dines, Jennifer M. "Amos." *The Oxford Bible Commentary.* Oxford: Oxford University Press, 2001.

Finkelstein, Israel and Neil Asher Silberman. *The Bible Unearthed: Archeology's New Vision of Ancient Israel and the Origin of Its Sacred Texts.* New York: Touchstone, imprint of Simon & Schuster, 2002.

———. *David and Solomon: In Search of the Bible's Sacred Kings and the Roots of the Western Tradition.* New York: Free Press, imprint of Simon & Schuster, 2007.

Geva, Hillel. "Ancient Jerusalem: The Town, the Village, the City," as published in Biblical Archaeology Review, May/June 2016, https://www.biblicalarchaeology.org/daily/biblical-sites-places/jerusalem/ancient-jerusalem/Heschel, Abraham J. *The Prophets.* New York: HarperCollins, 1962.

Hunt, Michael E. "The Significance of Numbers in Scripture." May 2012. Website Agape Catholic Bible Study. https://www.agapebiblestudy.com/documents/The%20Significance%20of%20Numbers%20in%20Scripture.htm

Israel Ministry of Foreign Affairs. Law of Return 5710–1950. https://mfa.gov.il/mfa/mfa-archive/1950-1959/pages/law%20of%20return%205710-1950.aspx

Joy, Anthony. *Exploring Gleanings: Commentary on Gleanings from the Writings of Bahá'u'lláh.* New Delhi, India: Bahá'í Publishing Trust, 2013.

Lambden, Stephen. "The Word Bahá: Quintessence of the Greatest Name." *Bahá'í Studies Review* 3:1, footnote 7. Association for Bahá'í Studies English-Speaking Europe, 1993.

Lendering, Jona. "The Siloam Inscription." Website of Livius, revised October 4, 2020. https:/www.livius.org/sources/content/anet/321-the-siloam-inscription/

McFall, Leslie. "Has the Chronology of the Hebrew Kings Been Settled?" website The Melios, vol. 17:1, https://www.thegospelcoalition.org/themelios/article/has-the-chronology-of-the-hebrew-kings-been-finally-settled/

Mírzá Abu'l-Faḍl Gulpáypání. *Miracles and Metaphors.* Translated from the Arabic and annotated by Juan Ricardo Cole. Originally published in 1900 in Cairo, Egypt. Los Angeles, CA: Kalamát Press, 1991.

Motlagh, Hushidar. *Lord of Lords.* Volume I, *Prophecies of the Second Coming.* Mt. Pleasant, MI: Global Perspective, 2000. http://www.globalperspective.org/

———. *I Shall Come Again.* Volume II, Time Prophecies of the Second Coming, 2nd ed. Mt. Pleasant, MI: Global Perspective, 2000. http://www.globalperspective.org/

Nabíl-i-A'ẓam [Muḥammad-i-Zarandí]. *The Dawn-breakers: Nabíl's Narrative of the Early Days of the Bahá'í Revelation.* Translated and edited by Shoghi Effendi. Wilmette, IL: Bahá'í Publishing Trust, 1970.

The Oxford Bible Commentary. Barton, John and John Muddiman, eds. Oxford: Oxford University Press, 2001.

The Oxford Companion to the Bible. Metzger, Bruce M. and Michael David Coogan, eds., 1st ed. Oxford Companions, New York: Oxford University Press, 1993.

Rabbaní, Rúḥíyyih (Mary Maxwell). *The Priceless Pearl.* London: Bahá'í Publishing Trust, 1969.

Schniedewind, William. *How the Bible Became a Book: The Textualization of Ancient Israel.* New York: Cambridge University Press, 2004.

Sears, William. *The Half-Inch Prophecy.* Johannesburg, South Africa: Bahá'í Publishing Trust, 2000.

BIBLIOGRAPHY

————. *Thief in the Night: The Strange Case of the Missing Millennium.* Oxford, UK: George Ronald, Publisher, 1961.

Selchert, Gary. "The Concept of Sacred Justice in Hebrew Eschatology." *Lights of Irfan,* Book 1. Wilmette, IL: Irfan Colloquia, 2000. https:// bahai-library.com/selchert_justice_hebrew_eschatology

Sours, Michael. *Preparing for a Bahá'í / Christian Dialogue,* Vol. 3, *Understanding Biblical Prophecy.* Oxford: Oneworld Publications, 1997.

Star of the West, vol. 10, no. 12: June 4, 1919. https://s3.amazonaws. com/starofthewest/SW_Volume10.pdf

Taherzadeh, Adib. T*he Revelation of Bahá'u'lláh.* Oxford: George Ronald, 1974-1987; vol. 1: *Baghdad 1853-1863*; vol. 2: *Adrianople1863-1868*; vol. 3: *Ákká, The Early Years 1868-1877*; vol. 4: *Mazar'ih & Bahjí 1877-1892.*

Thomas, J. Llewellyn. *The Assyrian Invasions and Deportations of Israel.* A reprint of the 1937 edition by Covenant Publishing Company, Britain. Publisher: Artisan Sales, Muskogee, OK, 1989.

Tyson, Jay, Blog #4. "End of the World"?? Possibly the world's greatest translation error, December 24, 2021, https://wisemenofthewest.com/ posts-for-the-wise-men-of-the-west/

United Nations Resolution No. 181, Adopted on the Report of the Ad Hoc Committee on the Palestinian Question Resolution. United Nations Documents. https://undocs.org/A/RES/181(II)

Younger, K. Lawson, Jr. "Israelites and Judahites in Assyria According to the Cuneiform Sources." https://www.laniertheologicallibrary.org/ wp-content/uploads/2015/01/Younger.pdf

Watts, John D. W. "The Book of Nahum." *The Oxford Companion to the Bible.* Bruce M. Metzger and Michael David Coogan, eds, 1st ed. Oxford Companions series. New York: Oxford University Press, 1993.

Weiss, Bari. "Can an Archaeological Dig Change the Future of Jerusalem?" *The New York Times,* March 30, 2019. https://www. nytimes.com/interactive/2019/03/30/opinion/sunday/jerusa-lem-city-of-david-israel-dig.html

Whybray, R. N. "Prophets: Ancient Israel," *The Oxford Companion to the Bible*. Bruce M. Metzger and Michael David Coogan, eds, 1st ed. Oxford Companions series. New York: Oxford University Press, 1993.

Worthington, Frances. *Abraham: One God, Three Wives, Five Religions*. Wilmette, IL: Bahá'í Publishing Trust, 2011.

Younger, K. Lawson, Jr. "Israelites and Judahites in Assyria According to the Cuneiform Sources." Lanier Theological School, Trinity International University, Deerfield, IL. https://www.laniertheologicallibrary.org/wp-content/uploads/2015/01/Younger.pdf

About the Author

EILEEN MADDOCKS GREW UP in Maine and graduated from the University of Kansas with a liberal arts degree. She worked in sales and raised two children.

She was raised in a Universalist church but as an adult became a spiritual seeker. In midlife, Eileen discovered and embraced the Bahá'í Faith. When first introduced to the Bahá'í Faith, she was seized by the fact that God has always been active in human history, that He was not only the Creator but had sent hundreds, perhaps thousands, of Prophets of God to educate humanity. Having majored in history during her university studies, Eileen was astonished to realize that the single most important factor in human history, God and His Prophets, was not recognized.

She subsequently served at the Bahá'í World Centre in Haifa, Israel, for sixteen years. Some of the positions that she held required extensive research and writing. Her avocation was arranging and leading day tours throughout Israel for Bahá'í World Centre staff.

Upon retirement, she chose to live in the bucolic state of Vermont where no billboards are allowed.

Eileen's first book, *1844: Convergence in Prophecy for Judaism, Christianity, Islam and the Bahá'í Faith*, was published in 2018. It explores expectations in the West for the return of Jesus Christ, and simultaneously in the East for the return of the Promised One of Shi'a Islam.

Her ten-year, current project is *The Coming of the Glory: How the Hebrew Scriptures Reveal the Plan of God*, three volumes that present a Bahá'í perspective of the Hebrew Bible and its prophecies and importance for today. This trilogy presents in a chronological, systematic manner the ministries and prophecies of the Hebrew prophets within the context of Israelite history.

By nature quite cerebral, Eileen balances her writer's lifestyle with a study of classical ballet for exercise and artistic expression. Two cats edit her work by walking across the keyboard and interrupting her with their plaintive insistence that it's mealtime.

Eileen's website can be accessed at eileenmaddocks.com.

www.ingramcontent.com/pod-product-compliance
Lightning Source LLC
Chambersburg PA
CBHW060252100426
42742CB00011B/1724